Somerset Paupers

"Yet I would rather know the histories of these humble unremembered lives than the great ones of the Vale who have left us a memory."

... from *The Shepherd's Life* by W.H.Hudson [1848-1922], quoted from the edition published by The Bodley Head in 1987. The 'Vale' refers to the Vale of the Wylye in south Wiltshire.

SOMERSET PAUPERS
Unremembered Lives

Thelma Munckton

Thelma Munckton

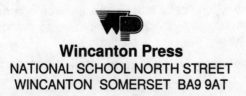

Wincanton Press
NATIONAL SCHOOL NORTH STREET
WINCANTON SOMERSET BA9 9AT

Publishing details. First published 1994.
Copyright Thelma Munckton © 1994. Published by the Wincanton
Press at the National School, North Street, Wincanton,
Somerset BA9 9AT (telephone 01963 32583) with distribution in
Somerset being undertaken by Rodney Legg.

Printing credits. Typesetting by Reg V. Ward, Holwell, Dorset (but until
1844 a Somerset parish), output by Daisywheel, Wallasey, Merseyside.
Printed by Redwood Books, Kennet Way, Trowbridge,
Wiltshire BA14 8RN.

International standard book number. ISBN 0 948699 28 0

CONTENTS

Author's acknowledgements.

The material for this study has been extracted during the course of compiling a personal name index to the Somerset settlement and bastardy papers.

This has taken eleven years; and I am most grateful to Irene Pendlebury whose help with the indexing has been invaluable.

I must also express my gratitude for much help and advice from the courteous staff at the Somerset Record Office; this, of course, includes Derek Shorrocks, retired County Archivist who asked me to compile the index, Adam Green the present County Archivist, who gave permission for the publication of extracts from the documents, and those used for illustrations.

I thank, too, Steven Hobbs, now the County Archivist for Wiltshire, for his encouragement; and Dr Robert Dunning for his interest.

My very special thanks go to Susan Berry, Senior Archivist at the Somerset Record Office, for her unfailing patience and help.

Some further research was carried out at the Dorset and Wiltshire Record Offices, whose assistance is hereby acknowledged.

To Rodney Legg, who undertook to edit and publish the book for me (and who had to unscramble my punctuation), I shall always be grateful, not only for his efforts on my behalf, but also for the opportunity to meet someone whose name I have long known, and whose writing is a delight.

Finally, all errors of transcription or interpretation are mine.

RECORDS OF THE UNREMEMBERED

Although the lives of the poor may be unremembered, as a social class they are well documented, surfacing from obscurity again and again through the pages of the parish and other records. Here we can find recorded the names of those who were too poor to pay the taxes levied by central government, such as the hearth tax which was imposed from 1663 to 1689.

Among the parish records the indentures of apprenticeship are a guide to the poor – those apprenticed by the parish officers, as well as those whose apprenticeship was arranged by a charity.

Charities were usually established for specific purposes such as supplying the needy with gifts of blankets, fuel or food. These donations followed the particular wish of the instigator of the charity. Some charity account books may have survived, naming recipients. William Penny had been the master of a charity school [case 85].

Cases of poaching and larceny dealt with at petty and quarter sessions may well indicate attempts by the poor to supplement their meagre diet. These cases can sometimes be followed up by reference to the records of the gaol or house of correction.

Some cases concerning settlement and bastardy could be dealt with at quarter sessions, especially if there was controversy between the parishes concerned. The documents dealing with these cases may be found in solicitors' deposits [case 182] as well as in the records of the court of quarter sessions.

The overseers' accounts are an important record of the treatment of the poor. Here will be recorded the moneys received from the poor rate, as well as the disbursements. These latter could be monetary provision, or expenses for items of clothing, payments to those who tended the sick, and those who nursed or fostered children.

Expenses incurred by the overseers in discharging their duties will likewise be entered into the accounts, though the cost of passing vagrants was paid by the county [case 41].

The casual or travelling pauper, discharged soldier or sailor, passing through the parish, would have received relief from the churchwardens. These payments may be found recorded in the churchwardens' account books.

The minute books of the vestry meeting will probably contain the decisions of the vestry regarding the poor. Such entries may be embellished by references to the character of the pauper.

After the Poor Law Amendment Act of 1834 the records of the poor law guardians will be found to contain a great deal of information about the inmates of the workhouse. These records may include settlement cases.

By the time of the 1851 census 'pauper' was to be entered under the heading of rank, profession or occupation; or a poor person might be recorded, as was Abraham Criddle, as "farm labourer, also in receipt of parish relief" [case 182].

The pauper does not escape that stigma even in death – the cost of the shroud and coffin provided by the parish will be entered into the overseers' accounts; and the word 'pauper' may be found beside the entry in the burial register.

All these records will show how the poor lived and how they were treated. However, the documents concerned with settlement and removal are even more revealing of the lives of the poor, and are probably the best example of any extant record.

It must be emphasised that the value of these records, as aspects of social history, lies in the detailed recital of the lives of the poor.

It is quite usual to find at least three generations noted in the examinations, as it may be necessary to establish the settlement of the parents or even the grandparents, in order to determine the settlement of the examinee and his family [cases 68 and 184].

The laws relating to the relief of paupers are numerous, tedious and complicated. This is especially true of the law concerned with settlement and removal, the administration of which often generated prolonged and expensive litigation between parishes, but which led to the creation of a wealth of documentary material.

Prior to 1572 the main provisions of poor law legislation were concerned with beggars, vagrants and vagabonds. Since 1388 it had been possible to return those found begging to their place of birth; in 1530 beggars who were incapable of working could be given licences to beg by the magistrates. In the act of 1572 licences were no longer to be issued. It was by this act that the office of overseer was created; although it was not until 1597 that the overseers were to be appointed annually by the magistrates.

In 1601 a temporary statute – made permanent in 1640 – enabled the parish officers to levy a poor rate. Previously alms giving had provided funds for the relief of the poor.

We consider now the act of settlement and removal. This became law in 1662, and was described as "an act for the better relief of the poor".

This act laid down that those who were unable to support themselves or their families, and had to seek relief from the parish officers, could only receive this relief if the parish in which the paupers were then residing was deemed to be their legal parish of settlement; if, indeed, it was found that the paupers' parish was elsewhere, then they could be removed to that parish. In fact any stranger found in a parish could be removed, pauper or not, if it was thought that he might become chargeable. It was not until 1795 that paupers had to become chargeable before they could be removed. At this date also the magistrates were able to suspend orders of removal if the pauper was too ill to travel. In those cases the receiving parish would be expected to contribute towards the maintenance of the pauper, who would still be liable to be removed when sufficiently recovered to travel.

It is important to remember that the act of 1662 referred only to England and Wales – Scotland, Ireland, the Channel Islands and the Isle of Man were excluded – therefore persons from outside England and Wales could only be dealt with under the vagrancy laws.

In 1834 the Poor Law Amendment Act was passed, being subsequently known as "the new poor law". The old poor law passed into history, unfortunately not taking the law of settlement and removal with it; paupers were still liable to be removed, if they became chargeable and were not in their legal parish. It had been possible since 1722-23 for parishes to join together to form a union and to build workhouses. After 1834 this unionisation became mandatory. Many rural parishes would have had a poor house for the aged and infirm, as distinct from a workhouse where the poor were to be housed and employed.

All parishes were now to be united into unions; workhouses were to be built; the administration of these would be entrusted to a board of guardians. These guardians were themselves responsible to the poor law commissioners. The individual parishes still had to provide the money to support their paupers, even if they were admitted to the union workhouse. After 1865, parish relief was charged to the union funds – i.e., the cost was spread throughout the union. Much of the 1834 act relates to the administration of the workhouse, the appointment and duties of the master, and the responsibilities of the guardians.

Although the reforms of 1834 were intended to stop outdoor relief, this was not carried into practice, and except in the case of able bodied men those in need could still receive relief without being admitted to the workhouse [case 183]. Some of the united parishes were quick to build their workhouses. Williton, for example, was soon ready to receive inmates, whilst in the neighbouring union of Dulverton the guardians took their time.

In fact twenty years were to elapse before their workhouse was built. Their story is told in *Rattle Their Bones* by Jack Hurley. The Dulverton workhouse is now the headquarters of the Exmoor National Park Authority.

In 1846 an act was passed which introduced irremovability – that is to say, any person who had resided in a parish or union of parishes for five years before obtaining benefit was deemed to be irremovable. In 1861 the period of residence was reduced to three years, and in 1865 again reduced, to a period of one year. However, these periods of residence did not confer settlement [case 188].

Various changes had also taken place in the administration of the poor law. In 1847 the poor law commission was replaced by the poor law board. In 1871 this board was in its turn replaced by the local government board, then in 1919 poor law administration was transferred to the Ministry of Health. In 1929 the poor law unions were abolished by the Local Government Act. In 1930 the functions of the guardians passed to public assistance committees set up by borough and county councils. Eventually, arising out of the Beveridge Report, administration at county level was taken over by central government in 1948. Another important change had taken place a century earlier, in 1848, as after this date cases of dispute could be referred to the arbitration of the poor law board, and not to lawyers.

Papers relating to settlement and removal have survived for many Somerset parishes until about 1860. Thereafter some may be found amongst the board of guardians records. Those for the Yeovil union [SRO, D/G/Y 48], dating from 1850 to 1884, contain removal orders with notices of chargeability.

Indeed the law of settlement and removal remained on the statute book until the middle of the twentieth century. S and B Webb, writing in 1927, note that it was then still the law that a person, not being a freeholder or renting a tenement worth £10 a year, if found outside their parish of settlement without an indemnity certificate, could be removed, but not if they fulfilled the criteria of residence noted above – i.e., irremovability.

Readers who wish to pursue in depth the poor law should see, in the first instance, the chapter on the poor law contained in *The Parish Chest* by W.E. Tate. Other books which are helpful will be found in the bibliography. For the real enthusiast there are, of course, *Statutes of the Realm*. A summary of the Acts of Parliament relating to the poor from 14 Elizabeth C5 (1572) to 11 & 12 George VI, C29 (1948) will be found in an appendix.

It may be useful to include here some notes, taken from *Archbold's Settlement Law*, showing how the administration of the law relating to settlement and removal operated at parish level.

The pauper would be examined by two justices of the county in which the removing parish is situated.

Overseers may compel the pauper to attend (but would need a warrant from the justice to do so).

The examination must consist of all the evidence given before the justices relative to the settlement.

A copy of the examination, together with a copy of the removal order and notice of chargeability to be sent from parish A to parish B.

The removal order must record the name of the pauper, and the names and ages of the family (if over seven years of age members of the family may have acquired a settlement of their own).

The removal may be carried out by the churchwardens and overseers of the removing parish, or by a contractor.

Types of settlement and removal papers

"Indemnity certificates" may also be called settlement certificates or discharges, but here will be referred to as indemnity certificates.

These were documents in which the churchwardens and overseers of parish 'A' promise to indemnify the officers of parish 'B', that is to say they will pay for the maintenance or receive back any of their parishioners or their families should the need arise.

The documents would have been signed by the parish officers and the principal inhabitants of the parish. They would then have been taken to a justice who signed them as being 'allowed'. Witnesses' signatures may also be recorded.

There is the case of Jacob Chaninge, who had been given an indemnity certificate, from Taunton St Mary, in 1684. Now, in 1719, he was old, weak and ill. The parish officers of Cheriton Fitzpaine, Devon, in which parish he had been living, request the parish officers of Taunton St Mary to provide relief for him [case 15].

In 1667 George Bartrume, together with his wife and family, had been given a certificate from Crowcombe so that they could live in Stogumber. By 1696 George, his wife and eight children – two with wives – and eight grandchildren, were all liable to become chargeable, and were to be removed back to Crowcombe [case 3].

It must be remembered that the issue of an indemnity certificate did not mean that the holder was a pauper, rather that it was a safeguard for those who were seeking to work or live outside of their parish of settlement.

There were also persons who could be allowed to reside in a parish other than their own; but who were maintained by their legal parish [cases 149, 177, 181 and 185].

It is interesting to note that Elizabeth England, with her son George, was given an indemnity certificate from Taunton St Mary to live in the parish of Taunton St James. Her husband William had been involved in the Monmouth rebellion of 1685, and had been banished beyond the seas [case 4].

In 1718 Joel Toop and his family had been given a certificate from Berkley to live in Beckington; his apprentice was included. Twenty-two years later we find both his sons, their wives and thirteen children also being given certificates from Berkley to Beckington [case 14].

Some certificates will be found to predate the act of 1662, as we can see from the certificate which enabled John Syme and family to move from Butleigh to Evercreech in 1658 [case 1]. It was not until an act passed in 1696-97 that the issue of certificates became general, allowing those seeking work to move into a parish other than that in which they were legally settled.

Although the act of 1691 laid upon the overseers the responsibility of recording the names and habitations of those coming into a parish intending to gain a settlement by residence, there is apparently, in Somerset, little surviving documentary evidence that this instruction was put into practice.

However, for the parish of Winsham there exists a register of discharges for 1697-1745, together with two loose sheets, for 1667-1699 [SRO, D/P/Winsh. 13/3/5 and SRO, D/P/Winsh. 13/3/4]. The book records the discharges both given and received, as well as the other parish involved. For example, in 1708, Thomas Grimster was given a discharge to go to Ilminster, whilst Charity Stone was received, having come from Knowle St Giles (Knole). The loose sheets appear to list the discharges which form the Winsham indemnity certificate deposit. The latter contains seventy-seven documents.

The indemnity certificates which survive for the parish of St James, Taunton, dating from c1662 to c1800, number 486 of which 154 (32 per cent) concern persons coming from Taunton St Mary, 238 (49 per cent) come from other parishes within the county, whilst 94 (19 per cent) came from parishes outside the county.

Many of these incomers were single men or men with wife but no family: some apprentices coming from outside the parish are also included. It would appear that the majority of those with indemnity certificates were seeking, or already had, employment in the woollen trade.

Settlement examinations

The majority of documents which survive are removal orders, though these may be linked to settlement examinations, and it is these examinations which can reveal many interesting details of the paupers' lives. The personal histories given later are largely determined by the questions asked; the answers to which will decide the pauper's legal parish of settlement. Here we can learn the pauper's name, age, place of birth, places of employment, when and where married and to whom, as well as the names and ages of any children. The document may recite names, ages and history of parents, and even grandparents. Although the date given in the document is the date upon which the pauper was examined, the information contained therein may go back many years and cover several generations.

James Phillis, who was aged seventy-three in 1829 and who was born at Canterbury, was apprenticed at the age of nine to Thomas Richmond of Shepton Mallet. His parents resided there. The examination gives details of James's movements around the country, and the lives of his seven children [case 148].

Three generations of the Templer (alias Templeman) family are to be found in case 125. The document is dated 1819, but contains a record of the baptism of Thomas in 1736.

In High Littleton the Chivers family figure prominently in the poor law records. For example Sampson Chivers's examination, taken in 1845, contains evidence concerning Sampson's parents, his grandparents and his grandfather's siblings, as well as Sampson's own family [case 178].

In fact there were so many paupers named Chivers in this parish that the clerk was apparently forced to make out a genealogical tree [SRO, D/P/High Littleton 13/3/5.24, 1731-1845].

We shall look later at the varied contents of the examinations.

Removal orders

Removal orders, signed by two magistrates, were documents which enabled the parish officers of parish 'A' to remove paupers, if necessary, to their legal parish of settlement. The parish officers of parish 'B' were required to receive and provide for those persons so removed.

The information given consists of the names of those to be removed, and will include the names and ages of any children.

An unmarried woman was always a target for removal if her settlement was in question. This was especially so if the woman was with child, and the child was likely to be born a bastard. These unfortunate women would also be subject to the bastardy laws [case 56].

An interesting series of removal orders can be found in the Croscombe parish deposit. Here, in 1736, we find four children of one family, named Cowell, all under six years of age. These children are to be removed – each child to go to a different parish – indeed three are to be sent to different counties [case 24].

It was possible for the parishes to lodge an appeal against receiving paupers into their parish. These appeal notices may be found amongst the settlement papers.

The bastardy laws

Under these, in 1732-33, the mother had to declare if she was pregnant, and she had to name the father. Bastard children took their birthplace as their parish of settlement.

By 1743, illegitimate children took their mother's settlement. Single women could be removed if they became pregnant, if

16

they were living in a parish other than their parish of settlement.

The overseers might try to get the father to marry the mother [case 9]. If the parents married within one month after the birth of a bastard child, then the child was considered legitimate. After 1750, if the father married the mother during pregnancy the child took the paternal settlement.

Bastardy papers

Bastardy examinations: Example, mother examined – names the father. Bastardy orders: mother names the father – who is ordered to pay maintenance and towards the mother's lying-in costs. Bastardy bonds: two persons put up a bond in a named sum, one of whom may be the father (the father is not always identified in the bond).

These documents may be found in deposits made by parish, petty and quarter sessions.

Vagrants' passes

Is there a collective noun for vagrants? A "Variation of vagrants" has a nice alliterative ring about it. Furthermore it is a true description; vagrants were indeed of many varieties. They could be classed as rogues, vagabonds, sturdy beggars, persons found wandering and begging, sleeping in the open air and not giving a good account of themselves, landless men, pedlars without a licence, fortune tellers and those calling themselves Egyptians (gypsies).

As noted above, vagrants could be returned to their own parish, from 1388. Subsequently numerous ways were tried to deal with the problem. This became acute following the disbandment of soldiers who had been engaged in the Civil Wars (1642-1646; second Civil War 1648; third Civil War 1649-1651). In the vagrant's pass we can follow the unfortunate wanderer as he or she is the parcel being passed by the constables or contractor from the parish in which they have been apprehended to the next tithing, and so on to that parish judged to be their parish of settlement.

In December 1754 Ann Smith, a widow, was apprehended in Camberwell, Surrey. She was then shifted off to Evercreech, where she probably arrived on 11 January, having been passed from Bathford on 10 January [case 47].

In 1818 Edith Scammell, who had worked for Mr Hoddinott in Evercreech, was found wandering about in Whitechapel, Middlesex. She was conveyed by the contractor to Colnbrook, Buckinghamshire, which was the first stop on her way back to Evercreech [case 124].

Even longer journeys were made by Sarah Willis, who was sent from Kirkby Lonsdale, Westmoreland, to Wedmore [case 80] and Ellen Tucker, who travelled from Edinburgh to Carlisle, from whence she went to Mells [case 48, but see also cases 41 and 50]. These passes may be accompanied by an examination.

Counsel's opinions

Complex cases of settlement could be referred to legal counsel for what is today a barrister's opinion. This of course led to greatly increased expense, as well as helping towards the accumulation of paper. The case of Edward Low was one which had created a headache for the parish officers. Edward had not gained a settlement for himself – he had been born at sea – and had no idea where his mother or father had been born, and he did not know the birthplace of his grandfather [case 96].

Angel Hyde's widow and family had caused a good deal of trouble to Easton-in-Gordano. They had already been removed twice, and now the case had to be referred to counsel to settle the question of their legal parish [case 68].

Both the above cases date from the late eighteenth century.

In 1827 the parish officers of Congresbury were much exercised about the fact that the ditch which divided the parishes of Puxton and Congresbury ran partly through the portion of the tenement occupied by the pauper William Nash. The document presented to the lawyer for his opinion included a plan of the property [case 147, but see also cases 13,17, 27, 33, 58, 80, 99, 105 and 118].

Information in settlement examinations

The place of birth might be the parish in which the pauper was residing at the time of the examination, or another parish in the county or elsewhere in the British Isles. However, some more exotic birthplaces have been noted. Edward Low was "born on the seas" [case 96]. Charlotte Mason was born in America, as was Caesar Jackson [cases 106 and 122]. The former's subsequent adventures seem almost incredible.

John Morel had been born in France [case 30]. John Brockett married a widow in Ghent. She already had two children by her former husband. Both were born on the continent [case 11].

Details of a marriage may be given. These are especially important when a woman is being examined. Sometimes, unfortunately, the marriage may be found to be illegal. If this was the case any children of the marriage would be illegitimate, and this would therefore affect their claim to settlement. Mary Hollard [case 21], Sarah Dyer [case 43] and Mary Hembury (Hellyar) [case 35] were all married at Bath, between 1736 and 1752, by a person pretending to be a clergyman.

One hundred years later Rebecca Rea married her soldier husband at the parish church of Stonehouse, near Plymouth – but the entry in the marriage register recorded Rebecca's name as Elizabeth Cornish [case 131]

Margaret Matilda Dudley had been married in a Roman Catholic chapel at a time when such marriages were not legal [case 152].

William Edwards returned from the West Indies, after twenty-five years, and found his wife married to another man [case 151].

In 1701 William Bennett was apprehended and taken to Butleigh where he was kept in custody until he was married to Hannah Cheeke, who was carrying his child [case 9].

There are several cases where the wife finds that her husband has a former wife still living [Cases 113, 141 and 164].

Marriages may have been contracted overseas. Charlotte Mason was married in New York [case 106], whilst Grace Vagg was married in Guernsey [case 143]. Stanford Birch and Abigail were married in Ireland [Case 12].

Two cases have been found where the wife was sold by her husband to another man [see appendices].

Dates and places of death and burial may appear. Sampson Chivers's examination gives this information for both his parents [case 178]. The father of Mary and Ann French was killed at the Battle of Waterloo [Case 153] and Rosanna Huntsmill's first husband was a mariner and died in a French prison [case 121]. Margaret Brockett died at Dunkirk [case 11].

Any apprenticeship that had been served was an important factor in claiming settlement. Paupers would be questioned about their apprenticeship. However, a considerable number of difficulties could arise to invalidate any claim.

Such problems might concern the actual document of apprenticeship. Had the indenture or contract been properly made out?

The case of William Clarke in 1807 required counsel's opinion, as to the validity of his claim, because the contract had carried only a six shilling stamp and no seal [case 105].

Since 1757, incidentally, it had not been necessary for the

contract to be indented.

Although some apprentices served out the whole of their apprenticeship, as did Thomas Simmons – who served from the age of seven until he was twenty-four [case 103] – others might run away. One such was John Snow, apprenticed in Queen Camel, who left his master and went to Poole in Dorset where he apprenticed himself to the Newfoundland fish trade [case 84]. Newfoundland was England's oldest colony, from 1491, and anyone serving there could legally claim to have settled in an English parish, even though it is more than 3,000 miles away.

There could be problems on the master's side. He might fail in his business, move to another parish, or die. The indentures could be lost, not given up on completion of the service, or destroyed.

It was inevitable that the parish officers would seize any opportunity of apprenticing the pauper children in another parish. This was possible as any substantial householder was liable to receive a parish apprentice, even if they did not reside in the pauper's parish but merely owned an estate there. Here we have the example of John Budd, aged eighty in 1812, having been born in West Hatch, but was apprenticed in Ilminster to Mr Orchard, "by reason of an estate Mr Orchard occupied in West Hatch" [case 115]. Joseph Martin was apprenticed in West Monkton, although born in Huntspill [case 89] and John Curry, also born in Huntspill, was apprenticed to John Smithfield of East Brent. After one year, however, he was turned over to another master in the parish of Mark [case 110]. John Hammers had gone as an indentured servant to America, in which country he served for seven years [case 71].

From this brief look at apprenticeship we pass to the subject of employment. Although the type of work followed by those who applied for parish relief was not important, the place, length of time served, and any contract made between the parties, were all factors which helped towards establishing settlement.

However, occasionally, interesting details of working practices have been noted – such as the conditions under which Ann Fussell worked for Mr Hoddinott, the latter being a silk throwster in Evercreech [case 118].

In Taunton Hannah Hillyar spent part of her time carrying milk. She also was engaged in quilling [case 136].

To supplement their incomes parishioners might rent some arable land on which to grow potatoes. For instance an agreement made in 1813 between William Watts and Thomas Channing is quoted in Watts's examination, and concerns the manuring of the land and the planting and harvesting of the crop [case 116, but see also cases 101 and 156]. Renting a dairy of cows was a West Country practice. We have the case of Benjamin Bulgin whose examination gives the number of cows that he rented and the amount paid to the owner for each cow [case 158; see also case 145].

Other occupations found in the examinations include miners. James Clare had worked underground as a coal miner in the Somerset Coalfield since the age of seven [case 137]. James Tucker also worked in the mines. He was born in High Littleton, Somerset, and had worked in Derbyshire and other places [case 117].

Abraham Harris became a plough driver. His earnings, when first employed, were three pence a day. Later he was impressed into the marines [case 26]. William Manners, born in Yorkshire, worked for horse dealers. He was married in Wells around 1760 [case 63]. John Brine worked for a confectioner in Wells and received commission on his sales [case 176].

A number of examinations relate to those employed in the woollen industry. Note, especially, Abraham Lane whose examination gives details of his work as a slubber [case 135]. Complications regarding their settlement could be encountered by servants employed by the aristocracy. Their masters would be moving around the country visiting, and residing in their town and country seats [cases 69, 88 and 102].

Wages received are often noted, as well as any payment in kind that had been made by the employer. John Clatworthy had worked at the Feathers Inn, Minehead, where he received two guineas a year. After four years he went to the Reverend Bradley and the wages then rose to £6 a year and a suit of clothes [case 167].

Sarah Miller had been employed as a cook/housekeeper. While she worked in West Coker she was paid £20 a year and had an allowance of two guineas for tea [case 130].

In 1846 Abraham Criddle had only tenpence a day – less than a shilling – to support himself, his wife and five children. Out of his wages he had to pay one shilling and eightpence a week in rent; his compensating payment in kind was three pints of cider daily [case 182].

The amount of rent paid for tenements was immaterial in establishing settlement – rateable value of the property was the criterion needed – but the rent paid by the examinee may be mentioned in the examinations. In 1839 Joseph Russell recounted the rent he paid for different houses over a number of years past [case 83].

Any consideration of occupation must, of course, include those who served in the armed forces. Besides those who volunteered, or who were drawn into the militia, some unfortunates were impressed, as was Stanford Birch, who was later discharged at Vigo in Spain in 1700 [case 12].

James Tucker, noted above as a coal miner, was impressed in Liverpool and served on a frigate. He had already served for two years in the 115th Regiment of Foot [case 117].

Amongst those who enlisted themselves we find James Annison, who was stationed at Axbridge while serving in General Wolf's regiment. James's wife had died leaving him with a baby girl, who was now, therefore, chargeable to Axbridge [case 51].

William Phillips led a colourful life. Born in Devonshire, he had gone about the country selling small articles, and then travelled with people showing wild beasts, until he came to Wells, "got into liquor" and enlisted [case 52]. Charles Meech who was living in Whitelackington in 1809, had been a lance sergeant in Lord Poulett's [de]fencible cavalry [case 112]. "Defence" was a marvellous word – one was liable only for home service.

Information regarding those who served in the armed forces, invaluable in tracing careers and exotic locations, may appear in the settlement examinations of wives and families who, for various reasons, might find themselves in need of assistance. Regiments could be sent abroad for very long periods, sometimes the wives and children were able to accompany their husbands – as did Elizabeth Purse. She went to New South Wales with her husband, Daniel Purse of the 46th Regiment, which later was transferred to Madras, where Elizabeth left him [case 128].

Those who were unable to travel with their husbands were entitled to assistance in order that they might return to their homes from the port of embarkation. The examination of Bridget Richardson shows that she was given assistance, by the parish officers of Curry Rivel, as she journeyed to Wales [case 90].

Travelling soldiers and mariners might need help. The churchwardens were responsible for the payment of casual assistance, and their accounts will often be found to contain entries reading: "given to a soldier with a pass".

In the pass given to Ann Cording by the military for her journey from Chatham to St Decumens (combined parishes of Watchet and Williton) we can learn details of James, her husband, the ages and sex of their children, her dress, route, mileage covered and the amount of relief given to her en-route [case 139]. This is indeed a rarity, for the pass is a unique survival among Somerset settlement papers.

William Cole had been born in London in 1750. He was to be found in Queen Camel, following the trade of a perukemaker. This was after his discharge from the navy. His examination contains a detailed account of his service, the ships in which he served being named together with the names of their commanders [case 40].

Besides the regular army there was, on home ground, the militia. Here men between the ages of eighteen and fifty could be chosen by ballot to serve in times of emergency. With the exception of Ireland – still totally part of the 'Kingdom' – the militia were not required to serve overseas, and it was usually the case that, if called up, they would be sent to a different county from that in which they had been embodied. Provision was made to enable those drawn by ballot to have a substitute serve for them. In these cases the bounty would be paid to the substitute by the parish; this was likely to happen if the balloted man had a large family, or if the family were likely to become chargeable. We have the case of Thomas Simmons who, in 1803, was given £5 by the parish to provide a substitute [case 103]. References may be found to men who had served in the Honourable East India Company, as did Joel Keemp [sic], who served for nine years [case 72].

Also noted are out-pensioners of Chelsea Hospital, such as John Standerwick, whose pension was one shilling and eightpence a day [case 142].

The marines came under the control of the army until 1755, at which date control passed to the admiralty. John Landford, who was back in his birthplace in 1796, had served in the Plymouth division of marines for over eleven years. He was then discharged, being "old and undersized" [case 91].

It was not only those in the armed forces who served overseas. For example, from Somerset in 1818, George Cook went as a plough boy to Antigua [case 166]. Also in 1818, George Taylor went to work for the Government, at the Cape of Good Hope [case 172].

The records of the army, the navy and the marines are at the Public Record Office in Kew, south-west London.

Early militia records may be found at the Public Record Office, Chancery Lane in central London. Eighteenth and nineteenth century records are at Kew. Some local records may be at the County Record Office under the lieutenancy deposit.

Ways in which settlement could be established

There were a number of ways in which settlement in a parish could be gained. Firstly, children born in wedlock took their settlement from their father or mother, until they had acquired a settlement of their own. A woman took her husband's settlement when she married. Base-born children took theirs from their birthplace until 1743-44, after which date they would take their mother's settlement.

From 1601 anyone who had resided in a parish for forty days could claim to be settled there. In 1662 it was established that persons coming into a parish, intending to inhabit, could establish a right to settlement if they occupied a tenement of the rateable value of £10 or over; the amount of rent paid was immaterial, and in fact no rent at all needed to have been paid. The tenant had to be resident for forty days. In reality it was necessary for him to have slept or resided in the property for forty nights, although this length of time did not need to be consecutive.

After 1819 the occupation was extended to one year, but settlements already established would still stand.

The owner of an estate, of whatever size, could claim to have settled in a parish until 1723. Thereafter the value of the estate had to be at least £30. We have the example of Samuel Holder's settlement in the parish of Hemington, where he had an estate (though the examination is concerned with the maintenance of his child) [case 17].

Legislation in 1691 introduced four more ways that could be used to claim settlement, such as by serving as a parish officer for one year [cases 38 and 146].

Paying the rates and taxes on a property worth at least £10 also entitled the parishioner to claim settlement. This right extended to the children; John Wheeler stated that his father had paid the poor and church rates [case 77]. Both the above categories were abolished in 1834.

We now explore the other clauses contained in the 1691 statute – namely claiming settlement by hiring and service, and by serving an apprenticeship.

Any person who served a year as a covenant servant, being unmarried and without children at the time of hiring, could be settled in the parish of his service [case 120]. Some people could be refused yearly work, or be turned off before the year was completed, in order that the employee did not gain a settlement [case 53].

It may be of interest to record that no instances have been found, in these documents, where those examined have stated that they were hired at a fair. It would seem that hiring fairs were not the custom in Somerset [*Old Somerset Fairs*. M. Walker].

Any agreement or contract between master and servant will be noted. These contracts were often entered into at Lady Day, on 25 March, and were to run for a year. In 1832 Elizabeth Flood, together with her three children, was able to take her husband's settlement, which he had gained from his father having served a year as a covenant servant in 1793. Elizabeth had been abandoned by her husband – who had married her under a false name, and had himself done no act to gain a settlement [case 160].

Serving an apprenticeship was often the means whereby a settlement could be gained. Apprentices retained their original settlement for forty days – then they took their settlement from the parish in which they were serving. Here again importance is attached as to where the apprentice slept [case 181]. In 1758 it was found necessary to amend the 1691 act regarding the settlement of apprentices because so many had been refused settlement or had been removed, on the grounds that the document recording their apprenticeship had not been properly indented.

From 1758 any apprentice bound by any deed, writing or contract, which had first been legally stamped, could claim to be settled in the parish of their apprenticeship if they had been resident there for the required length of time [case 105]. William Clarke's apprenticeship details have been given in full to illustrate the terms and conditions under which children were apprenticed.

Sometimes absurd situations arose which posed difficulties for the parish officers, especially when parish boundaries were involved. Such is the bizarre case of John Rose, whose bed was situated over the drain dividing the parishes of Taunton St Mary and Bishops Hull. The bed was longwise over the drain, and John did not know in which parish he slept [case 129].

A good example of the tortuous way in which settlement could be established can be found in the records of Edwin and Sabina Cattle [case 186].

We should, perhaps, define a tenement. This could be any legal holding – that is to say, renting part of a house, an outhouse, a mill, a coney warren, a ferry, fishery of a pond, the occupation of a school house by a schoolmaster, and the right of feeding cows on a master's pasture. These cows were to be fed on some particular land of the value of £10 per annum.

However, no gate keeper or toll keeper of any turnpike road, or persons renting the tolls, or residing in the toll house, could claim settlement. Here we have the example of Ebenezer Merriot, who acted as toll gate keeper for twelve years but was unable to gain a settlement thereby [case 59].

After the act of 1819 [59 Geo. III, c.50], when the period of renting was increased to one year, a tenement was held to consist of a separate and distinct building or land, or both. For example, renting a dairy of cows would no longer confer settlement.

As for the "coney warren" qualification, on 2 May 1717 at Ilchester sessions, the barrister Abraham Gapper stated: "I am of the opinion that a warren of £20 per annum is a tenement within the statute of 13 and 14 Charles II, and if any person rents such a tenement or warren and has it on forty days undisturbed is a good settlement in the parish where the warren lies."

Social aspects and value of documents

Although we have looked at the ways in which settlement in a parish could be claimed, consideration must also be given to the social background and conditions which caused those unable to support themselves to seek relief.

It is now accepted as a fact that the population was much more mobile that was previously thought to be the case. This applied to all strata of society. It was in an effort to immobilise the poor that the law of settlement and removal was introduced – and it was the failure to do so that generated the vast amount of documentation that emerged as a result of the attempts by magistrates and parish officers to administer the act.

What were the factors that produced such poverty, and caused the working population to move around the country? Many were indeed seeking work and travelling perhaps only a few miles in order to obtain employment. Provided that they had an indemnity certificate from their legal parish of settlement this should have presented no problem to the receiving parish. In the countryside harvest workers would need to bring a certificate from their home parish; ditto other itinerants such as hawkers, pedlars, carriers and coach drivers, drovers and horse dealers, canal and railway workers, miners engaged in coal or iron ore mining. Those engaged in mining might have migrated from other mining areas such as Cornwall or Wales.

All these workers might be travelling around the country, working or seeking employment.

Wives and families of those in the armed forces, including the militia, might be in need of assistance. Other wives and families might be left to the care of the parish should their husbands have absconded, be languishing in gaol, awaiting transportation on the hulks, or have been actually transported [David T. Hawkings, *Criminal Ancestors*, Alan Sutton 1992]. For references to transportation see cases 4, 123, 149, 169 and 187.

Transportation to America and the West Indies took place between about 1615 and 1775. Thereafter those sentenced to be transported were sent to Australia and Tasmania. The "First Fleet" sailed to Australia in 1787, and transportation ceased in 1868.

The male prisoners awaiting transportation were confined in hulks – disused naval vessels moored off various ports – and some prisoners may even have served out their entire sentence in a hulk.

As for mainland living conditions, the reality behind the picturesque would have been extremely squalid. We can imagine a small – maybe cob – dwelling, perhaps erected on the waste or common land encroachment, with an earthen floor, small window with only a shutter, and an open fire on which to cook (that is if there was any food to cook). Water had to be fetched from a nearby river, well or pump. Wood for fuel had to be gathered. Sanitary arrangements were probably lacking.

Any parishioner might be in need of relief if they met with some disaster such as loss of employment, illness or accident. It is disappointing to find that few details of illness or accident appear in the examinations, although many removal orders will have been suspended because of infirmity. Abraham Criddle, however, gives a graphic description of his urticaria [case 182].

Let us consider what these documents do not tell us – as the examinations contain the answers to specific questions which would be slanted towards the establishment of the pauper's correct parish of settlement, very little of the examinee's personality emerges. Their thoughts and feelings are not revealed. Just occasionally, and probably through correspondence, we may perceive some human interest, such as the letter written by Joseph Smith to his wife [case 28].

Dwellings might be shared between two or more families. Such applied to Eleanor Tucker, who with her five children lived for three years in one room, for which she paid one shilling and twopence a week in rent; though this was in Derbyshire [case 117].

As an extreme occurrence we note that Judith James lived for two weeks in an oven stack [case 45].

Factual evidence of the conditions under which the population lived and worked can be found in official reports. Here we quote from the 1869 report, by R.F. Boyle, on the employment of women and children. In Somerset it was found that the weekly wage of farm labourers in the west of the county was about eight shillings. It was therefore necessary that every farm labourer's wife should be employed. Boys and girls started work at an age which could be as low as six or seven years, although eight or nine years was more usual.

The first employment of these children would most likely be that of bird scaring. During the time that the corn was ripening they might start work at 5 a.m. and continue until sunset. At seven or eight years boys could be leading the plough horses – this was called plough driving. Abraham Harris started his working life in this fashion "as soon as he was old enough to labour"; and he received three pence a day [case 26].

James Clare, in his examination, stated that he had worked underground as a miner from the age of seven years [case 137]. Farmers might supply their workers with cider or ale each day.

The labourers might live in a rent-free cottage, or have part or all of the rent paid by the parish [case 82]. Various charities existed from which the poor might receive bedding and clothing. Although these "hand-outs" could help towards alleviating some of the day to day misery, they did nothing to alleviate the indignity of having to exist without a fair wage.

The role of the overseer

The parish as it existed up to the nineteenth century was a self-sustaining self-regulating community, where much would have depended upon the abilities, character and compassion of those responsible for the administration of the laws relating to the relief of the poor and impotent.

We have an occurrence which although not strictly a settlement paper, gives an idea of the varying treatment received from the officers of the parishes through which those travelling had to pass, and where they might have applied for relief. In this case it is likely that Thomas Protherow came across the Bristol Channel from Wales. He could have landed at Watchet and from there come to Doddington [case 61].

The duties of the overseers must have greatly increased after the Act of Settlement and Removal. They were now not only responsible for the relief of paupers, but also for bringing before the justices any of the poor whose legal settlement was in question. Orders of removal made by the justices had to be carried out – those to be removed had to be escorted to their correct parish or to the next tithing along the route.

This duty might be carried out by the parish constable or a contractor appointed for the purpose; many removal orders will carry an endorsement "delivered the within named pauper to . . . ". Women and children might be delivered to the wife of the overseer or churchwarden.

Families might be removed only to return of their own accord the following day, as did William Needs [case 157].

As well as distributing the poor rate, the overseers were the collectors, and an account of moneys received and disbursed had to be kept. The parish poor rate was set by the vestry and the overseers' accounts were 'allowed' by the vestry before being submitted to the local magistrates.

Some of the records show how the relief was administered: these may be in the form of directions to the overseers from the magistrates, or letters concerning paupers.

James Wyatt, overseer of Combe St Nicholas, is summoned by the magistrate to answer a complaint that William Slade has been refused relief. Wyatt is directed to give Slade the amount of relief that is linked to the price of bread. This is an example of the Speenhamland system of poor relief, introduced from Berkshire in 1795 [cases 114, 177 and 184]. Note that a loaf of bread at this time would probably have been of quartern size, weighing four pounds.

In 1667 Henry Gitto had gone away from Minehead and left his daughter there. The overseers are directed to seek ways of providing maintenance for her [case 2]. Twenty years later, also in Minehead, two women – one with three children – complain to the magistrate that they are not receiving relief [case 5].

J.Halliday, a local magistrate, sent a letter to the overseer of St Decumans ordering him to provide Ann Cording "with what is absolutely necessary" until the next meeting of the magistrates [case 139].

After the passing of the Poor Law Amendment Act in 1834 there was the added problem of whether relief could be given outside of the workhouse. We give here two examples of outdoor relief. Henry Foster had been transported for ten years and in 1840 his wife and four children were removed to the Clutton union workhouse. After four months his wife applied for outdoor relief. This was allowed and she received six shillings a week [case 169].

Eliza Rapps, a child who had been in the workhouse, was in 1844 allowed to go and live with her aunt, receiving relief of one shilling and sixpence weekly [case 183].

When the parishes were formed into unions, applications for relief had to be made to the relieving officer, although the parish officers were able to grant relief in an emergency. The fact of so doing had to be reported to the relieving officer. Thus was lost, to a large extent, the personal contact between the overseers and the poor.

Sources of the Somerset settlement papers

The Somerset records of settlement and removal survive for various parishes all over the historical pre-1974 county limits. This rich source of social history has been used to give some indication of the vast and mostly untapped material which is available for the study of the pauper classes in the eighteenth and nineteenth centuries. It would, of course, have been impossible to publish all of the Somerset documents in one volume or indeed dozens of volumes. They number approximately 50,000 and cover dates from approximately 1662 to 1862, and yet later records may be found with the Board of Guardians' deposits.

The selection given here is an attempt to provide examples of the working of the settlement laws as they relate to the daily life of the parish and the poor. They show how the examinations can provide unparalleled insight into the social history of those seeking relief, and the administration thereof.

The documents used have been chosen from as wide an area across the county as surviving records provide and will be found to have been drawn from the larger towns – such as Taunton, Wells and Shepton Mallet – as well as the smaller centres and rural parishes. The area around Ilminster, which includes parishes on the Dorset border, is particularly well represented.

Surviving records of cases which came before the Ilminster petty session court number about 3,500. Yet more must occur in the records of the court of quarter sessions.

Although the majority of the remaining documents appear to have emanated from the parish chest, a number were subsequently transferred to successor authorities, or removed into private hands, before passing to the Somerset Record Office in recent times. An exception is those records generated by the poor law unions, which may be found to include settlement papers.

Settlement and bastardy papers have also been found amongst the estate records of the Wyndham and Luttrell families.

Parish records may have been transferred to the parish council and by that body deposited at the Somerset Record Office. There are, as well, the Bridgwater records which were transferred to the borough council, and later sent to the record office.

The Somerset Archaeological Society and Wells Museum have both made deposits of previously acquired papers, as have some private individuals. For example, those for North Cadbury can be found in the Penrose deposit, as well as others for the same parish which were acquired from Suffolk. The archives of local solicitors, who handled the legal cases, have produced some very interesting examples, the two major deposits being Couch of Stogumber and Foster of Wells.

The parish deposits of settlement papers are to be found catalogued under *"Parish records"*, with the sub division being "Civil records, the office and function of the overseers of the poor".

The quantity of the documents will be given in the catalogue, as are the dates covered.

Other deposits concerned with a parish will be cross referenced under the system detailed above. Examples of this are the Bridgwater borough records and the East Coker parish council deposit.

Those records not primarily concerned with a single parish can be retrieved through the "Settlement and bastardy index".

Editorial notes

As the language of the documents is very repetitive the information has been processed mainly in the form of abstracts. Where the whole or part is quoted in the original form inverted commas have been used. It is hoped that the abstracts will be found to be easily readable – it is to this end that abbreviations have been kept to a minimum.

The ages and periods of time usually given in the documents, for example "six years and upwards" or "six years or thereabouts" have been given as six years, and the expression "as I have heard and believe", which may be used when the examinee is reciting parts of his history which is beyond his recollection, has been omitted.

The headings of the documents – excepting as they relate to the case – have been ignored, as have the names of the parish officers where they are noted in the document; however the names of the justices have been included. This posed considerable difficulty as many names appear only as signatures.

Forenames and surnames have been given as spelt in the paper, but modern spelling has been adopted for placenames. Where this differs from the original, the latter has been given in brackets in the first instance.

Forenames have been used for the examinee and family; surnames for the other persons noted. All dates are given as found in the document, i.e., uncorrected for year-end conventions or calendar changes.

Monetary items have been expressed as given – that is to say, pounds, shillings and pence, as well as guineas.

Abbreviations used in headings or notes are listed below. Abstracts have been arranged in chronological order, except where two or more documents relate to the same person or family.

Missing or illegible words have been indicated by dotted lines.

Where a 'thorn' has been encountered in a document this has been transcribed as 'th'. Derived from a Scandinavian rune, this is 'Thorn', which became the Saxon 'Th' and later the 'y' of documents for phrases such as "ye parish" which should be read and transcribed as "the parish".

Take note, in considering the date, that before 1752 – at which date the Gregorian calendar was adopted in England and Ireland – the new year commenced on 25 March. From 1752 the new year was to commence on 1 January. Thus prior to 1752 an examination taken on, for example, 3 February 1690, if 'corrected' would read 3 February 1690-91, January, February and March being the last months of the old style calendar.

Some documents will have been dated by the Regnal year, i.e., the year of the monarch's reign. These dates have been converted in the text.

Note that Ursula Burgess, in her examination, speaks of "old Christmas eve" [case 53], which means 5 January in the new style calendar. See C.R. Cheney, *Handbook of dates for students of English history* (Royal Historical Society guides and handbooks No 4, reprinted 1970).

Abbreviations

D.R.O. – Dorset Record Office
S.R.O. – Somerset Record Office
W.R.O – Wiltshire Record Office

Wee the parishioners of Butleigh whose names are subscribed according
to an order made by the Justices of the peace at the last generall Sessions
holden at Wells for the County of Somsett doe acknowledge John Syms and
his wife with fower small children to belong and be of the parish of Butleigh
aforesayd in the sayd County of somsett, and doe hereby promise and agree
to and with the parishoners of Evercreech, & if at any time hereafter
they shall become chargeable to the parish to receive them backe againe
into the parish of Butleigh as parishoners of the same. In witnesse
whereof wee have hereunto sett our handes even the thirteenth day
of Aprill in the yeare of our Lord God One thousand five hundred fifty
eight.

Richard Willins   Tho: Gyncocke   John Locke Minister

Walter   Hogges   Robert Talbott Churchwarden

Thomas   I T Gaylott   Edmund Ballew

margreat M Goose   Thomas Budden

walter   Parry

Nich: Pope
H

william Collins

Thomas Locke

william   Jour

John Perry

Richard King

John Burgham

1806
1558
248

Evercreech
13/3/1. 1.

Y

Indemnity Certificate for John Syme and family, 1658 (case 1).

[Case 1] **13 April 1658. John Syme.**
"We the parishioners of **Butleigh** whose names are subscribed (according to an order made by the justices of the peace at the last generall sessions holden at **Wells** for the county of Somerset doe acknowledge John Syme and his wife with fower small children to belong and be of the parish of Butleigh aforesayd in the sayd county of Somerset, and doe hereby promise and agree to and with the parishioners of **Evercreech**, [that] if at any time hereafter they shall become chargeable to the parish to receive them backe againe into the parish of Butleigh as parishioners of the same: In witnesse whereof wee have hereunto sett our handes even the thirteenth day of Aprill in the yeare of our Lord God one thowsand six hundred fifty eight."
Signed by
John Rocke, minister, Robert Talbott, churchwarden, Edward Catlow, Thomas Burdham, ?[Nicholas] Pope, William Collins, Thomas Looke, William Pery, John Perry, Richard King, John Burdham, Thomas Symcuks, Richard Billine, Wallter Parry.
The following names also appear, but with a '*mark*' beside them: Peter Hogges, Thomas Jasklett, Mergreat Cooke.
[S.R.O., indemnity certificate D/P/Evercreech 13/3/1.1]

[Case 2] **20 May 1667. Henry Gitto, otherwise Jenkins.**
William Wyndham and John Malet, magistrates.
Complaint has been made to the magistrates that Henry Gitto, otherwise Jenkins, has gone from **Minehead** and left his family. It is feared that his daughter will be chargeable to the parish, the overseers are directed to see that those persons who have any goods belonging to Henry Gitto, otherwise Jenkins, in their hands or custody are to provide for and maintain the child.
[S.R.O., miscellaneous poor law document D/P/Minehead St Michael 13/3/1.21.]

[Case 3] **1681. George Bartrume.**
George Bartrume, his wife and children, residing in the parish of **Stogumber**, have been given an indemnity certificate from the parish of **Crowcombe** dated 8 February 1667, at which date the statute of 14 Car. 11. c12.[1662] was in force, all certificates given before the expiration of that statute shall be good, legal and binding.
[S.R.O., D/P/Crowcombe 13/3/2.6.]
4 January 1696. George Bartrume and family.

Before P. Malet and G. Musgrave.

Complaint made by the churchwardens and overseers of Stogumber that the persons named below had intruded themselves into the parish intending to inhabit as parishioners, and as they may become chargeable they are to be removed to **Crowcombe**, which is understood to be the place of their last legal settlement:

George Bartrum senior, Jane his wife, Henry, Robert, Sarah and Prissilla his sons and daughters.

George Bartrum, son of the said George Bartrum the elder, Frances his wife, George, John, Richard, Elizabeth and Frances, his sons and daughters.

John Bartrum, another son of the said George Bartrum the elder, Sarah his wife, Elizabeth, Sarah and Mary their daughters.

Elizabeth Bartrum, another daughter of George the elder. Ann Bartrum, the youngest daughter of George the elder.

[S.R.O., Indemnity certificate D/P/Crowcombe 13/3/3,52.]

[Case 4] 30 August 1687.Elizabeth England.

"Elizabeth England, wife of William England of our said [**Taunton St Mary**] parish, barber, who is banished beyond the seas for being concerned in the late rebellion [of the Duke of Monmouth, 1685] and George England her son, for their better advantage and livelyhood are desirous to take their residence within your parish."

(Rodney Legg, who has studied the Monmouth episode, tells me: "The England family was deeply involved in the Western Rebellion, losing one member among the 257 who were executed judicially, and five among the 850 transported to the Caribbean. In all probability the Englands also figured among the 900 or so unknown victims of the Battle of **Sedgemoor** and subsequent instant 'justice'. Jonathan England was among the nineteen executed at Taunton on 30 September 1685, condemned by Lord Chief Justice Jeffreys at his Bloody Assize which toured the west. William's name occurs in the list of those transported, along with Allen England, John England, Philip England and Thomas England.")

[S.R.O., Indemnity certificate from Taunton St Mary to Taunton St James. D/P/Taunton St James 13/3/8.51.]

Consent given by Samuel Bindon, mayor. Benjamin Poole, alderman. Signed by, Walter Harte, vicar, Thomas Gale, Thomas [?Pirkes.], churchwardens. Nicholas Cross, John Smith, and Joseph Way, also signed.

[Case 5] 2 February 1688. Joane Jenner and Grace Griffith.

Francis Luttrell, magistrate.

Joane Jenner, widow, with three small children, and Grace Griffith, widow, a lame woman, both of the parish of **Minehead**, have made complaint to the magistrates that they are not receiving maintenance.

The churchwardens and overseers are ordered to give Joane Jenner one shilling and sixpence a week, and Grace Griffith is to be given one shilling each week, unless the parish officers can "show cause to the contrary".

[S.R.O., miscellaneous poor law document. D/P/Minehead St Michael 13/3/1.48.]

[Case 6] 1690. **Richard Hickes's family**.

Justices: W. Coward, Edward Berkley and George Long. Year and month not given.

The parishioners of **Baltonsborough** (Baltonsbury) complain that they are burdened with the three small children of Richard Hickes, who has absconded and left the children. The parishioners acknowledge that one of the children was born in Baltonsborough, but the other two, Mary and Jane, were born in **Worle** (Worll).

They were born at the time that Richard Hickes was serving, (being concerned in the late rebellion in the West.) [the Monmouth rebellion, 1685]. At that time his legal parish of settlement was not known, but was since discovered to be in Baltonsborough.

The parishioners of Baltonsborough are asking that Worle should contribute to the maintenance of the children.

[S.R.O.,miscellaneous. D/P/Baltonsborough 13/3/1.12.]

[Case 7] **11 May 1694. William Barnard and others.**

The churchwardens and overseers of the parish of **Wrington** have made complaint that several persons have lately intruded themselves into the parish, and are likely to become chargeable if they are allowed to continue to reside therein. The constables and tithingmen are to summon and warn these persons to depart out of the parish to the place of their last lawful abode, and if they refuse they are to be brought before the justices on Saturday 19 May, at the sign of the 'Kings Arms' at Wrington.

Signed by the justices, John Pigott and Edw. Baber.

A list of names follows, some of which have been deleted; these have not been transcribed:

William Barnard senior, and his wife. Charles Weaver. John Williams and his wife. Jonathan Briant. Sarah the horse rider (sic). Widow Baggs. [?Emanuell] Williams. Sarah Dobbs. Joseph Butt.

[S.R.O.,miscellaneous settlement paper. D/P/Wrington 13/3/7.1.]

[Case 8] **18 April 1699. William Godfrey and family**. This concerns an indemnity certificate from Cornwall.

William Godfrey, Hannah his wife, Samuell his son, and Hannah his daughter, have come from St Thomas by **Launceston** (Street of St Thomas) **Cornwall** to live in **Minehead**. The parish officers of St Thomas promise to receive the family back should they become chargeable to the parish of Minehead. They certify that William has an estate within the parish of St Thomas, and that he has always been a payer to the poor rate.

"And further we do certifie for his behavior and carrage when living among us in said Street to be so honest and just so quiet and peacable toward every person and so well able to instruct and bring up youth that it is a loss to us by his departure."

[*Signed by*] Francis Downing, mayor and John Bewes, and Henry White, churchwarden, William Parsons and Ruben Kingdom, overseers.

[S.R.O., Indemnity certificate, D/P/Minehead St Michael 13/3/1.60.]

[Case 9] **31 December 1701. William Bennett.** Heard before John Gilbert and Robert Balch.

William Bennett and Hannah his wife were removed from **Huntspill** to **Butleigh**, which parish was his birthplace and where he had his last legal settlement. Butleigh have given notice of an appeal.

William was born and lived most of his life at Butleigh, "about two or three days before the first of November last was twelve months" (sic) William came to the parish of Huntspill and made a covenant with Robert Leaker of Huntspill to serve him until Michaelmas following, which he did, and at Michaelmas agreed with Leaker again, and served until St Andrews tide [St Andrew's day, 30 November] following; and was paid by the week.

And having got one Hannah Cheeke with child, [William] went away, so that Hannah went before a justice of the peace, and swore that she was with child and that William Bennett was the father.

William was then apprehended and taken to Butleigh and kept in custody until he was married.

[S.R.O., settlement examination D/P/Huntspill 13/3/6.24.]

[31] December 1701. William Bennett and wife Hannah removed from Huntspill to Butleigh.

[S.R.O., D/P/Huntspill 13/3/1.50.]

[Case 10] **26 February 1710. John Paddon.** Heard before John Gilbert.

John Paddon, son of Simon Paddon, mason, late of Cannington, states that he was born at **Cannington**, he was aged twenty two years on 3 March 1703. In 1704 John contracted with William Rowe of **Enmore**, mason, to work with him weekly at seven shillings and sixpence a week (except Sundays, Holy days and rainy days, when he did not work). On 4 April 1805 he bound himself apprentice, by indenture, to William Rowe for four years. John lived with Rowe for over one year, he was then indisposed and Rowe cancelled the indenture, which he delivered to John Paddon who gave up the counterpart of the indenture to Rowe.

Whilst serving as an apprentice John Paddon had worked in the parishes of **Huish, Westonzoyland** and **Othery.** Since discharged from his apprenticeship John had worked mostly with Rowe, sometimes by the day and sometimes by the week.

On 25 March 1708 John contracted, in writing, with Rowe to serve him either as a covenant servant or as an apprentice for three years, he was to receive as much by the week as any other servant; he worked until the end of July, at that time, as Rowe had no work for him. John worked for Edward Needs and Thomas Davis in **Bridgwater** until St Andrew's day [30 November], when he was married. Since then he has worked for various people, but has made no contracts.

[*Mark.*]

[S.R.O., settlement examination D/P/Cannington 13/3/5.3.]

[Case 11] **7 November 1712. John Brockett, junior.**

Before Robert Strode, mayor and Robert Taylor. Examination taken at **Wells.**

John Brockett states that when he was serving as a soldier in Flanders he was married, at **Ghent,** to Margaret the widow of James Allen. Margaret had two children by two former husbands, Henry, now aged seven years, by James Allen and Archibald, aged nine years by Alexander Mackbrane, Henry was born in **Holland** and Alexander at the Moselle, or thereabouts, as John Brockett has been informed.

John had also made the above declaration to a justice in London before he was examined.

John and Margaret had one child of their own named Alice, aged two and a half years; Margaret died at **Dunkirk** about eleven weeks ago.

John further states that he had been informed that James Allen, father of Henry, was born at **Wicksworth** (Waxworth) in the Peak (Peack) of **Derbyshire** (Darbyshire), in **New Street** near **Warmwell.**

[*Mark.*]

[S.R.O., settlement examination D/P/Wells St Cuthberts 13/3/16.2.]

[Case 12] **13 May 1715. Stanford Birch.**

The justice taking the case is not named.

Stanford Birch states that he was born at **Bristol** as his father, who was a soldier under King William, was going for Ireland. Stanford was bound apprentice to Anthony Hutchinson of **Dublin,** clothier. Stanford served six years, then went into the Queen's service for three quarters of a year, he then returned to his master to finish his apprenticeship, his master refused to take him and turned him over to James Hustis of Dublin, where he stayed a year. As Stanford was going to visit his brother who lived in **Salisbury, Wiltshire**, he was prest into the Queen's service; and served until he was discharged at **Vigo** in **Spain**, which was about five or six years ago. Has since then lived about **Clutton**, with Abigail his wife, whom he married two years ago in **Cork, Ireland**.

[*Mark*.]

[S.R.O., settlement examination, D/P/Clutton 13/3/4.19.]

[Case 13] 29 March 1717. Robert Hinton, or Hetton.

Heard before Henry Strode and William Applin.

Robert Hinton states that he was born in the parish of **Mells**, where he lived and worked several year at scribbling [the first process in preparing wool for spinning, before carding]. Three years ago Robert made an agreement with Samuel Allen of the parish of **Temple, Bristol**, to serve him as a covenant servant for a year, his wages were to be £6 the first year. Robert served two more years, during which he received £7 a year.

The whole time that Robert served Allen he dwelt at **Frome** (Froom Selwood), where he looked after several work people who worked for Allen at the clothing trade.

Robert further states that he has done no other act to gain settlement; also that while he worked for Allen he had received his wages but not meat, drink, washing or lodging.

[*Signed*.]

2 May 1717. Ilchester sessions.

Opinion given by Abraham Gapper regarding the settlement of Robert Hinton.

Robert Hinton is not a parishioner of Mells. Frome should be his parish of settlement, although the agreement was made with Allen who lived in Bristol, as master Allen was able to send his servant to any place, and Robert had been living in Frome the whole of his three years service.

[S.R.O.,settlement examination D/P/Mells 13/3/3.46.]

[Case 14] 26 December 1718. Joel Toop.

Joel Toop, senior, Jane his wife, Abel and Jeremiah his sons and Jane his daughter, and Elizabeth Seirine his apprentice.

Indemnity certificates from **Berkeley, Gloucestershire** to **Beckington**.

[S.R.O., D/P/Beckington 13/3/5.26.]

30 September 1740. Abel Toop.

The churchwardens and overseers of the parish of Berkeley own and acknowledge Abel Toop, his wife Martha, John, Lydia, Sarah, James and

Elizabeth, to be parishioners settled in Berkeley.

[S.R.O., Indemnity certificate from Berkeley to Beckington. D/P/Beckington 13/3/5.1.]

Names of witnesses given, and document signed by churchwardens and overseers.

Two magistrates certify that Edward Pierce, one of the witnesses to the execution of the above certificate, made oath that he saw the churchwardens and overseers sign the above certificate, and the magistrates allow and confirm the same.

30 September 1740. Jeremiah Toop.

Jeremiah Toop, Mary his wife, William, Elizabeth, John, Anne, Abel, Sarah, Rachel and Hannah.

[S.R.O., indemnity certificate from Berkeley to Beckington. D/P.Beckington 13/3/5.23.]

See Alice Toope [case 50].

[Case 15] 22 March 1719. Jacob Channinge.

From the churchwardens and overseers of the parish of **Cheriton Fitzpaine, Devon**, to the parish officers of **Taunton St Mary**, requesting relief for Jacob Channinge, who is now residing in **Cheriton Fitzpaine**, and where he has lived for several years, and "by his honest labour maintained him selfe and famally but now being growne old and weake and of late visitted with sickness by reason whereof he cannot gett a sufficient mantainance nor suport him selfe but is forced to crave releef and we have releeved him with fair money".

Jacob is living in Cheriton Fitzpaine under an indemnity certificate from the parish of Taunton St Mary, dated 6 November 1684, and the parish officers of Taunton St Mary are asked to "order sufficient releef for the said Jacob Chaning and not suffer him to perish for want, in doing which you may save both yourselves and us from moor greater and unnecessary charges and performe the dutyes both of charitie and justice, desiring your answer wee subscribe ourselves".

[*Signed.*] Thomas Gibbs, churchwarden. John Kingston, Henry [?Bagtor] overseers.

[S.R.O., Poor law document. D/P/Taunton St Mary 13/3/10.6.]

[Case 16] 9 August 1721. George Buckland. Before George Thynne, mayor at Bath.

George Buckland, a cordwainer, states that he was born at **Tiverton, Devon**, and is lawfully married to Elizabeth, late Elizabeth Coles, by whom he has one child, also called George, who was born in the parish of **Temple, Bristol**, on 29 December last, and was christened at the parish church.

George further states that he has gained a legal settlement in Bristol, having lived there for five years and upwards until last May, and that he kept a cobblers stall in Redcliff Street and elsewhere in the city.

[*Signed.*]

[S.R.O., settlement examination. D/P/Bath St Michael 13/3/2.10.]

[Case 17] **23 May 1728. Joseph Holder.** Concerning the settlement of an infant, before Thomas Strangways Horner and William Long.

The parish officers of **Laverton** wish to remove Joseph Holder, an infant of the age of seven months, from Laverton to **Hemington**. It is likely that he would become chargeable to Laverton, and that Hemington is his legal parish of settlement.

The circumstances causing the infant to be removed: Joseph is the child of [blank] wife of Samuel Holder, and was clandestinely left at Laverton by her. Samuel Holder is legally settled at Hemington, and has an estate in that parish of £30 per annum, although it is under mortgage to Michael Holder, father of Samuel and grandfather of Joseph.

This estate is now in Michael's possession, Samuel having absconded three or four years ago. Joseph was born so lately that the grandfather would feign bastardise the child, which it is presumed cannot be done as the child was born in wedlock.

Michael Holder is a man of very good substance, he rents two farms and has an estate of his own.

The case is set out for counsel's opinion:

As any person leaving their wife and family on the parish enables the parish officers to seize his goods and chattles, rents and profits in order to provide for the child.

Does this apply to a freehold estate for life? (as the statute does not say lands and tenements as well as goods and chattles) [5 Geo.1.c8].

As the parish of Hemington cannot (without an appeal) fix the pauper on the grandfather, how are the parish officers to proceed?

Can the parish officers (by a summons under the hand of one justice) summon the grandfather to appear at the quarter session, or can the bench make an order upon him? (To relieve the pauper) [43 Eliz.1.c2].

Is it necessary to prove the marriage of the mother and father, to fix it on the grandfather?

29 June 1728. Counsel's opinion. Given by H. Colman.

As the pauper is under seven years of age, and therefore cannot gain a settlement for himself, the order of removal is wrong. The question should be, where was the father's settlement? As there is no account of cohabitation between the husband and wife for three or four years, such child, although

46

born in wedlock, is naturally a bastard, in which case the place of birth is the place of settlement (there should have been a bastardy order made).

The grandfather is bound to relieve the child, and the rents and profits of the freehold estate are liable to seizure by a warrant from the justices. It is not necessary to prove the marriage of the mother and her husband.

[S.R.O.,Removal order and counsel's opinion. D/P/Hemington 13/3/2.13.]

17 July 1728. Maintenance order.

Michael Holder ordered to pay two shillings a week for the maintenance of his grandson Joseph, son of Samuel. Order made at general quarter sessions, **Bridgwater.**

[S.R.O., D/P/Hemington 13/3/3.12.]

[Case 18] 7 August 1731. Felix Phillips and wife Elizabeth.

Indemnity certificate from the churchwardens and overseers of the parish of **St Mary Magdalen, Taunton** to the churchwardens and overseers of the poor of the parish of **Silverton** (Sylverton) in the county of **Devon.**

The parish officers of St Mary Magdalen certify that Felix Phillips and his wife Elizabeth are legally settled in the parish of St Mary Magdalen.

Signed by: George Stibbs, John Paine, Robert Culverwell, Joseph Case, Thomas Rowswell.

Above certificate allowed by:

Signed by: Thomas Graunt, mayor. Jo. Hassum, jun. justice.

[S.R.O., Indemnity certificate D/P/Taunton St Mary 13/3/8.288.]

5 February 1759, Ann Phillips.

Examination and vagrant's pass from **Exeter, Devon**, before Richard Densham, mayor.

Ann Phillips, apprehended wandering and begging in the parish of **St Martin, Exeter**, states that she was born in the parish of **St Thomas the Apostle** [Exeter].

Five and a half year ago she was married in the church of **St John**, Exeter, to Felix Phillips, sergeweaver. Her husband had told her that he was a freeman of **Taunton Dean**, and that his legal parish of settlement was in **St Mary Magdalen, Taunton**. Ann further states that she has begged and received charity in the parish of St Martin, Exeter.

Ann is to be conveyed to the parish of St Thomas the Apostle and from there to be sent to Taunton.

[S.R.O., settlement examination and vagrant's pass D/P/Taunton St Mary 13/3/4.32.]

[Case 19] 1735. Thomas Davis.

Before William Portman. Date and month not known.

Thomas Davis, residing at **Croscombe**, states that he was born in that parish; he was bound apprentice to William Clark of Wells Forum, but Clark lived under a discharge [indemnity certificate] lawfully given by the parish of Croscombe. Robert Board was one of the parish officers that gave the certificate but Thomas has forgotten the other officers' names.

[*[Mark.*]

S.R.O., settlement examination D/P/Croscombe 13/3/1.21.]

[Case 20] **21 August 1736. James Gillard.**

Before William Peirs.

James Gillard, husbandman, on his oath, states that eighteen years ago John Hollard of **Ditcheat** (Ditchet) and Mary Brown of **North Wootton** (Wooten) desired him to go with them to be married. They went to a place near **Bath**, where a man in a black coat who was reputed to be a parson read over the matrimony to them, and James Gillard gave John Hollard in marriage to Mary Brown.

They afterwards lived together as man and wife; but for some years past John Hollard has left the parish, supposedly on account of debts. James also declares that sixteen years ago he was summoned concerning the marriage and at that time gave the same account.

[*Mark.*]

[S.R.O., witness gives information. D/P/Ditcheat 13/3/7.1.] See case 21.

[Case 21] **30 September 1736. Mary Hollard alias Powell.**

Before William Peirs.

Mary Hollard alias Powell on her oath declares that about eighteen years ago she was married, near **Bath**, to John Hollard of **Ditcheat** (Ditchett) by a man she believed to be a clergyman, for he wore a gown and declared himself to be a parson. They returned to Ditcheat and lived some months as man and wife.

[*Mark.*]

[S.R.O., gives information. D/P/Ditcheat 13/3/7.2.] See case 20.

[Case 22] **28 September 1738. Elizabeth Shears, otherwise Jelly.**

Before John Bailey.

Elizabeth,the wife of Henry Shears, now residing in **Bruton**, states that twelve years ago she married Thomas Jelly of the parish of **Pitcombe**. Thomas lived with her about eighteen weeks, he then enlisted as a soldier, she has heard and believes that he went to **Gibraltar**.

Elizabeth had not heard from her husband for eleven years, and thinking him to be dead many years, she married Henry Shears, this was two and a half years ago. Elizabeth is now expecting a child by Henry.

[Mark.]

[S.R.O., settlement examination D/P/Bruton 13/3/8.8.]

22 April 1751. Elizabeth Jelly, otherwise Woods.

An inventory of goods seized and distrained by Thomas Mogg, in the house of Elizabeth Jelly otherwise Woods, for a sum of seventeen shillings, for rent due to Thomas Mogg at Lady Day last:

"One square tableboard and form, 1 small iron crock and pott hookes, 1 water pail, 1 bed, bolster and 1 green rugg, 1 pillow, 1 box iron heaters, 1 spinning turn and reel."

Subscribed: Note addressed to Elizabeth Jelly otherwise Woods.

Moggs locked the goods in the house where John Jelly lately lived and died, and if Elizabeth does not pay the rent or reply the goods will be sold in five days time.

Signed by Thomas Mogg.

[S.R.O., D/P/Pitcombe 13/3/5.1.]

15 February 1752. Elizabeth, wife of Thomas Jelly.

Before Thomas Coward and Hill Dawe.

Elizabeth Jelly states that her maiden name was Elizabeth Davidge, she was born in Pitcombe. Twenty six years ago she was married by licence to Thomas Jelly at **Horsington**.

Thomas, a linenweaver, and Elizabeth had cohabited at Pitcombe and other places for about a year, they had a son born in **Bristol**.

About three months after they were married her husband enlisted as a soldier; a year later he was sent to Gibraltar, and remained beyond the seas for nineteen years.

After Thomas had been gone for nine years Elizabeth married Henry Shears, at **Wincanton**, they cohabited for three years, she had a son, born at **Bruton** and christened Leonard Shears, who was now aged fourteen.

A year after Henry died Elizabeth married George Woods of Pitcombe. They were married by licence at **Shepton Montague**, they cohabited and Elizabeth had by him a son, named Thomas, who is now aged seven, and a daughter Mary aged nine years, both children were born at Bruton.

Elizabeth believes that Thomas Jelly is now living in the garrison at **Plymouth**.

[Mark.]

[S.R.O., settlement examination D/P/Pitcombe 13/3/4.2.]

14 March 1752. Leonard Shears.

To be removed from Pitcombe to Bruton. Leonard's mother named as Elizabeth Jelly.

[S.R.O., removal order D/P/Bruton 13/3/2.20.]

23 September 1759. Elizabeth Shears, or Sheers, otherwise Jelly.

The churchwardens and overseers of Pitcombe do own and acknowledge Elizabeth Shears otherwise Jelly to be legally settled in Pitcombe.

John Bishop and William Baker witnessed the churchwardens and overseers signing the above certificate.

Certificate allowed by Thomas Coward and W.Rodbard (JPs).

[S.R.O., indemnity certificate D/P/Bruton 13/3/6.92.]

[Case 23] **20 March 1739. Mary Henley, wife of Robert.**

Before George Bisse. She was late of **Windsor**, Berkshire.

Mary Henley states that she was born at **Halwell** (Holwell) **Devonshire**. When she was eleven years old she was placed by her parents to Robert Brown of **Harburton** (he was a near relation). Mary stayed with him until she was aged twenty one years. During that time she was provided with wearing apparel, but did not receive any wages, her parents not having made any agreement that she should be paid.

At the beginning of June past she was married to Robert Henley, a cordwainer, at **Windsor**, in which parish her husband had told her he was legally settled, but she later learned that this was not so. Robert and Mary lived together for two weeks, then Robert left her and she does not know where he has gone.

Mary, who was with child by her husband, intended to return to her relations and friends in Devon, as she was returning there on foot, on Shrove Tuesday last [18 February 1739] being on the road between Bristol and **Berrow**, Somerset, she was overtaken by one Charles Page who was driving two horses, and with whom she bargained to carry her on horseback to **Bridgwater**, for which she would pay two shillings.

Page took her to his dwelling in **Chapel Allerton** where she "lay that night and was then unexpectedly taken with travell, and called to the said Pages wife to make her all the assistance she could in order to her delivery, but she was doing her no service at all".

The next morning Page, at the instigation of his wife, took Mary on horseback to **Blackford** [near **Wedmore**], he put her down a little way before the village, and directed her to go to the public house, where soon afterwards she was delivered of a female child; and where Mary has remained until this time, and has been maintained by the parish of Wedmore.

[*Mark.*]

[Case 24] **19 October 1739. Cowell family.**

Before James Strode and Thomas Coward.

Charles and Rebecca Cowell, residing at **Croscombe** in 1739 had four children. Removal orders exist for all these children, they are to be removed, each child to a different parish. The information contained in these orders was obtained from the mother Rebecca.

Rebecca, aged five years, to be removed to **Claines, Worcestershire.**

Charles, aged four years, to be removed to **Ledbury, Herefordshire.**

William, aged two years, to be removed to **St Davids, Exeter, Devon.**

Rose, aged threequarters of a year, to be removed to **Shepton Mallet.**

There is no indication that these children have been born out of wedlock.

The parish register for Claines shows that Rebecca daughter of John (sic) Cowel and Rebecca his wife, was baptised 13 October 1734. (Information from the Hereford and Worcester Record Office, which is hereby gratefully acknowledged.)

[S.R.O., Removal orders D/P/Croscombe 13/3/2. nos. 4,5,6,7.]

(Prior to 1743-44 bastards took their settlement from their birthplace. It was not until 1781-82 that children under the age of seven could not be separated from their mother.)

[Case 25] **4 March 1740. Edward Felton.**

Before George Bisse.

Edward Felton, a tailor, residing at **Mark**, states that he was born in that parish, where his parents lived. When Edward was about eleven years old his father died, and Edward went to live with his uncle John Felton, clothier, in the parish of **Stogursey**, his uncle treated him as a relative and not as a hired servant, finding all neccessaries for him.

After two years Edward was apprenticed by his uncle to John Dyer of Nether Stowey, tailor, for a term of nine years, which apprenticeship Edward served for six years, he then ran away "deserted his masters service and strolled about the country in a loos idle way of life about ten yeares".

Edward then came to **Bristol** where he worked as a journeyman tailor for several masters, but never for a whole year. He was married at **Clifton** three years ago.

[*Mark.*]

[S.R.O., settlement examination D/P/Mark 13/3/4.8.]

[Case 26] **29 May 1740. Abraham Harris, labourer.**

Before Dodington Sherston, mayor, and John Tutton. Examination taken at **Wells.**

Abraham Harris states that he was born at **Bishops Hull**, and lived there until he was old enough to labour, he then went to **Ilminster** and drove the plough for Mr Humphrey Pitts. He was paid three pence a day and had his victuals. Abraham then hired himself to Mr Thomas Dorster [sic, probably Mr Dorchester] of **Isle Brewers**, his wages to be four pounds and ten shillings a year, which employment he followed for over three years. After that service, Abraham, with others, went about the country mowing.

At **Glastonbury** he was impressed to serve as a marine under Brigadier Hull, Abraham was then about eighteen or nineteen years of age. He served as a marine for nearly eleven years, and has done no act to gain a settlement since he served Mr Dorster.

[*Mark.*]

S.R.O., settlement examination. D/P/Wells St Cuthberts 13/3/16.74.]

[Case 27] **1 July 1740. Concerning J.D.**

In the following abstract, which is a case requiring legal opinion, the protagonist and the parishes are identified only by initial letters. As it is included in the **Portbury** parish deposit it is reasonable to suppose that the parish designated by the letter 'P' refers to Portbury.

'J.D.' had a wife and five children. He rented a farm at 'P', after several years it failed, whereupon the landlord seized his stock (except two cows, two heifers and a mare, which 'J.D.' had clandestinely moved off), but the stock was not enough by £40 to pay the rent.

At Lady Day 1739 'J.D.'s wife, by lease parole [an unsealed contract, probably verbal] took an estate in 'W', for three years at an annual rent of £28. She had the key of the house, and all the profits of the estate from that time, but 'J.D.' and his family did not go there to live until midsummer 1739, they stayed until 25 January following (being half a year) and paid fifty shillings in rates and taxes.

On 25 January his landlord at 'W' seized his stock and effects (which were more than sufficient to pay the half year's rent), thereupon 'J.D.' absconded and left his wife and children, who returned to 'P' from whence the parish officers drove them back to 'W'. The family were relieved by the parish of 'W' until 26 June 1740, at which date they were brought back to 'P' by an order; although the husband was included in the order he was still absent, and therefore could not be brought back.

When 'J.D.'s wife took the lease her husband never saw the landlord; his stock only consisted of two heifers, two cows and a mare. 'J.D.' was still in debt to his former landlord.

'J.D.' then applied to the parish officers of 'P' to advance him £12 to enlarge his stock, and as the landlord insisted upon the rent due to him being paid, the parish officer did advance the £12.

When examined before the justices 'J.D.' swore that his stock was not worth £10 a year, his wife first having declared that it was, 'but at length she was prevailed upon to swear that they had not'.

Question to counsel:

Has 'J.D.' gained a legal settlement in 'W' or not, and can the advance of £12 by the parish of 'P' defeat 'J.D.' and family gaining a settlement in 'W'?

1 July 1740. Counsel's opinion.

Given by W. Cann, **Bristol**.

"'J.D.' would have gained a settlement in 'W' had he come to reside there at Lady Day in 1739 when the parole lease commenced, but "however as 'J.D.' appears to be an obscure person sometimes residing in one place, and sometimes in another (besides him being incompetent to stock an estate to the value of £10 per annum) I am of the opinion that it will be fruitless to appeal from the order of the [two justices] and that the advance of the £12 by the parish of 'P' was plainly a crafty device to ease themselves of this pauper and his numerous family, and to fix them on the parish of 'W', but the law will not establish settlements grounded on such kind of artifices, and it has been expressly held that when the residence of the pauper is obscure and uncertain he cannot gain a legal settlement".

[*Signed by* W. Cann.]

[S.R.O., Counsel's opinion D/P/Portbury 13/3/3.28.]

[Case 28] **27 October 1740. Elizabeth Smith, wife of Joseph.**

Due to a misunderstanding the unfortunate Elizabeth and her two children have been sent from **Durham** to **Bridgwater** – they should have been sent to **Bridgnorth, Shropshire**.

Document No.1.

Elizabeth Smith, wife of Joseph Smith and their two daughters, Ann aged seven and Jane aged four years, have been apprehended in the parish of **St Nicholas**, Durham, where Elizabeth was found wandering and begging. She is to be sent to Bridgwater in the county of Somerset, where her husband was born.

[S.R.O., D/B/bw. 1918. folder 5. (Bridgwater borough archives). Vagrants pass.]

Document No.2.

15 November 1740. Letter from Joseph Smith. Written from Birmingham: "My dear I reeryed yrs from **Worcester** (Woster) but itt was 4 days after you left itt and was glad to hear of yr being in health and the childer. But am grived to the hart to think what truble and hardship you have had and I wonder what took you to that Bridgewater so fare out of your way and to be so mestaken to call itt Bridgewater insteed of Bridge North which you have oftims heard me speak of my frends that lived between Birmingham and Bridgnorth so as I found you wear mestaken in the place of my parish I went to my officer and he has writt to the mair or Justice of the place to send you hear so do not be desmaied for if they do not send you hear when they geat this send me a letter derectly and if you do for eather (sic) Bridgnorth send me a letter befor you sett out and if you com to Bridgnorth I will meat you there but beg the Majgestrats to send you to Birmingham for it is 12 miles nearer for you and not have to com back again so how ever itt hapen send me a letter and derect for me at the signe of the windmill in **Digbeth** (Digdbalh) Birmingham the Lord derect you and be with [you] which is the harty desir of him who is your loveing and affecatent husband till death."

[*Signed.*]

[S.R.O., D/B/bw. 1918. folder 2.]

Document No.3.

15 November 1740. Letter from ? Moses Moran Esq. From Birmingham; ? Constable:

"Worshipfull, I do under stand that there is a solders wife bee longing to our Ridgmet that is com to your toun through a mistake by us here, she not knowing rightly her husband's parish calling it 'Brigg Watter' in stead of Bridgnorth shee never being in England with her husband as I doo supose did not know the differance, and often hearing him say that hee would goo to see his father and mother with other frends that hee has there. And I can asure you, sir, that it is his parish because I listed him there my own self about twelve years a gow. Hee be heaving his selfe hoistly and soberly as also his wife bearing an extroedaery good cracter among us.

"Sir the man is very uneasy about his wife and tow childer and I am afraid that hee will take liberty of his own accord to go in search of her there for Sir I desire the faver of you that you would send her to her respectouf parish to Bridg North or Birmingham where hee intends to send her to his parents and in so doing you will oblidge. Sir your most humble servant."

[*Signed.*]

[S.R.O., D/B/bw. 1918. folder 2. (Bridgwater borough records.)]

It would appear that the 3rd Regiment of Foot was the most likely one in which Joseph Smith could have been serving, also known as The Buffs. The regiment was stationed in **Scotland** 1729 to 1731, and 1738 to 1740. As it was stated that Elizabeth "was never in England" it is probable that Joseph and Elizabeth were married in Scotland.

Assistance in researching this case has come from the National Army Museum, and The Buffs Regimental Museum, Canterbury, and is gratefully acknowledged.

[Case 29] **24 November 1740. Thomas Harrison.**
Before Joseph Houlton and . . . Hayward.
Thomas Harrison, residing in **Rode**, states that he is aged forty eight years, he was born in **Manchester, Lancashire**, where he lived with his parents until he was twelve years old. At that age he was apprenticed by indenture to John Tomlinson, a barber surgeon, in the town of **Ashbourne** (Ashbornham) in the **Peak, Derbyshire**. Thomas lived with Tomlinson for six and a half years.

He then entered the late Queen's service, General Macartney Regiment of Foot, and served therein until the peace of Arleuk [5 August 1711]. Thomas then entered in Brigadier Kerr's Regiment of Marines, and went to Ireland, where he stayed until 1721.

Thomas then came to Rode, and has resided there and in the neighbouring parish of **North Bradley, Wiltshire**, ever since. Sixteen years ago he was married to Mary Payne, by whom he has three children, Betty fourteen years old, Charles twelve and James six. Thomas further states that he has done no act to gain a settlement since serving his apprenticeship.

[*Signed..*]
[S.R.O., settlement examination, D/P/Rode 13/3/1.14.]

[Case 30] **14 April 1741. John Morel.**
Before Richard Champneys and Thomas Baynard.
John Morel, a dyer, residing at **Frome** (Froom), states that he is aged seventy one years, and was born in **Vitry-le-Francois** (Vitre) in the Province of Britannia in the Kingdom of **France**. He lived there with his mother and father. At the age of fourteen as his father was dead, he and his mother went to live in Jersey, where they stayed seven years, then removed to **Guernsey**.

After about two years there John was sent, by his mother, to **Plymouth, Devonshire**, to learn the "English tongue".

John lived in Plymouth with his English tutor eleven months. He was then pressed as a sailor to go on board the *Victory* man of war.

John was discharged after eleven months, and then travelled about the country asking for work until he came to **Mells**, here John worked for twenty two months as a journeyman dyer, his master being Mr Thomas Snook, from whom John received three shillings a week and his victuals.

John then went to Frome and hired himself as a covenant servant to Samuel Norman, dyer, at the yearly wages of £8 and meat, drink, washing and lodging. After two years John returned to Mells and again worked as a covenant servant for Mr Snook for a year. John was then hired by Mr Snook to serve him as a dyer of wool at the same wages and conditions that he had received from Mr Norman.

John served two years under this covenant and then married his present wife Margarett, by whom he has two sons, John and Mathew who are both living in London, and a daughter Mary, who is living with them in Frome. John has not gained a settlement in any parish except Mells.

[*Signed.*]

The *Victory* in which John Morel was pressed, c1692, had previously been known as *Royal James*, becoming the *Victory* in 1691. In 1714 the vessel was again renamed, this time as *Royal George*. In 1715 the name reverted to *Victory*.

The vessel was burnt by accident in 1721, and was not repaired.

John Morel would have served during a period of intense naval activity, which culminated in the peace of Ryswick in 1697.

This information is from the National Maritime Museum, whose help is gratefully acknowledged.

[S.R.O., settlement examination DD/LW. 7.50. (Lewis of Frome)]

[Case 31] 9 June 1741. Samuel Jeans.

Before Edward Jones and George Bisse.

Samuel Jeans, residing **Huntspill**, states that he was born in **Burnham**. At the age of nine years he went and lived with his mother Ann (the wife of Thomas Leaker) in Huntspill.

Four years ago Samuel agreed with William Body, gentleman, of Huntspill, "for a piece of meadow or pasture ground containing eight acres (more or less) which Samuel was to hold from All Saints Day [1 November] to Candlemas [2 February] come twelve month following". The rent of the land was £10.0s.0d., but William Body valued this piece of ground at £8 per annum, and the grass to be worth £2.

Body had told Samuel that he would only allow him to rent the ground if he would continue his tenancy for a further year to the next Candlemas.

[*Signed.*]

[S.R.O., settlement examination D/P/Huntspill 13/3/6.21.]

9 December 1741. Samuel Jeans, or Janes. He and his family removed from Huntspill to Burnham.

[S.R.O., Huntspill 13/3/1.47.]

[Case 32] 15 October 1741. Haines Ryall.

Before George Dodington Esq.

Haines Ryall, shopkeeper, states that he was born at **Thornford, Dorset** and is now of the age of forty two years.

When he was fourteen years old he was bound apprentice for seven years, by indenture, to Joseph Tuck of Thornford, linenweaver. He served out his apprenticeship and then worked as follows:

Two years as a journeyman at **Fordingbridge, Hampshire**. One year as covenant servant with Mr Shatfield, a tea merchant in **London**.

Two years with Mr Wyat, a turkey merchant in **Charterhouse Square, London**. Four to five years with Madam Torriano in **Putney, Surrey**, at the wages of £10 a year. Two or three years with Richard King, his brother-in-law [step brother, probably], with whom he lived as a tabler [getting meals for services rendered].

Next to **Charleton Horethorne** where Haines married the Reverend Mr Edgar's daughter, and lived with him as a tabler over a year.

Four to five years ago rented a house and a pair of leases [meadows, possibly with common rights] in **Horsington** from Mr Robert Wadham, for which he paid £4.14s.0d. a year.

From 1736 until 1739 he rented a ground in Horsington from Martin Wadham at the rent of £3 a year.

In 1738-39 he also rented a house and orchard from Mr John Wadham, senior, paying £3.5s.0d. In 1738 Wadham gave him back £1.5s.0d.,as apples were scarce that year.

In 1738 Haines let John Wadham's house to Mary Pierce and Anthony Waite junior for twenty shillings a year each.

[*Signed*.]

[S.R.O., settlement examination D/P/Horsington 13/3/6.15.]

[Case 33] **4 May 1742. John Stacy.**
Before George Dodington.

John Stacy, linenweaver, states that he was born at **Horsington**, and is aged forty-seven years.

At the age of fourteen his father covenanted with John Brine, son of James Brine of **Combe Throop, Templecombe** (Comb Throop), linenweaver. John Stacy was to serve three years with Brine in order to learn the trade of a linenweaver, at the end of three years he was to have £12 for his work and service. John did whatever Brine required of him, such as tending masons, and working in the garden. John served over two years, when they had some small differences and John left Brine's employment, he had received several sums of money during his service which amounted to over £4.

John then worked as a journeyman linenweaver to the following employers:
Richard Leir of **Cucklington** for three years.
Jonathan Ryal of Whitchurch, **Henstridge** for two years.
William Ellory of **Stallen** at **Nether Compton** (Compton Staling), **Dorset**, for two years.
John Helliar of Whitchurch, Henstridge for over two years.

During all his services his employers provided lodging and small beer, whilst he was with Brine his father found him in victuals, clothes and washing, when working as a journeyman John found himself in victuals. When a journeyman John worked "by the piece".

Twenty-one years ago John was married, and has lived in Horsington working as a journeyman weaver and other labouring work ever since.

[*Signed*.]

11 June 1742. Counsel's opinion. Regarding John Stacy's settlement, given by William Churchey.

Unless a derivative or subsequent settlement in his own right can be found, he is settled by birth in the parish of Horsington, and that settlement has not been destroyed by any of the facts stated in the examination.

[S.R.O., settlement examination D/P/Horsingston13/3/6.23.]

[Case 34] **8 June 1742. Benjamin Browne.**

Before George Doddington.

Benjamin Browne, carpenter, states that he was born at **Shaftesbury** (Shaston), **Dorset**, and is now aged twenty eight.

When he was thirteen years old, the trustees of Mr Lush of Shaftesbury bound him by indenture to Thomas Hannam of **Horsington**, carpenter, his period of service to be seven years.

Benjamin served over one year, he then returned to Shaftesbury and lived with his friends there, working at his trade and as a sawyer, and remained there until ten years ago, at which time he married; and rented a house there from John Parrot, which house was of the value of twenty eight shillings.

Benjamin further states that he paid, in his own right, the king's tax, church tax and poor tax for six years and up to last Easter. He has also voted several times for members of parliament as a parishioner and inhabitant in Shaftesbury. He has gained no other settlement, except as stated above.

[*Signed*.]

[S.R.O., settlement examination D/P/Horsington 13/3/6.17.]

[Case 35] **1744. Eleanor Hellyar.**

An order for the removal of Eleanor, wife of William Hellyar from **Symondsbury**, Dorset, to **Lovington** (Luffington). Undated, apart from the year.

Eighteen years ago William was married to Mary Hembury of **Curry Rivel**, spinster, at the city of **Bath**, by a person in a black coat and band, whom the said Mary Hembury apprehended to be a clergyman, but has since been informed that he was a layman.

The matrimonial ceremony of the Church of England was read over and a ring was properly made use of, and the same was performed in a private room in a dwelling house and not in a church or chapel.

William and Mary lived as man and wife for nine or ten years, but have not lived together since. On 10 June 1742 William Hellyar was married to Eleanor in the parish church of Symondsbury by licence (during the life of Mary).

Taken from *Decisions of the Court of King's Bench*. Sir Jas Burrows, London 1786.

[S.R.O., DD/X/JF. 15.]

[Case 36] **12 February 1745. Thomas Node.**

Examination taken in Gloucestershire, before Robert Cann.

Thomas Node states that he was born in the parish of **Mells**, he had not gained a settlement in any other parish. For the last five years he had "travelled about the country gathering raggs and buying and selling rabit string" [noose traps] for a livelyhood.

Last Monday sennight (seven night) he was very sick and weak, and had no money, this was in the parish of **Henbury**, where some persons took care of him.

He further states that six years ago he was married to his wife Mary, in the church of St Mary Magdalen, **London**.

[*Mark*.]

[S.R.O.,settlement examination D/P/Mells 13/3/3.86.]

[Case 37] **4 November 1747. William Parfit.**

William Parfit, residing **Mells**, states that he is thirty five years old, and was born at **Shepton Mallet**, in his infancy he was carried to his grandfather John Snook, at Babington, where William lived until his grandfather died.

He then worked at the coal pits until about five years ago, when he went to **Leigh on Mendip**, where he also worked at the coal pits, for two years, then he and his family moved to Mells. At Leigh on Mendip, William had married Anne Turner, they had two children, John three years old and Mary two years.

[Blank]

[SRO., settlement examination D/P/Mells 13/3/3.9.]

[Case 38] **16 June 1748. John Hillard.**

Before Thomas Coward and Samuel Hill.

John Hillard, residing **Ditcheat** states that he was born in the parish of Ditcheat and is now aged twenty eight. He lived for several years in Ditcheat, and then went to **Melbury Bubb, Dorset**, where he was hired by Fitz Walter Foy to serve him for a year. John served for two and a half years.

While in Melbury Bubb he was sworn to and served the office of tithingman for two years. John further states that he has done no other act to gain a settlement.

[*Mark.*]

The above document also contains a declaration by John Hillard that: "On 16 June Abra Clare of Ditcheat, widow, sold to him one pint of cyder, for which he paid Abra Clare one penny farthing."

[S.R.O., settlement examination D/P/Ditcheat 13/3/3.5.]

[Case 39] **1 March 1749. Robert Coombe.**

Before Jno. Pigott and Ed. Jones.

Robert Coombe, residing **Meare**, states that he was born at **Mark**, and lived there with his parents until he was seventeen years old; at that age he agreed to serve Ferdinando Board of Mark for a quarter of a year. Robert then made a contract with John Jennett of **Stone Allerton**, whom he served from the beginning of May until the following Lady Day, his wages were £2.17s.6d.

Robert next went to Richard Westover of **Chapel Allerton**, where he served one year from Lady Day, and where his wages were three guineas a year. However, as he fell sick for two weeks during that time his master kept back two shillings and sixpence from his wages to pay another person to do Robert's work.

Soon after this service Robert was married, at Meare. He then rented an estate there for which he paid £13.10s.0d. a year, and lived there two years.

During the first year Robert only had three heifers and a mare of his own with which to stock the estate, as well as six [co]ws which he hired from his landlord. The second year Robert stocked the same estate with nine beasts and the mare, all of which were his own property. He also rented some more land, for which he paid twenty-seven shillings yearly; he now resides at the latter property.

[*Mark*]

[S.R.O., settlement examination D/P/Meare 13/3/1.6.]

[Case 40] **30 May 1750. William Cole.**

Before A. Gapper, Thomas Medlycott and James Chaffey Cowper.

William Cole, perukemaker [a wigmaker], residing **Queen Camel**, states that he is thirty years old and was born in the parish of **Botolph, Allgate,** in the manor of **East Smithfield, Middlesex.**

At the age of fourteen years he was bound apprentice, by indenture, to his father William Cole, which apprenticeship he served, and afterwards worked with his father for three years at the wages of £16 a year.

For half a year he rented a house (at £20 per annum) in the parish of **Allhallows, London Wall**, but only paid one quarter's rent. Sometime later he went as a volunteer on board the *Chatham* man of war, after four months he fell sick and was taken to **Deal Hospital, Kent**, for one month, from there William was removed to **Guys** (Guises) **Hospital, Southwark**, where he remained six weeks.

Several times since he had served His Majesty as a sailor, until two years ago when he was discharged.

William then came to Queen Camel, where he lived as a lodger and carried on the business of perukemaker.

[*Signed*.]

Further examination in the form of questions and answers regarding William Cole's service:

[Questions]

The time he entered the **Chatham** man o' war was he made over or discharged. The name of the commander.

The names of other men o' war on which he served, and the names of their commanders.

The time he entered and the time he was discharged.

How was he removed from the King's Hospital at Deal to Guy's Hospital.

The name of the last man o' war on which he served.

The name of the commander.

The time he entered and the time he was discharged, and did he receive his pay.

[Answers]

The beginning of March [17]42-43 went on board the *Chatham* man o' war. Discharged and sent to Deal Hospital in July. Captain Townshend, commander.

He removed himself from Deal to Guys for "the sake of his recovery" 1743.

The last man o' war on which William Cole served was the *Barfleur*; Mr West, commodore, Captain John Orme, commander.

Discharged at **Hill House, Chatham,** 7 June 1748.

A note in this document refers to the Act under which William Cole claims protection to live anywhere unmolested [5 Elizabeth, 1562-63]. It is pointed out that although any soldier or sailor may do so whilst exercising their trade, it does not give a settlement, and if the parish has reason to expect that a soldier or sailor will become chargeable they have the power to remove him.

Also it is necessary that all details of his service should be given as deserters cannot claim such protection.

Further information regarding William Cole:

William Cole rented a house in Broad Street, Allhallows, for six months, from Mr Cook, who was a hatter in the Borough of Southwark, between Mr Gambal's, a butcher, and the sign of the 'White Bear'.

In [17]43 William entered on board the Chatham, after four months service, as he was sick, he was put ashore. When recovered William entered on board the *Friends Adventure*, a tender on the *Pearl* man o' war, after three months the ship was put out of service, and William was discharged. He then entered on the *Royal Sovereign*, a guard ship, where he served twenty months, then served on the *Barfleur* for nine months, until he was paid off at **Chatham**, by Commodore Brown.

[S.R.O., settlement examination D/P/Queen Camel 13/3/2.26.]

[Case 41] **Isaac Everson.**

Before John Madox Esq. and Giles Hall, clerk.

Isaac Everson, apprehended as a rogue and vagabond, in the parish of **Frome**, states that he is aged twenty three years, he was born in **Cripplegate, London**, and where he had lived for five years after his parents died; since which time he has travelled the country, grinding razors and knives. Last Christmas he married Ann Sutton, widow, who had two children by a former husband.

[*Mark*.]

2 July 1750. Isaac Everson, his wife Ann and her children Eleanor, ten years old, and James, three years, were apprehended on 30 June 1750 in the parish of Frome (Froom), they are to be removed to the parish of Cripplegate.

To be conveyed on horseback to **Corsley, Wiltshire**.

The tythingman to be allowed seven shillings and sixpence [account endorsed].

The justices then direct the constables of Frome to pay a reward of twenty shillings to John Sheppard for apprehending and conveying the vagrants (that is to say ten shillings each). This sum is to be paid within one week after demand, this will be allowed by the treasurers of the county upon production of this order and a receipt from John Sheppard.

John Sheppard received his reward on 6 July 1750, paid to him by Mr William Parsons, one of the constables of Frome.

The cost of apprehending and passing vagrants was paid by the county.

One single horse 4 miles at 1½d. per mile	6d.
Sustaining 3 vagrants 4 days and nights [presumably two children counted as one vagrant] when not travelling	4s
When travelling	1s.
Provision for the officer	6d.
Provender for the horse	6d.
Certificate	1s.

[S.R.O., Q/FA.23.13. (Quarter sessions deposit, treasurers accounts.] (I am grateful to David Hawkings for drawing my attention to this deposit.)

[Case 42] **15 July 1751. Joseph Willmott.**
Before George Somerville.

Joseph Willmott, a blacksmith, residing at **Shepton Mallet** (Mallett), states that in 1742, when he was aged fourteen years, he bound himself apprentice to John Bacon of **Wincanton**, blacksmith. Joseph had worked for John Bacon for about three years, until Bacon was arrested for debt and became a bankrupt.

Joseph further states that the parish of **Dinder** gave him £8 which he had paid to Bacon, and signed the indentures. The indentures were left in the hands of Mr Hughes, attorney, at Wells. Joseph had worked at several places as a blacksmith, but had never hired himself for a year.

[*Mark*.]

"Upon examining the parish books of Dinder I find the following articles in the year 1742."

For indentures for Joseph Willmott and expence	£0.6s.0d.
Gave with Joseph Willmott	£8.0s.0d.
For carrying him to Wincanton	£0.3s.0d.

"Sworn before me at Dinder the 15th day of July 1751."

[*Signed* Geo. Somerville.]

[S.R.O., settlement examination D/P/Shepton Mallet 13/3/3.10.]

[Case 43] **18 November 1752. Sarah Dyer, wife of Richard Dyer.**

Regarding the settlement of her children, heard by John Tripp, mayor, and J. Doman, alderman. Examination taken at **Taunton**.

Sarah Dyer states that Bartholomew Dyer, otherwise Stowell, was born at **Burlescombe, Devon**, fourteen years ago.

Michael Dyer, otherwise Stowell, was born at **Charterhouse upon Mendip** ten years ago.

Rebecca Dyer, otherwise Stowell, was born at **Langport** three years ago.

Sarah further states that she was lawfully married to Richard Dyer at **Shipham** on 28 April last, also that sixteen years ago she was married to Richard Dyer at the 'Three Blackbirds' at Bath, in the "publick kitchen there by one Crese who was dressed in a clergyman's habit but at such marriage no ring was made use of nor did any person give her in marriage".

[*Mark*.]

[S.R.O., settlement examination D/P/Taunton St Mary 13.3.5.19.]

[Case 44] **29 September 1753. Mary Page.**
Before William Swymmer.

Mary Page, a single woman residing at **Brent Knoll** (South Brent) states that she was born at South Brent and lived there with her father until five years ago, at that time her father agreed with Mr Tuthill, who lived at the sign of the 'Fox and Goose', to serve him as nurse to his child "if born sometime before midsummer day until Lady Day next after following" (sic). Mary did serve for that time but does not know how much wages were given.

At Lady Day she agreed with Mr Tuthill to serve him for a year, her wages to be twenty shillings and half a crown, and such vails [gratuities] as were given to her by the guests.

Mary served Mr Tuthill for a further year, although during the second year she was "ill of the mezzles", and went home until Michaelmas. After next Lady Day, Mary went to **Bath** and was hired by Farmer Deverall, of **Newton St Loe**, for half a year at thirty shillings, after which she contracted with Thomas Somerell of Bath, to serve him for a year from Lady Day, for standing wages of three guineas. She served Somerell until Christmas. Mary then lived "at her own hands" until Easter when she returned to South Brent.

[*Signed*.

[S.R.O., settlement examination D/P/Brent Knoll 13/3/4.3.]

[Case 45] **28 October 1753. Judith James, widow of John James.**

Case set out by lawyer acting for **Ashwick** (Ashweek), appellants and **Shepton Mallet**, respondents. The date is that of the removal as no other is given in the document.

By an order of the above date, Judith James was removed from Shepton Mallet to Ashwick. The latter parish had not received any notice that application for such removal had been made by Shepton Mallet.

Judith James is the widow of John James, who died twelve years ago at **Oakhill** in the parish of Shepton Mallet; he had been a coal carrier by trade.

John James had been born in Ashwick, and it was claimed by Shepton Mallet that Ashwick was, therefore, his parish of settlement. However, thirty four years ago John had been living in the parish of **Stoke St Michael** (Stoke Lane) and had there rented a house and paddock (parrock) for which he had paid rent of two pounds, fifteen shillings a year for the holding.

John also rented in the parish of Shepton Mallet:

Two fields at £5.10s.0d. a year.

Two pieces at £6.0s.0d. a year.

One close at £2.0s 0d. a year.

The total amount that John had paid in rent being £16.15s.0d. At that time John James kept nine or ten horses for carrying coal.

The case seems to be based on the premise that although John James resided in Stoke St Michael, his settlement was in Shepton Mallet, owing to the fact that he was paying over £10 a year in rent for his horse pasturage, whereas in Stoke St Michael he only paid £2.15s.0d. for the house and paddock.

The case continues:

"The pauper is desirous of being settled with the appellants, that about two years since she was brought in a chair into Ashweek parish and there left, but upon the parishioners threatening to prosecute those that brought her, she was carried back again. Not long after she came again there and got into an 'oven' stag [oven stack, i.e., a large open fire place with a bread oven or curing chamber attached; it is reasonable to suppose that this could have been the only shelter in a derelict building]. There she stayed for a fortnight till she was almost starved and then returned to Shepton Mallet again and there have remained ever since."

Several persons are named who could be called as witnesses if necessary:

To prove notice of appeal, Mr Samuel James.

To prove pauper's husband living in Stoke St Michael, and renting as stated in the case there and in Shepton Mallet:

Thomas Atwood and James Atwood.

Thomas Atwood had worked with the husband in all or most of the grounds.

[S.R.O., settlement examination D/P/Shepton Mallet 13/3/1.11.]

[Case 46] 13 April 1754. Charles Burges, otherwise Risly.

Before Thomas Coward and W.Rodbard.

Charles Burges, residing in **Shepton Mallet**, states that he was born at **Bruton** (Brewton). He was a base born child, his mother at that time was called Hannah Burges.

At the age of eleven years he went around the country selling knives, buckles and other things. When he was seventeen he enlisted into the Foot Guards and served for fifteen years.

Charles further states that he has done no act to gain a settlement since he lived in Bruton. He has a wife called Isabela and a daughter Ruth, aged twenty weeks.

[*Mark*.]

[S.R.O., settlement examination D/P/Bruton 13/3/3. 14.]

13 April 1754.

Charles Burges otherwise Risly and family to be removed from Shepton Mallet to Bruton.

[S.R.O., removal order D/P/Bruton 13/3/2.22.]

26 March 1755. Hannah Young.

Wife of John Young, of Fiford, tanner. Before W. Rodbard and Thomas Coward.

Hannah Young, residing Shepton Mallet, states that she had been told by her friends that she was born in that parish.

When she [document torn] young she travelled around the country with James Rusly (sic) by whom she had one child, who was born and christened at Bruton (Brewton). She was never married to Rusly, but travelled around with him and Charles Burges otherwise Rusly their son, for about four years.

Then James left her and took the child with him; Hannah has only seen James once since then.

[*Mark.*]

[S.R.O., settlement examination D/P/ Shepton Mallet 13/3/3.15.]

[Case 47] 27 December 1754. Ann Smith.

Ann Smith, apprehended in the parish of **Camberwell, Surrey**, states that she is the widow of George Smith, who had rented and lived in a house and premises in the parish of **Evercreech** (Avacruch) at the yearly rent of £10. She had never gained a subsequent settlement.

[*Mark.*]

The constables of the parish of Camberwell are instructed to convey the vagrant to the first parish in the next precinct through which she has to pass on her way to Evercreech, this parish being **St Magnus, London Bridge**.

28 December 1754 Ann conveyed to **Colnbrook, Buckinghamshire**.

30 December 1754 Ann conveyed to **Maidstone, Berkshire**.

31 December 1754 Ann conveyed to **White Waltham**, Berkshire.

1 January 1755 Ann conveyed to **Reading**, Berkshire.

2 January 1755 Ann conveyed to **Tilehurst**, Berkshire.

3 January 1755 Ann conveyed to **Charnham Street, Wiltshire**.

6 January 1755 Ann conveyed to **Bathford, Somerset**.

10 January 1755 'To the tithingman of Bathford in the said county, convey the within named vagrant to the parish of Evercreech in the said county and deliver her to a proper officer there, taking his [receipt] for the same.'

[S.R.O., settlement examination and vagrant's pass. D/P/Evercreech 13/3/5.3.]

[Case 48] 18 June 1755. Ellen Tucker.

Wife of John Tucker, now a soldier in H.M.Regiment of Foot under the command of General Seelton, quartered at **Canterbury**. Heard before Lionel Seaman and Gyles Hill, clerk.

Ellen Tucker states that she is aged thirty six years, she was born in **Sheriffmuir, Perthshire**, she lived there until she was twelve years old, At that age she went to **Edinburgh** and dressed linen and did other business for her living.

When she was about thirty three years old she married John Tucker, who was a soldier in Edinburgh, and with whom she has lived until five weeks ago, when Thomas Tucker their child, who was two years old, became ill, and Ellen was left at a place called **Leskar**, between Edinburgh and **Stirling**, to take care of the child, John Tucker being about to march to England.

After two days stay Ellen followed her husband to **Carlisle**, but he was gone from there before she arrived. Ellen, being in distress and want applied to the Mayor of Carlisle for relief, who sent her by his warrant or pass as a vagrant to the parish of **Mells**, it being the parish of her husband's birth.

[*Mark.*]

[S.R.O., settlement examination D/P/Mells 13/3/3.90.]

[Case 49] **19 July 1755. Ananias Webber.**

Letter from J. Boswell at **Taunton**, to the Reverend Mr Hall at **Hemington**.

J. Boswell writes that he is making the best enquiry regarding the settlement of Ananias Webber. Boswell's clerk knew Ananias very well as he had worked with the clerk's father, and says that Ananias was born at **Stogumber**, but he does not know where he served his apprenticeship.

Philip Cross, aged over sixty years, who also worked with the clerk's father at the same time as Ananias agrees with the details:

"James and Samuel Cridland seem to know the whole affair, but will not speak out, they are both very poor and fellows of no very [great, deleted] extraordinary character."

James and Samuel had stated that they had heard of the affair before and had been offered two or three guineas to discover where Ananias Webber had served his apprenticeship. However Boswell does not believe them and intends to get them summoned before the magistrate to get the truth, "after which he will trouble you with another letter".

"Your affectionate, humble servant."

[*Signed.*]

"The mayor this moment sends me word that the Cridlands have promised to speak out."

[S.R.O., miscellaneous settlement document D/P/Hemington 13/3/3.13.]

[Case 50] **29 September 1756. Alice Toope.**

Settlement examination and vagrant's pass, taken at **Harrow**, Middlesex, before L. Bever.

Alice Toope, apprehended in the parish of Harrow, wandering and begging, lying in out houses, states that she is the wife of Onesipherous Toope who is now a soldier in the First Regiment of Foot Guards. She has heard her husband declare that he was born in **Taunton**, and where he had served an apprenticeship to Stephen Baker, tailor, soon afterwards he enlisted as a soldier, and has not done any act since by which he could have gained a settlement.

[*Mark.*]

Alice is to be conveyed from Harrow to **Colnbrook**, then to **Maidenhead, Berkshire**, from thence to **Charnham Street, Wiltshire**, then to **Bathford, Somerset** and from Bathford to Taunton. Dated at Bathford 9 October 1756.

[S.R.O., settlement examination and vagrants pass. D/P/Taunton St Mary 13/3/11.1.]

(See [Case 14]. Another family of Toop, who also have a predilection for Biblical names.)

See Somerset and Dorset Notes and Queries. Vol.XXXI. pp 37, 72, 433 for notes on Onesipherous and Alice Toop.

[Case 51] 1 April 1757. James Annison.

Before William Walker, mayor and Eldridge Aris, alderman.

James Annison states that he was born in **Norwich**. He lived there with his mother under a certificate from the churchwardens and overseers of the poor of the parish of **Flegg** (Flagburrow in Flag) in the county of Norfolk.

After eight years he and his mother removed to **Hassingham** (Hazinhane), also in Norfolk, where they still received relief of one shilling a week, from Flegg. Three years later they returned to Norwich, where James worked for William Freeman, worsted weaver, but not as an apprentice, he worked as a journeyman for about a year and a half, at the end of which time James enlisted in General Wolfe's regiment.

A year ago he was married to Judith Pilsher of St Pauls, **Canterbury**.

In 1757 James was stationed in **Axbridge**, here on 9 March his wife died, having been delivered of a female child; who has been baptized Mary, and who is now chargeable to the parish of Axbridge.

[*Mark.*]

[S.R.O., settlement examination D/P/Axbridge 13/3/4.20.]

[Case 52] 3 July 1762. William Phillips.

Now a private soldier in Colonel Erwin's regiment of Foot. Heard before Charles Tudway, mayor and William Nichols.

William Phillips, quartered in the City of **Wells**, states that he is aged twenty-three, and was born at **East Allington, Devonshire**. He was the son of William Phillips, miller,and Grace his wife. His father died when William was seven years old, and he was apprenticed by the parish officers to Roger Diston of **Pit** in the parish of East Allington.

William served for five years then ran away as he was being ill used. William's mother Grace was at that time travelling around the country selling lace, pins and other small wares.

William also went about the country, sometimes he begged and at other times worked for anyone who would employ him; he then "travelled with people who carried and travelled about several parts of the country showing wild beasts".

At length he saved some money and bought buckles, buttons and other hardwares, four or five years ago he met Ann Francis, who also travelled about selling the same kind of things. Banns were published in some parish church at **Exeter**, where also they were married.

William also states that his wife died at Wells a month ago, he has lost the marriage certificate, he and his wife had travelled together in several counties, and whilst in **Surrey** she was delivered of a child who is about three quarters of a year old, and is named William.

William, the father, had come to Axbridge, where he "got in liquor" and enlisted in the above regiment, this was nineteen weeks ago, since when his wife's sister, Jane Francis, has taken care of the child.

[*Mark.*]

S.R.O., settlement examination D/P/Wells St Cuthberts 13/3/16.39.]

[Case 53] **12 March 1763. Ursula Burgess.**
Before Thomas Dyke Acland and N.Poole.

Ursula Burgess, singlewoman, residing at **Hawkridge**, states that she was born at Winsford; about a week before Shrovetide 1762 [The period comprising Quinquagesima Sunday and the following Monday and Tuesday]. She was sent for by Elizabeth Bale, an old infirm woman of the parish of **Withypool**. She was a widow and Ursula was asked to stay and assist her, and if she did so she would be "no loser".

Ursula then lived with Mrs Bale from Shrovetide until old Christmas eve [5 January, in the new style calendar] following; she received her meat and drink, and when at leisure she spun worsted for her own benefit.

Being dissatisfied and not knowing what further advantage she was to receive she threatened often to leave Mrs Bale, but was assured that she would not lose by staying, so Ursula continued to serve until old Christmas eve, at which time she was turned away by Mrs Bale so that she should not gain a settlement in Withypool.

[*Signed.*]

[S.R.O., settlement examination D/P/Winsford 13/3/11.]

[Case 54] **15 July 1756. James Parfectt.**
Before Thomas Prouse and Henry Harris.

James Parfectt, a broadweaver, residing at **Frome** (Frome Selwood) states that he is now aged thirty three years, and was born in Frome, where he lived with his father, Joseph Parfectt, until he was five years of age, then his father died.

Some time before Joseph died he had made a will in which he gave to Lionel Morris of Frome, broadweaver, "divers household goods, wearing apparel and some money", this legacy was given to Morris so that he would take care of James, and be responsible for him until he was sixteen years of age. Morris also instructed James in the trade of a broadweaver; no covenant or agreement was made between them, neither did James receive any wages.

James then worked as a journeyman broadweaver for two or three years, after which he enlisted as a soldier, and served twelve years, at the end of which service James returned to Frome. He has done no act to gain a settlement, and believes that his father's settlement was in the parish of **Mells**, which settlement he had gained by serving an apprenticeship with Richard Doddimead.

[*Mark.*]

[S.R.O., settlement examination D/P/Mells 13/3/3.12]

15 July 1765.

James Parfecct, broadweaver, to be removed from Frome Selwood to Mells.

[D/P/Mells 13/3/2.24.]

[Case 55] **23 July 1766. Mary Caddell.**

Wife of Lewis Caddell of **Dublin**. Heard before Robert Tudway, mayor, and Thomas Miller. Examination taken at **Wells**.

Mary Caddell states that she is the daughter of Mr John Boulton and Mary his wife, both now deceased. Mary was born in the **Liberty of St Andrews**, Wells, her father being one of the Vicar's Choral. At the age of twenty she hired herself to Dr Willes "then and now Bishop of Bath and Wells" [Edward Willes, bishop from 1743-74].

Ten years ago she went with the Bishop's family to **James Street, Westminster**. In the February following she was married to her husband (out of the Bishop's service), at **St Margarets** church, Westminster.

Lewis Caddell lived in Mr Whitfield's house, which together with the coach house and stables, was in James Street, **Grosvenor Square**, and the rent of which was £10 a year. Lewis and Mary lived there for nearly six months after they were married, then they went to **Ireland**, both going into service.

Mary quit after six months, but being unable to obtain maintenance she returned to England, and was brought by the **Bristol** waggon to Wells, where some of her relatives live, she is now ill and chargeable to the parish of **St Cuthberts**.

[*Signed.*]

[S.R.O., settlement examination D/P/Wells St Cuthberts 13/3/16.31.]

[Case 56] **25 March 1767. Sarah Jones.**

Before Robert Balch and Benjamin Allen.

Sarah Jones, a single woman, residing at **Hunstspill**, states that she was born in that parish and lived there with her parents until she was fourteen years old. Sarah then hired herself to William Wride of Huntspill for a year, her wages were £1.10s.0d. a year.

The next year she again served Wride at the wages of £1.15s.0d. a year.

Returned to her father for two years.

Sarah then worked as follows:

Hired herself for a year to John Edwards of **East Brent**, wages £2.0s.0d.a year.

Hired herself for a year to Thomas Colestone of East Brent.

Hired herself for a year to William Wride of Huntspill, wages £2.10s.0d a year, served two years.

Returned to her father for six months.

Hired herself for half a year to Francis Giles of East Brent, yeoman, and later made a contract for a year. However Sarah only served Giles about three quarters of a year, for during that time she was gotten with child, which child was born in Giles's house in East Brent, from whence four days later, Sarah was removed to the poor house in East Brent, where she stayed for seven weeks.

Since then Sarah has lived with her father in Huntspill, and with her kindred in East Brent; she has done no other act to gain a settlement.

[*Mark.*]

[S.R.O., settlement examination D/P/Huntspill 13/3/6.1.]

[Case 57] **22 October 1767.Michael Weare.**

Before H.Harris and H. Edgell.

Michael Weare, residing at **Mells**, states that he is aged sixty years and was born in the parish of **Chard**.

At the age of twenty he came to the parish of **Longleat, Wiltshire**, the seat of Thomas, Lord Viscount Weymouth. Michael made an agreement with his Lordship's steward Mr Palmer, to serve for a year as smith and farrier, his wages to be £15, and two new aprons, also meat, drink and lodging.

Michael served out his year, during that time he lodged in part of the workshop that was situated in the parish of **Longbridge Deverill**, Wiltshire. Michael served his Lordship another six months, but did not make a new agreement.

For six weeks before he left his Lordship's service he had lodgings appointed for him over the slaughter house, which is in the parish of **Horningsham**. But he frequently went to **Maiden Bradley**, Wiltshire, ("in an affair of courtship") and lodged there. So he is unable to affirm that he lodged over the slaughter house for forty nights in the whole. He has done no further act to gain a settlement. Michael has a wife named Betty.

[*Signed.*]

[Case 58] **16 March 1768. Hester Willis.**

Before Henry Harris and H. Edgell.

Hester Willis, residing at **Rode** (Road), states that she is aged thirty six years, she was born at Rode. When she was twenty seven she made an agreement with Daniel Jefferies of **Tellisford** to live with him and do his household work. Jefferies was to find her in all necessaries, and anything that she and Jefferies daughter might earn at spinning and carding [brushing out the wool] was to belong to Hester. No length of time had been attached to the agreement.

Hester served Jefferies six and a half years at Tellisford, during that time she worked as a servant, milking cows, making butter and cheese, and "the like". She was found in all necessaries but never received any wages, although Jefferies paid for her wearing apparel.

Nearly three years ago Jefferies moved to Rode, and Hester went with him, and stayed with him until Jefferies died about six weeks ago.

Hester further states that she has done no act to gain a settlement. Her father, Richard Willis, is residing at Rode under a certificate from the parish of **Beckington** dated 4 June 1729.

[*Mark.*]

The case regarding Hester Willis required legal opinion on the facts as set out below:

March 1768. In June 1729 Richard Willis, his wife and three children, arrived in Rode (Road) with an indemnity certificate from Beckington. Hester is the daughter of Richard Willis, and was born after they came to Rode; she is now aged about thirty six.

Daniel Jefferies married her elder sister, they had children, the mother died, whereupon Hester went and lived with Daniel in the parish of Tellisford, this was about ten years ago.

Extract from the Examination of Hester Willis:

72

Daniel and Hester lived in Tellisford for six and a half years, during which time they had five bastard children (not being allowed to marry) ["a man may not marry his wife's sister": Table of Kindred and Affinity, *Book of Common Prayer*].

In 1766 they removed to Rode, and had another bastard child born in that parish.

In 1766 the parish of Tellisford gave a certificate to the parish of Rode, concerning the five bastard children born at Tellisford, Hester and the child born at Rode were not included.

Daniel died in January 1768, Hester and the children are still living in Rode. Hester is expecting another bastard child by Daniel.

The opinion given is that Hester Willis has established settlement in Rode, by reason of her being in service with Daniel Jefferies for eight months under the same conditions as her service in Tellisford. Daniel and Hester stood in the relationship of master and servant.

Opinion given by J. Morris, dated at Bath 2 April 1768.

[S.R.O., case and opinion D/P/Rode 13/3/5.14.]

[Case 59] **Ebenezer Merriot.**

Before Thomas Coward and Gerard Martin.

Ebenezer Merriot, residing at **Croscombe**, states that he was born in the parish of **St Sepulchre, Middlesex**. At the age of seventeen or eighteen he went to the **West Indies** in a merchant vessel, and "was out about a year and a quarter".

After his return to England he lived in service with his brother for one and a half years, this was in the parish of **St Giles, Holborn**, Middlesex. Ebenezer then went shopkeeping on his own account, in the parish of **St James**, also in Middlesex. Here he had rented a house in which to carry on his business, at the yearly rent of £14.

After one and a half years Ebenezer went to sea again, and served in the sea service three to four years.

On returning to England Ebenezer went to **Haselbury Plucknett** (Hasleburough Plucknet), where he kept the school for sixteen years, he then went to **Beckington** and "taught school" about fifteen years. During his time at Haselbury and **Beckington** he had never paid more than thirty five shillings a year in rent.

At the end of his time at Beckington, Ebenezer went to **Downton** (Downson) in Wiltshire. Here he was made a toll gatherer at the turnpike gate, and stayed there about eight years. He then moved to the turnpike gate called **Fromefield Gate** in **Frome**, where he remained four years.

Ebenezer then resigned on account of his age and infirmity, and came to the parish of Croscombe about four months ago. Not being able to sustain himself without help, he went to St James for relief and obtained an allowance of two shillings a week for himself and Patience his wife.

[*Mark.*]

We note here that although Ebenezer "taught school" he was only able to make a mark at the foot of his examination. This, of course, could have been due to his infirmity.

Ebenezer Merriot's residence in Haselbury Plucknett and Beckington did not qualify him to claim settlement in either parish, as it is probable that the property that he was renting was not rated above £10. Neither could he claim to be settled in either Downton or Frome, as toll gate keepers were specifically excluded from gaining settlement.

[S.R.O., settlement examination D/P/Croscombe 13/3/10.8.]

From the overseers accounts of Croscombe we find that the overseers received two guineas from St James out of which they paid Ebenezer the sum of one pound seven shillings.

[S.R.O., D/P/Croscombe 13/2/5/]

[Case 60] **27 October 1768. John Butler.**

Soldier in 15th Regiment of Foot. Before T. Horner.

John Butler, residing **Mells**, states that he is aged thirty one years, and was born in **Shepton Mallet** (Shepton Malet). When he was eighteen years old he enlisted in the above regiment, and in which he has served ever since. John understood that his father's settlement was in Mells, although he resided in Shepton Mallet under a certificate from the parish of Mells.

John further states that six years ago he was married in an English church, at **Philadelphia** in **North America**, to Katherine Gordon, widow, by whom he has two children, John aged three years and Hannah aged one year. John and his family are now living at Mells.

[*Signed.*]

[S.R.O., settlement examination D/P/Mells 13/3/3.91.]

[Case 61] **25 February 1770. Thomas Protherow.**

This example is taken from the parish register of **Doddington**:

"Was buried Thomas Protherow (a Welchman), as he was travelling from **Caernarfon** (Carnarvan) to Westminster in **London**, his parish. Being eaten up by lice through the inhumanity of the parish officers through which he came. All possible kindness being shown in this parish, but he lived in it a few days, and died a most miserable spectacle as was ever seen. Aged 67."

[S.R.O., burial register. D/P/Doddington 2/1/2.]

[Case 62] **27 April 1771. William Dryal.**

Before Thomas Millard, mayor, and Joseph Lovell.

William Dryal, papermaker, residing in the **In parish of St Cuthberts, Wells**, states that he was born at **Wookey Hole**, which is in the **Out parish of St Cuthberts**; his parents William and Mary Dryal are both deceased.

William, the son, learnt the business of a papermaker under William Willey of Wookey Hole, but there was no indenture or written agreement between them.

About fifty three years ago he was married, in the parish church of St Cuthberts, to Mary, by whom he has one son living. Fourteen years ago he removed with his wife to **Stoke St Michael** (Stoke Lane), where he made an agreement with Henry Fussell, papermaker, to give him six shillings a week for a dwelling house and the half share, or part of, a paper mill, they were to be partners in the trade of papermaking, the profits of the business to be shared between them. They continued in this way for three and a half years, William then worked as a journeyman for half a year, at the end of which time he and his wife returned to Wells.

William further states that he has done no other act to gain a settlement.

[*Mark.*]

[S.R.O., settlement examination D/P/.Wells St Cuthberts 13/3/16.104.]

[Case 63] **16 October 1771. William Manners.**

Before Robert Tudway, mayor, and Thomas Millard.

William Manners states that he was born at **Beverley, Yorkshire**, and is the son of Thomas and Elizabeth Manners, he lived with his parents at Beverley, and latterly at **Kingston upon Hull**, until he was nine or ten years old. William then went to **Northampton** and lived with John Easton, a horse dealer, for about two years, during which time he received his clothes, victuals and drink as well as a shilling for every horse that his master sold. William then went to live with Samuel Smith of Northampton, also a horse dealer, with whom he stayed three years, his wages were two shillings and sixpence a week during the first year, and three shillings a week for the second year. For the remainder of the time he was to receive £5 a year. However William left this service after eleven months as he was ill.

Soon afterwards William went to **Langham** in the county of **Rutland**, where he worked for William Hubbard, a horse dealer, at the yearly wages of seven guineas, here he stayed over a year, and then went to **London** and lived as a weekly servant at the 'Queen's Head' in **Greasing Lane**. Later William returned to Langham and worked for Hubbard as a weekly servant, but at no stated wages.

A year later William came to Wells, where he was married to Jane, daughter of Joseph Bendall, woolcomber. William and Jane have two children, Thomas aged twelve year and Robert who is nearly six years old.

[*Mark.*]

[S.R.O., settlement examination D/P/Wells St Cuthberts 13/3/16. 102.]

[Case 64] 3 April 1772. William Brookman.

Before H. Edgell and H. Harris.

William Brookman, residing at **Rode**, states that he is twenty-three years old, and was born in **Burnett**. Two years ago he hired himself for a year, to serve Samuel Selway of **Wellow**, yeoman, at the yearly wage of five pounds, fifteen shillings, and he was to have his meat, drink, washing and lodging.

William had served for ten months, then he was married to Sarah, they have one child named Joseph. After his marriage, William continued to serve Selway, lodging still in Wellow, except sometimes on Saturday or Sunday night when he lodged with his wife in the parish of Rode. William had done no further act to gain a settlement.

[*Mark.*

[S.R.O., settlement examination, Rode 13/3/1.34.]

[Case 65] 3 April 1772. Jeremiah Tucker.

Before H. Edgell and H. Harris.

Jeremiah Tucker, a clothworker, residing **Rode** (Road) states that he was born in that parish, and that he is now aged forty years. Fourteen years ago he hired himself to serve William Hale of **North Bradley, Wiltshire**.

Jeremiah was to be Hale's servant, Sundays included, at the weekly wages of two shillings and sixpence, he would also receive his meat, drink and lodging. Jeremiah served Hale for a year, he then hired himself to Mr Whitaker, also of North Bradley, to learn the art of shearing cloth, and work shearman's hours only [shearing woollen cloth].

Jeremiah served Whitaker for two years, since when he has done no act to gain a settlement.

Jeremiah is married, his wife is named Mary and they have four children, Mary eight years old, Ruth seven, Rachel five and Juda aged six months.

[*Mark.*]

[S.R.O., settlement examination. D/P/Rode 13/3/1.71.]

[Case 66] 3 April 1772. Edward Greenland.

Before H.Harris and H. Edgell.

Edward Greenland, a clothworker, residing at **Rode**, states that he is twenty-seven years old and was born in Rode. His father, Edward Greenland, was a legal parishioner of **Tellisford**. When Edward junior was fourteen years old he agreed to serve Mr Barnes of Rode, scribbler [preparing wool for spinning] for three years at agreed weekly wages.

Mr Barnes was to teach Edward to scribble wool on the working days, and on Sundays Edward was to clean Mr Barnes's shoes, and to look after his horse; also on Sundays Edward was to have breakfast and dinner with Mr Barnes, but for the rest of the week Edward was to find himself in meat, drink, washing and lodging.

Edward lodged in Rode while he was serving Mr Barnes, who died two years after Edward started to work for him. Edward then agreed with John Wickham of Rode, clothworker, to serve him for four years, he had actually served for upwards of a year when Wickham failed in his trade.

Edward's wife was named Martha, they had three children – Ann aged five years, Samuel two years, and Betty four months.

[*Mark*.]

[S.R.O., settlement examination D/P/Rode 13/3/1.46.]

[Case 67] **1 January 1773. Mary Tyler.**

Before H. Harris.

Mary Tyler, a single woman, residing at **Rode** (Road), states that she was born a bastard in the parish of Rode, and that she is now twenty-two years old.

When Mary was aged fifteen she went to live with William Pool of **North Bradley, Wiltshire**, fuller [one who fulls cloth, by beating and washing]. Pool's wife was sister to Mary's mother.

Mary lived with Pool for eight years, during that time she worked at or assisted with the domestic business, and when that was done she sometimes worked at spinning wool. Mary was found in all necessaries by Pool, but she received no wages, although sometimes Pool gave her some pocket money.

[*Mark*.]

[S.R.O., settlement examination D/P/Rode 13/3/1.77.]

18 April 1775.

Mary Tyler had been delivered of a male bastard child on 6 April 1773, in the parish of **Rode** (Road). William Bishop, late of North Bradley, Wiltshire, is the father of the child. He is ordered to pay £1 towards Mary's lying in, and one shilling weekly towards the maintenance of the child, as long as the child is chargeable to the parish.

Mary is to pay ninepence weekly if she does not nurse and take care of the child herself.

[S.R.O., Bastardy order D/P/Rode 13/5/2.7.]

[Case 68] **5 February 1773. Angel Hyde.**

Before Cann Wilkins and T.W. Morgan.

Angel Hyde, a labourer residing at **Easton-in-Gordano** (St Georges) with

Mary his wife, states that he was born in **Milborne Port**, that he has never gained a settlement of his own; the last legal settlement of his father Angel Hyde, deceased, was in the parish of **St Nicholas, Bristol**; his occupation being that of tideman [customs officer, working shifts dependent on the tides] and where he was rated and paid the King's tax.

[*Signed.*]

Extract from the parish register of **Compton Pauncefoot**:

"Angel Hyde, the base born son of Ann Pinn was baptised January 22 1741 at Compton Pauncefoot. Angel the father was married there to the said Ann Pinn September 28 1742. Note. Angel the father in the register is called of **Westminster** in the county of **Middlesex**."

[*Signed Richard Hunt.*] (Rector of Compton Pauncefoot).

Martha Oliver, Angel Hyde's aunt, states that his father went to **London** and lived with a Mr French, who had been a member for Milborne Port, but did not gain a settlement there.

Ann Pinn, his mother, was a native of **Charleton Horethorne** (Charlton). She and Angel Hyde, the father, both lived with Parson Hunt at Compton Pauncefoot.

By January 1782 Angel Hyde is dead and the parish officer writes to Mr Hallet, the overseer of Milborne Port, to say that they will not try the notice of appeal against removal of Mary Hyde and children to Milborne Port, also that an account of money that has been disbursed for the family should be sent by Mr Messiter to Wells, where it will be paid to him.

[*R. White, for the parish officers of Easton-in-Gordano.*]

[S.R.O., settlement examination D/P/ Easton-in-Gordano 13/3/1.84 & 84a.]

13 July 1781. Mary Hyde, widow of Angel Hyde.

Before Cann Wilkins and T.W. Morgan.

Mary Hyde, residing Easton-in-Gordano (St Georges) states that Angel Hyde, the father of her late husband, was legally settled in the parish of St Nicholas, Bristol, by being a boatman in the service of H.M. Customs, all of whom are deemed to belong to the parish of St Nicholas. Her husband, Angel Hyde the younger, never gained any other settlement. Mary has three children by her late husband, who are Ann aged six years, Sarah five years, and John three years.

[*Signed.*]

[S.R.O., settlement examination D/P/Easton-in-Gordano 13/3/1.97.]

29 January 1782. Counsel's opinion.

This would be given by H.Hobhouse, Clifton.

The case set out:

This document recites the above details of the birth of Angel Hyde, and the subsequent marriage of his mother and father. Also the fact that Angel Hyde, the son, was married in the parish church of Easton-in-Gordano by that name. Angel Hyde is now dead leaving a widow and three children who are all chargeable to the parish of Easton-in-Gordano, which parish has had a deal of trouble with the widow and children, having already removed them twice.

Question.

Is not Compton Pauncefoot the parish of settlement of the widow and her children, where her husband and the father of the children was born, and therefore should not the family be removed, as the widow of Angel Hyde Pinn, otherwise Angel Hyde, having been married by the latter name?

Opinion.

There can be no doubt that the paupers are settled at Compton Pauncefoot, and as the husband was baptised and married by the name of Angel Hyde, this is the proper name to be used in the order of removal.

Question.

Whether the affidavit of the person who has the register of baptisms will be sufficient grounds for the order of removal?

Opinion.

Such an affidavit, with a copy of the register of baptisms and the wife swearing to his having been her husband, will be sufficient for the justices to make an order of removal; should there be an appeal, then the copy of the register must be produced at sessions, by some person who has examined it with the original, and can confirm that Angel Hyde was the widow's husband.

[S.R.O., D/P/Easton-in-Gordano 13/3/7.15.]

[Case 69] **5 August 1774. James Wilson.**

Before W. Rodbard and Gerard Martin.

James Wilson, servant to John Donne Esq., residing at **Batcombe**, states that he was born at **Elford, Staffordshire**. When he was fourteen years old James hired himself to Lord Donegall [Arthur, 5th Earl and created Marquess of Donegall, 1739-99], then of the parish of **Greenhill**, Staffordshire, whom he served for two and a half years.

James then went to **London** and was hired by Mr Robert Harris (who was a coachman to Lord Berkeley). James was to receive seven shillings a week, he served Mr Harris for four years. James then left this service for eleven months, however he then returned to serve Mr Harris (who was still a servant to Lord Berkeley, and living in **Berkeley Square**).

James served for two years under this hiring during which he lived as Lord Berkeley's other 'domesticks', during the summer, residing at **Bruton**, and in the winter season at Berkeley Square. James served the last seven or eight months of his service with Harris at Bruton Abbey. [The Berkeley family held the manor of Bruton from the dissolution of the monasteries until 1776.]

A month before his service expired James was married at Bruton to Betty, they have one child called Mary.

James further states that he has been a servant to Mr Donne for over fourteen months.

[*Mark.*]

[S.R.O., settlement examination D/P/Bruton 13/3/8.21.]

[Case 70] **1777. Amy Clogg.**

Name of justice not given, nor the precise date.

Amy Clogg, a widow, residing in **West Monkton** (Monckton), states that she was born at **Creech St Michael**, and is now aged eighty-one years. About the year 1727 Amy married Robert Clogg. Robert had been born in the parish of **Taunton St James**. Amy had heard him say that before marriage he had lived for a year at **Bathpool Mills** with Mr Gudderidge, but Amy does not know if he had been hired by the year or by the week.

Amy had heard that her husband had been bound apprentice to Mr Bicknell, a dyer in the parish of Taunton St Mary; also that about thirty-nine years ago he had kept house in the parish of Taunton St Mary, and had voted for members to serve in Parliament for the Borough of Taunton.

About thirty-seven years ago Robert had enlisted as a soldier, and when he left her she had applied to the overseers of the poor of Taunton St Mary, who at that time relieved her and her four children, and continued to relieve her until lately.

The overseers then refused her relief giving as reasons that she did not reside in the parish of Taunton St Mary, and also that she had sufficient property of her own with which to maintain herself. Amy declares this is not true for she is "not in possession of anything to the value of nothing".

[*No mark or signature.*]

[*Endorsed*] "All useless."

[S.R.O., settlement examination DD/DP 7/10. 2. (Doveton papers.)]

[Case71] **22 April 1777. John Hammers.**

Before Cann Wilkins and T.W. Morgan.

John Hammers states that after the decease of his mother and father he was brought up in the poor-house belonging to the parish of **St Philip and Jacob [Bristol]** in the county of **Gloucester**.

He does not know where he was born but has heard that he was born near the new church otherwise **St George's** in the county of Gloucester.

He was bound out apprentice, by the parish of St Philip and Jacob, to Thomas Ross of Hannam in the same parish; Ross had served the office of overseer of the poor.

John Hammers left Ross a short time after he was apprenticed and went as an indented servant to **Philadelphia** in America, where he stayed seven years.

He came from America to the port of London, and from thence to **Pill** in the parish of St George in the county of Somerset [Easton-in-Gordano].

John further states that he has never gained a settlement by renting or service; he has a wife named Elizabeth; he had applied to Robert (sic) Ross for his indentures, who told him that he had burnt both parts.

[*Mark.*]

Incidentally, interesting articles by J. Wareing and D. Galenson, about indentured servants who went to America, can be found in the *Genealogists Magazine,* vol. 18 no.5; and vol.19 no.2; no.6; no.8.

[S.R.O., settlement examination D/P/Easton-in-Gordano 13/3/1.72.]

[Case 72] **11 September 1777. Joel Keemp.**

Before Francis Gwyn and John Helliar.

Joel Keemp a soldier, residing at **Combe St Nicholas**, states that he is aged thirty, he was born in Combe St Nicholas and had lived there with his father.

When he was aged twenty-one Joel went to **Bath**, where he worked for a short time, he then went to **London**, where, after two weeks in the city, he enlisted as a soldier in the East India Company. He served nine years, and then returned to Combe St Nicholas. Joel further states that he has done no other act to gain a settlement.

[S.R.O., settlement examination D/P/Combe St Nicholas 13/3/4.27.]

The archives of the Honourable East India Company are at the India Office. The Oriental and India Office Collections now form part of the British Library. There is no trace of Joel Keemp/Kemp in the above record office. However, a Joseph Kemp appears in the **Madras** Muster Roll. He enlisted in 1769, and arrived in **India** on the ship *Havana* from England [IOR Madras Muster Rolls 1771-73]. Unfortunately the recruitment registers only commence in 1817, so that there is no record of his enlistment.

I am most grateful to the India Office for supplying the above information.

No baptism of a Joseph Kemp can be found in the Combe St Nicholas register recorded during the relevant period. There was, however, a Joel Kemp, son of George and Joan Kemp, baptised on 19 July 1747.

[S.R.O., D/P/ com. n. 2/1/1.]

[Case 73] **19 September 177[7?]. Thomas Ray.**

Before Cann Wilkins and T.W. Morgan.

Thomas Ray states that he was born in the parish of St Philip and Jacob in the county of Gloucester [**Bristol**]. Seventeen or eighteen years ago he lived with

Samuel Shepherd of **St George's [Easton-in-Gordano]** for twelve months. In May 1775 he went to the parish of **Barry**, in **Glamorganshire**, where he rented a house from Robert Jones Esq., of **Fonmon Castle**, Glamorgan. Thomas paid £3 a year in rent, and also rented a quantity of stones lying on the shore, one half of which stones lay in the parish of Barry and the other half in **Porth Kerry** and **Rhoose**, Glamorgan, for which stones he agreed to pay £27 per annum.

In March 1776 he left Barry and returned to St George. He has a wife called Sarah and eight children, William aged fourteen years, Sarah thirteen years, Elizabeth eleven years, Hannah eight years, Mary seven years, Thomas five years, Ann four years and John fifteen months.

Thomas further states that he has not gained a settlement anywhere since he left Barry.

[*Mark.*]

[S.R.O., settlement examination, D/P/Easton-in-Gordano 13/3/1.1.]

[Case 74] **11 October 1780. James Robins**. Regarding the settlement of Dinah Robins.

No justices named.

James Robins states that Dinah Robins, residing at **Mells**, is aged one and a half years, she was born in Mells, her father, Benjamin Robins, was born in **Frome**, but James is unable to say if Benjamin had gained a settlement. Benjamin is now a private in the **Porstmouth** marines.

[*Signed.*]

[S.R.O., settlement examination D/P/Mells 13/3/3.85.]

[Case 75] **24 January 1781. Ann Foot.**

Before H.Harris and H. Edgell.

Ann Foot, residing **Mells**, states that she was married thirty years ago to Thomas Foot. Thomas, who was a legal parishioner of Mells, died eighteen years ago, they had three children living at the time of his death, and the children had resided with them. When the youngest child was of the age of fourteen years, Ann was asked by her sister's husband James Turner, who rented a dairy of thirty cows in the parish of **Mere** (Meer) in **Wiltshire**, to assist him in his business.

Ann then left her children at Mells and went to Mere where she stayed three years and five months, during which time she helped to milk the cows and attended the children and did other business of a servant, but she never hired herself to Turner except for the last six months, at which time she made an agreement for a year, her wages to be £3, meat, drink, washing and lodging.

However, after six months under this agreement, Turner was "put out of the dairy". Ann then hired herself to Betty Jupe, widow (who lived at **Burton** (a hamlet a mile east of Mere). This hiring was under the same type of agreement. After Ann had served the year with Betty Jupe she returned to Mells, where she resides in a tenement for which she pays twenty six shillings a year in rent.

While Ann was living in Wiltshire her children in Mells were frequently sick and incurred some debts, which Ann has discharged; she states that all the children were able to maintain themselves from the time that she left them at Mells, except when they were ill.

[*Mark.*]

[S.R.O., settlement examination D/P/Mells 13/3/3.77.]

[Case 76] 21 November 1782. Sarah Gould.

Wife of George Gould, labourer ("gone from her"). Before R. Scudamore.

Sarah Gould apprehended as a vagrant in the parish of St **Philip and St Jacob [Bristol]**, in the county of **Gloucester**, states that her husband's last legal settlement was in the parish of **Huntspill**, where he was born and served his apprenticeship. Sarah also states that she is "very poor and did wander and begg."

Sarah Gould, wife of George Gould (gone from her), and his children, Constant aged six years, Mary four years and an infant aged one year are to be removed from Bristol to Huntspill.

[S.R.O.,vagrant's pass D/P/Huntspill 13/3/2.12.]

2 March 1784

Sarah Gould, widow, to be removed from **Bridgwater** to Huntspill.

[Endorsed, George Gould's widow.]

S.R.O., D/P/Huntspill 13/3/2.15.]

3 August 179[?] John Winn.

Pass from the county of Gloucester to Huntspill.

To all Justices of the peace, Mayors, Sheriffs, Bailiffs, Constables, and other officers whom these may concern.

These are to desire you, and every of you, to permit and suffer the Bearer hereof.

[Note: the words in italics have been handwritten onto a printed form.]

Thomas Winn labourer, Betty his wife, and Mary Gould aged about ten years their grand daughter, to pass to the parish of Huntspill in the county of *Somerset.*

Without any of your let, Hinderance, or Molestation whatsoever, *they* demeaning *themselves* orderly, keeping the common and direct Roads, and not exceeding a reasonable time, from the Date hereof, to accomplish *their* said Journey allowing them what necessary Relief and Assistance as to you shall seem requisite and meet.

Given under my hand and seal (being one of His Majesty's Justices of the Peace for the County of *Gloucester* the *Third* Day of *August* 179..

William H. Winstone.

[S.R.O., D/P/Huntspill 13/3/7.]

[Case 77] **29 August 1785. John Wheeler.**

Before Cann Wilkins and T.W. Morgan.

John Wheeler, now residing in the parish of **Easton-in-Gordano** (St George's) late an invalid under the command of Major Watson at **Plymouth** [see below] states that he was born at Easton-in-Gordano, where his father had a leasehold house worth between £8 and £9 a year, if not more; his father had paid to the church and poor rates. When John was six years old his father removed to **Abbots Leigh**, where he rented a public house called 'The George' and where he died.

His father had paid the poor rate at Abbots Leigh, but John does not know if he had paid the church rate. John has not gained a settlement in his own right by renting or service.

[*Signature*.]

The reference to his 'invalid' posting is interesting. Soldiers or sailors disabled by illness or injury from being employed on active service could be employed on garrison duty, or be in a reserve force.

[S.R.O., settlement examination D/P/Easton-in-Gordano 13/3/1.67.]

[Case 78] **2 February 1786. Thomas Newton.**

Before James Bernard and John Acland.

Thomas Newton, a mason, residing **Crowcombe**, states that he was born in that parish. In 1765 he went to **London** and hired himself to Lady Frances Elliot, in the parish of **St George's, Hanover Square**, and then in **Chiswick, Middlesex**, until Michaelmas 1766.

He then left Lady Frances and worked as a mason in **London** for one and a half years. Thomas then served King George in 67th Regiment of Foot for five years, after which he returned to the parish of Crowcombe and married his present wife, by whom he has five children – Alexander ten years old, Abraham eight years, Patience six years, Tryphena five years and Isaac aged one and a quarter years.

[*Signed*.]

[S.R.O., settlement examination. D/P/Crowcombe 13/3/1.3.]

[Case 79] **5 October 1786. Benjamin Boynton.**

Before T. Horner.

Benjamin Boynton, a gardener, states that he is aged thirty-seven and was born in **Mells**, where his father was legally settled.

At the age of eighteen Benjamin made an agreement with Mr Dowding of **Trowbridge, Wiltshire,** to serve him as a gardener. His wages were to be half a guinea a week and the superfluous produce of the garden, Benjamin served Mr Dowding about a year under the agreement; he cannot remember if it was more or less. During his service he found himself in meat, drink and other necessaries. He did not lodge in Mr Dowding's house.

Benjamin then went to **Frome**, where he rented a public house known by the sign of the 'Griffin'. He cannot remember if he paid rent of £8, £9, or £10 a year.

After six months Benjamin returned to Mells, where he thinks that he is entitled to a house for some term of years determinable upon his decease. This house was given or made over to him by his late father, by some writing which Benjamin understands is in the custody of his mother-in-law, one Elizabeth Moore, who lives at **Witham Friary** (Witham Frary).

Benjamin has a wife named Elizabeth and four children.

   [*Signed*.]

   [S.R.O., settlement examination D/P/Mells 13/3/3.34.]

[Case 80] **1 November 1786. Sarah Willis.**

   Settlement examination and vagrant's pass, sent from **Kirkby Lonsdale, Westmoreland,** to **Blackford** in the parish of **Wedmore.** Sarah Willis, together with her children Mary and Thomas, was apprehended in the town of Kirkby Lonsdale as a vagabond, wandering and begging. Sarah states that she was born at Blackford in the parish of Wedmore, in which parish she has her legal settlement. She is aged twenty three years, and she has two children, both born in Wedmore – but not in wedlock.

Her journey starts on 17 November 1786, from Kirkby Lonsdale to **Dalton-cum-Hutton, Lancashire.**

18 November 1786 to be conveyed through the county of Lancashire.

22 November 1786. Conveyed to **Talke** (Talk-O'-Th' Hill), Staffordshire.

23 November 1786. Conveyed to **Stembury** (Stembridge), **Worcestershire.**

25 November 1786. Conveyed to **Clent**, Staffordshire, and the Constable of Clent, to convey her and her family to **Belbroughton**, Worcestershire.

27 November 1786. Conveyed to **Twyning** (Twining), Gloucestershire.

28 November 1786. Conveyed from the city of **Gloucester** to the hamlet of **Littleworth**, and from there to the parish of **St Philip and Jacob [Bristol].**

30 November 1786. Conveyed from St Philip and Jacob to **Bedminster.**

The pass ends at this point. It may be presumed that Sarah and the children finally reached Wedmore at the beginning of December.

   [S.R.O., settlement examination and vagrant's pass. D/P/Wedmore

January 1787. Samuel Willis.

Husband of Sarah Willis, above. Case for Counsel's opinion:

"Samuel Willis was sent to Aberdeen by a pass, on his arrival at Aberdeen he ran away and left his wife and family, his wife was afterwards sent by a pass by the parish of [blank] to Wedmore, from where she and her husband had before been sent. Willis's wife says that she imposed upon the Justice by not informing him of the whole affair, as **Aberdeen** appeared to be Willis's place of settlement and which his wife knew from the information she received from her husband."

Cannot the Justices in the neighbourhood of Wedmore send her and her family to her husband's parish by a pass, as she has committed acts of vagrancy?

"The woman being married to a Scotchman who has in a legal sense no settlement, I am inclined to think that she cannot be moved from her maiden settlement, without her husband, though she might be moved with him. Her examination in Westmoreland seems to have been a gross perjury, for which she would be indictable if it were worth while to send her to Westmoreland for the purpose."

Opinion given at Wells sessions, by H. Hobhouse.

[S.R.O., D/P/ Wedmore 13/3/1.87.]

[Case 81] 20 April 1788. John Watkins.

Before J. Durbin, T.W. Morgan and S.Webb.

John Watkins, a sailor residing in the parish of **Easton-in-Gordano** (St George's) states that he was born at **Westbury-on-Trym, Gloucestershire**. He apprenticed himself to Captain Thomas Jackson of the *Aurena* of **Whitby** in Yorkshire, the term of service to be six years, and for which Captain Jackson was to give him £30. John had never gained a settlement in his own right except as aforesaid. He was aged twenty on 6 April; he has no family; and has served Captain Jackson only three and a half years.

[*Mark.*]

[S.R.O., settlement examination D/P/Easton-in-Gordano 13/3/1.62.]

[Case 82] 12 March 1789. Martha Simons, or Symonds.

Before James Tooker and Alexander Adams.

Martha Symonds states that thirteen years ago last February, she married her late husband at **High Littleton**. Three or four years ago her husband had been examined, at **Wells** petty sessions, as to his parish of settlement, should it be **Litton** or High Littleton.

It had been decided that Litton was his legal parish of settlement, the parish officers at Litton had acknowledged him as such by having given him relief to pay his house rent once or twice; also admitting him to receive some of the charity money arising from lands given to the second poor of Litton.

Martha further states that she has four children, Anne aged twelve years, Elizabeth ten, Thomas eight and Richard four years old.

[S.R.O., settlement examination D/P/High Littleton 13/3/7.37a.]

[Case 83] 1 December 1791. Joseph Russell.

Before John Hanning and Alexander Hood.

Joseph Russell, a shearman residing in **Chard**, states that he was born at **Broadwindsor, Dorset**. At the age of five and a half years he was removed, with his father and family, to **Thorncombe**, [then in **Devon**; transferred to Dorset in 1844]. At the age of fourteen Joseph was hired by his father to Samuel Hitchcock of **Stoke Abbott**, Dorset, nine months later, Joseph and his master having had a dispute, he went to his father's house, but returned to Hitchcock after one week, and stayed there until the end of the year.

After staying with his father for five months Joseph hired himself, as a stable boy, to Robert Durden who kept a public house at **Upwey**, Dorset.

Here Joseph served for sixteen months, after which he went to William Fudge, also of Upwey, for two months. His next moves were to John Allen of **Fleet**, Dorset, for three months, and then nine months in the parish of **Hillsill** [Hilfield, possibly], Dorset. The next place Joseph went to was **Porstmouth Common**, where he lived with his uncle for three months, and then went as a sailor to **Newfoundland** where he served one year and nine months in the fishery.

On his return to England Joseph went to **Tatworth** in **Chard** parish and worked as a journeyman weaver. On 8 March last he was married in Chard parish church, to Sarah Warry of **Hawkchurch** [then in Dorset; transferred to Devon in 1844].

[*Mark.*]

[S.R.O., settlement examination D/P/Chard 13/3/9.2.]

27 February 1839. Joseph Russell.

Before R.W. Spicer and John Toms.

This examination must relate to the same Joseph Russell as the previous document. Here Joseph states the he was born at Thorncombe, Devon, he names the ship in which he went to Newfoundland as being the *Winchelsea*. Details are also given for the years following 1791.

On returning from Newfoundland to Chard, Joseph Russell worked for Mr George Berry in the clothing business, for about two years, it was during this time that he married his present wife Sarah, subsequently Joseph worked for various persons in husbandry, and then in Messrs Coles and Co., clothing factory.

He then served in the supplementary militia from which he was discharged in 1802, having served for four or five years. After his discharge he again worked in husbandry for different persons for two or three years.

Afterwards he went to Tatworth for one or two years, and where he rented a house and orchard from Mr Thomas Pitts for £9 a year. He also rented a field from Mr Jacob Larcombe for £12 a year. The next move was to **Martock** where Joseph worked as a labourer for about three years, he then removed to **Chardstock**, Dorset [since transferred to Devon] for four years, went back to Chard parish for three years, and then in 1827 he went into Chard borough and rented a house from Mr John Gunn for five shillings a week, after two years the rent was reduced to four shillings a week for two years.

Joseph then rented a house from Mr Fry for ten shillings a week, after a year Mr Fry reduced the rent to five shillings a week for two or three years, during this time Joseph let part of the house to his son-in-law Samuel Plyer.

Later Plyer took over the tenancy and sublet part of the house to Joseph Russell who lived there for about three years. After the house burnt down Plyer took another house from Mr Lemon, part of which Joseph rented for one shilling a week.

Joseph states that he has done no act to gain a settlement. He and his wife are now chargeable to Chard parish.

[*Mark*.]

[S.R.O., settlement examination D/P/Chard 13/3/9.29.]

[Case 84] **19 September 1792. John Snow and family.**

Mary his wife, John aged twenty one years and Mary twelve years, their children, are all to be removed from the parish of **St James, Poole, Dorset**, to the parish of **Queen Camel**.

Removal order sent from Poole. Justices: John Lester, mayor and George Garland.

[S.R.O.,D/P/Queen Camel 13/3/3.35.]

12 October 1792.

John Snow, mariner, residing Queen Camel, states that he was born in that parish, where his father, Thomas, had been legally settled. When John was eight or nine years old he was placed as a parish apprentice to Mr Constantine Crowbrow, after six or seven years he ran away and went to Poole, where he apprenticed himself to Mr Benjamin Lester for five years, to work in the **Newfoundland** trade.

No indentures were executed, but Mr Lester agreed to give John £5, and a suit of clothes, at the end of his apprenticeship. John stayed at Poole between thirty and forty days before he went to Newfoundland; where he served the whole of his apprenticeship.

He then agreed with Mr Isaac Lester (Mr Benjamin Lester's partner) to serve him as a yearly servant, at the wages of £15; which he did for one whole year and then left the service.

He has two children living with him – John aged twenty-one years and Mary of the age of twelve years.

[*Mark*.]

[S.R.O., settlement examination D/P/Queen Camel 13/3/2.20.]

A removal order has also been found amongst the settlement papers for Poole [D.R.O., PE/PL. OV.12.]. This orders that John Snow and the two younger children should be sent to Queen Camel. The baptism, in 1770, of an older child, Susanna, is recorded in the Poole register [D.R.O.,PE/PL. RE.4.].

Endorsed. A note states thaat the family had been left at Queen Camel with James Sealey, churchwarden, at the 'Sign of the Cock'. The mother, Mary, does not appear to have been with them.

[Case 85] **19 December 1793. William Penny.**

No justice named.

William Penny, born **North Bradley, Wiltshire**, went to **Babington** and was employed as master of the charity school there. His salary was £15 a year, and he had a house for his residence, he does not know if the house is in the parish of **Mells** or Babington.

[Signed.]

[S.R.O., settlement examination D/P/Hemington 13/3/5.11.]

20 April 1797.

Before T. Horner and Thomas S. Jolliffe.

William Penny, residing in Mells, states that he is aged thirty and was born at North Bradley, Wiltshire. William's father, also called William, is a legal parishioner of Hemington. In 1789 William junior was chosen by Mrs Knatchbull (since deceased) to take care of the charity school at **Vobster**, in the parish of Mells, his salary was to be £15 a year, William has continued to live at Mells ever since,

In 1790 Mrs Knatchbull had asked William to act as parish clerk at Babington for John Berriman (who through age and sickness was unable to serve that office), William officiated as parish clerk until December 1795, when John Berriman died, and continued to do so until John Berriman's son, also called John, was appointed to the office in February 1797.

William further states that he has done no other act to gain a settlement, his wife's name is Mary and they have five children, William ten years old, Ann eight, John six, Mary three years and Sarah of the age of nine months.

[Signed.]

It is probable that the school referred to in the above examination was that for which Elizabeth Long, of **Babington House**, had created a charity. By a deed enrolled in Chancery in 1763, a sum of £15 was to be paid annually to a schoolmaster to teach and instruct the poor children of Babington in reading and writing. The schoolmaster was to be appointed by the heirs of Babington Manor [Charity commissioners report].

[S.R.O., settlement examination D/P/Hemington 13/3/5.16.]

[Case 86] 1794. Elizabeth Baulch.

She is now the wife of William Long, otherwise William Harvey. No justice is identified, nor the precise date given.

Elizabeth Baulch states that prior to her marriage to William Long, otherwise Harvey, she was delivered of a bastard child, now called Mary Ann Long Baulch, born in July 1789 in the parish of **Cudworth**; in which parish Elizabeth had a settlement, and where she had received relief.

In March 1791 Elizabeth married William Long, otherwise Harvey, and they went to reside at **Winsham**. William was at that time, and still is, serving as a substitute in the **Dorset** Militia, he has been in actual service for two years, and Elizabeth has been with him.

Elizabeth had left Mary Ann in Winsham, in which parish the child had been receiving relief.

[No mark or signature.]

3 December 1794. William Long, otherwise Harvey.

Before J. Michell and John Hanning.

William Long, otherwise William Harvey, now serving in the Dorset Militia as a substitute for John Wheller of **Dorchester**.

William states that he was born a bastard in the parish of **Knowle St Giles**. His mother was Susanna Long, deceased. At the age of sixteen weeks he was taken to their home at **Axminster** by his aunt, Ann Seward, wife of Edward Seward.

William had lived there until he was aged between nine and ten years old, he then worked as a day labourer for Francis Denning of Axminster for several years. During the time he worked for Denning he lived at Denning's house.

When work was short he worked for other persons, and then he lodged at the house where he worked or in private lodgings.

He worked one whole year for Denning without leaving his service, and done no other act to gain a settlement.

In February 1792 (sic) William says he was married to Elizabeth Baulch at Axminster, by whom he has one child called William, now aged two years. His wife and child are now residing in the borough of **Chard**.

[S.R.O., settlement examination D/PS/ILM. 6/42.2. (Ilminster petty sessions).]

[Case 87] **28 March 1795. Thomas Cox.**
Before John Turner.

Thomas Cox, a labourer, states that he was born in the parish of **Meare**, and lived there until he was fifteen years old, at which age he hired himself as a servant to Mr Rocke of **Glastonbury**. His wages were to be three and a half guineas a year. Thomas stayed with Mr Rocke for two years, he then returned to Meare and lived with his father for a year.

Thomas then hired himself as a servant to the following:
Mr Symes of **Brent Knoll** (South Brent) served one year, wages six guineas.
James Reed of **Chilton**, served one year, wages £6.
Mr Willmott of **Lovington** (Lavington) served one year, wages six guineas.
Returned to Meare and lived with his father. He has done no other act to gain a settlement.

[*Signed.*]
[S.R.O., settlement examination D/P/Meare 13/3/1.12.]

[Case 88] **21 August 1795. Joseph Rumbold.**
Before W. Phelips and S.Farewell.

Joseph Rumbold residing in **Bruton**, states that he was born in **Hounslow, Middlesex**. At the age of eight or nine years he went to live as a yearly servant with the Earl of Rockingham [Charles Watson Wentworth, 1730-82, succeeded his father, Thomas, who was created Marquess 1746] in the parish of **Wakefield, Yorkshire**.

His wages were five guineas the first year, and an additional guinea each succeeding year. Joseph served the Earl about nine years, after which he was hired by Captain Torr of His Majesty's 4th Regiment of Dragoons, the hiring was as a yearly servant, for which Joseph was to receive twenty guineas a year. He served Captain Torr for five years at different places; the last forty days of his service being at **Ansford**.

Joseph then went to **Bath**. There he was married to Elizabeth, they have four children, Henry, Joseph, Sarah and Elizabeth.

[*Signed.*]
[S.R.O., settlement examination D/P/Bruton 13/3/8.48.]

[Case 89] **1 January 1796. Joseph Martin.**
Joseph Martin, residing at **Huntspill**, states that he was born there. He is now aged twenty-eight years. Joseph was bound out by the parish as an apprentice to Thomas Jeane Esq. of **West Monkton**, this apprenticeship was in respect of

Jeane's estate in the parish of Huntspill.

Joseph served Jeane for two years and then was turned over to Thomas Grabham, Jeane's tenant, with whom Joseph lived in Bridgwater for five years. Joseph, who was at that time of the age of fourteen years, then ran away and hired himself to various people in **Hampshire**.

Six months after his apprenticeship expired, Joseph was married to Mary, by whom he had one child of the age of nine months. Joseph further states that he has done no other act to gain a settlement.

[*Mark*.]

[S.R.O., settlement examination D/P/Huntspill 13/3/6.11.]

[Case 90] **29 March 1796. Bridget Richardson.**

Before John Michell, clerk.

Bridget states that she was born at **Holywell**, Wales. At the age of sixteen she went to live with her brother who kept the 'White Hart', Temple Street, **Bristol**. She stayed a year, then married William Richardson, sergeant in 119th Regiment of Foot.

She went with her husband in his marches from place to place. Six weeks ago her husband was ordered to embark for the West Indies, the commanding officer refused to give Bridget a passage with her husband. So they parted, at **St Helens**, near **Portsmouth**.

Bridget understood that her husband had gained a settlement in **Curry Rivel** by service. As she had no money she is applying to the overseers of Curry Rivel to assist her on her way to **Bristol** and then to **Wales**.

[*Mark*.]

[Endorsed] Bridget is correct and she is to be given 12s to enable her to reach her friends [here meaning relatives], who appear to be in a line of life to receive and provide for her.

[S.R.O., settlement examination, D/P/Curry Rivel 13/3/4.40.]

[Case 91] **14 January 1797. John Landford.**

Before W. Phelips and C. Phelips.

John Landford, residing at **Pitcombe**, states that he was born there, though his baptism has not been found in the Pitcombe registers. When he was aged fourteen he went to work as a blacksmith for Philip Beck of **Stoney Stoke**, he worked for his victuals only. John stayed there for six months, he then went to **Bristol** and other places for two and a half months.

He then went to **Rodney Stoke** and worked for William Weeks, dairyman and carpenter, he received one shilling a week, and his victuals and lodging 'sometime'.

John's next moves were to **Compton Dundon**, working for George Edgar as a blacksmith, stayed two months.

Then employed by Thomas Randell, at **West Coker**, working as a journeyman blacksmith, stayed three months.

From West Coker John went to **Shepton Mallet**, where he enlisted into the **Plymouth** division of Marines, under the command of Colonel James Burleigh. John served in the Marines for eleven years and two months; for nine years he was on board His Majesty's ships *Kingston, The Dublin* and *Prince Edward*. John was then discharged, being "old and undersized".

Returning to Pitcombe he resumed working as a journeyman blacksmith and weaver, for different persons. He has done no other act to gain a settlement.

[*Mark.*]

[S.R.O., settlement examination D/P/Pitcombe 13/3/4.12.]

[Case 92] **30 December 1797. William Stacey.**

Before W. Medlycott.

William Stacey, residing at **Horsington**, states that he was born in the city of **Westminster**, but he cannot state in which parish.

He was bound apprentice to the parish of **Maperton**, to Michael Pitman of the same parish, farmer. When Pitman died his widow married Mr John Longman of **Milborne Port**, and William was taken there by his mistress, and served Mr Longman until two years before his indentures expired.

William then went to **Newfoundland**. He then enlisted into His Majesty's service, from which service he has lately been discharged. He has done no further act to gain a settlement.

[*Mark.*]

[S.R.O., settlement examination D/P/Horsington 13/3/6.6.]

[Case 93] **5 January 1798. Jane White.**

Before C.Hobbs and G.Templer.

Jane White, residing at **Ashcott**, states that two years ago she was hired for a year by William Nicols, of **Mark**, her wages to be two and a half guineas. Jane served her year and received her wages, less eleven shillings and sixpence, which sum her mistress retained for articles of household furniture which Jane had broken whilst in service, and for "other causes".

Jane further states that she has done no other act to gain a settlement.

[*Mark.*]

Subscript, "she has a child named Ann"

[S.R.O., settlement examination D/P/Mark 13/3/4.62.]

5 January 1798. Jane White, single woman, to be removed from Mark to Ashcott.

[S.R.O., removal order, D/P/Mark 13/3/3.41.]

[Case 94] **31 March 1798. Jeremiah Bacon.**

Before W. Phelips and C. Phelips.

Jeremiah Bacon, aged forty two years, and residing in the parish of **Horsington**, in which parish he states that he was born and where his parents were legally settled. When he was aged sixteen years he hired himself to Mr Peter Martin of Horsington for a year, his wages to be £6. He served Mr Martin for the year and received his wages.

Since the above service Jeremiah has been serving as a private soldier in the 27th Regiment of Foot. The regiment was stationed in **Gibraltar**, where he was wounded with a musket shot in his right leg, in consequence of which he was discharged as being unfit.

He further states that he has worked as a day labourer only, and has not worked as a yearly servant, neither has he done any other act to gain a settlement.

[*Mark.*]

[S.R.O., settlement examination D/P/Horsington 13/3/6.3.]

[case 95] 13 December 1799. John Hockey.

Before W. Medlycott.

John Hockey, a butcher, residing in the parish of **Horsington**, in which parish he states that he was born, and where his father was settled. When John was twenty years old, he went to **Henstridge**, where he rented a dwelling house, a slaughter house and a piece of ground, for which he paid six pounds six shillings a year.

John stayed in Henstridge for ten years, he then returned to Horsington, and where he has lived ever since in a cottage, which was given to Betty, his wife, by the late Mr Spencer, in lieu of a debt that was owed to her. John has done no act to gain a settlement in his own right.

[*Signed.*]

Note by Justice of the Peace:

"Allow nine shillings a week for the man and his wife."

[S.R.O., settlement examination D/P/Horsington 13/3/6.2.]

[Case 96] 26 December 1799. Edward Low.

Before [Lord] Paulett and Richard Thomas Combe.

Edward Low, residing **Curry Rivel**, states that he was born on the seas, his father and grandfather were both soldiers, and he does not know where they were born, neither does he know where his mother was born. Edward had continued with the army since his birth until he enlisted as a soldier. He was discharged about eight years ago. He had never lived as a servant or apprentice or done any act to gain a settlement.

About five years ago he was married at **Yeovil** to Mary Gillard, widow, whose settlement was at **Drayton**, by birth and by right of her former husband

Francis Gillard. The pauper and his wife, together with their two children Betty and Jane, who are both under the age of seven, are now chargeable to the parish of Curry Rivel.

[Mark.]

Counsel's opinion is now sought:

The parish of Curry Rivel wish to remove the pauper and family to Drayton, and the two parishes submit their case. Can the pauper be removed or not?

Can the wife be removed to Drayton, whilst the husband remains in Curry Rivel, or if the pauper runs away and leaves his family chargeable to Curry Rivel can they be removed to Drayton?

Or if they remain at Curry Rivel can an order be made for the maintenance of the wife and children, and if so will the parish of Drayton be obliged to reimburse the parish of Curry Rivel such part of the expenses as relate to the wife and children?

If it can be proved that the pauper was born in Ireland, and has gained no legal settlement in England, can he and the family be removed to Ireland as vagrants?

Opinion given by John Lens, Lincolns Inn, 14 February 1800:

If the husband had left the wife and children then they could be removed to the original settlement of the wife before marriage, but no authority can be found for sending the wife and children away from the husband, he cannot be removed with them as Drayton is not the place of his settlement. No order can be made on the parish to which a pauper belongs to reimburse the expenses

occasioned by his maintenance in another.

The Vagrant Act of 17 Geo. 11 c5 provides for sending Irish vagrants back to their own country, but some positive act of vagrancy must be committed by the party who is so removed.

[S.R.O., settlement examination D/P/Curry Rivel 13/3/2.19 & 19a.]

[Case 97] **3 February 1800. John Hockey.**

No justices named.

John Hockey, now aged thirty-four years, and residing in the parish of **Horsington**, states that he was born in that parish, where his parents were settled. When he was thirteen or fourteen years old he went to **Sherborne, Dorset**, and hired himself to Mr Robert Clarke, who kept the 'Plume of Feathers' public house.

John was to work under the ostler and to go errands, for this he was to receive the vails [gratuities] that were given to him, and if these were not sufficient he would be given some old clothes. After thirty or forty weeks John fell out with his master as he was only receiving sixpence or a shilling a week.

John then returned to Horsington and hired himself to Mr John Knight, of **Horsington Marsh**. Mrs Knight was John's cousin. After a year John hired himself to Mr John Knight (sic) of **Wilkinthroop**, also in the parish of Horsington, carpenter. John was to receive three shillings a week from Lady Day to Michaelmas, and two shillings a week from Michaelmas to Lady Day. Nine years ago John was married in **Henstridge** to Elizabeth.

[*Mark.*]

[S.R.O., settlement examination D/P/Horsington 13/3/6.10.]

[Case 98] **7 May 1801. Thomas Wise.**

The justices are not named.

Thomas Wise, a shearman [cloth cutter] residing in **Mells**, states that he was born in that parish and is now aged fifty-eight years.

At the age of twelve he was apprenticed for five years, to Richard Poyntz and Richard Durbin, clothiers. Thomas had served three years when Durbin died, shortly afterwards Poyntz also died. Thomas then agreed to serve, for three years, Charles French of **Whatley**, clothier. Thomas was to work shearman's hours, that is about seventy-two hours a week.

French, who also carried on the business of a brandy merchant, wanted Thomas to work for him at other times as needed, to do such work as looking after his master's horse; for this "overwork" Thomas received clothes and victuals.

Thomas usually lodged with his father, but occasionally stayed in French's house at Whatley.

At the end of the three years service Thomas agreed to serve another six months. During this time he "eloped from his service" but returned after six weeks and served over the time that he was away.

Thomas further states that he has a wife named Elizabeth, and that he is chargeable to the parish of Mells.

[*Mark.*]

[S.R.O., settlement examination D/P/Mells 13/3/3.39.]

[Case 99] **30 July 1801. William Manning.**

Before R. Combe, John Hanning and W. Hanning.

William Manning, a staymaker residing at **Curland**, states that he was born in **Buckland St Mary**, and is now aged forty-eight years. His father was Robert Manning, who was settled at Buckland St Mary by birth.

At the age of nine years William went as an apprentice to his uncle John Stembridge of Buckland St Mary, staymaker [stays were formerly of leather, worn by working women outside their clothes]. He lived with his uncle until he was twenty-one. William had never seen any indentures, although he heard Stembridge say that he had been bound by his father by indenture, neither does William know if any consideration was paid.

When the apprenticeship had expired William agreed to serve Stembridge as a yearly servant, which he did for six or seven years, receiving an increase in wages every year. William then carried on the business of staymaker in Buckland St Mary for two years, after which he moved to **Staple Fitzpaine**, and there stayed about one year, lodging with John Cross.

William then married his present wife Ann; they rented a house in Curland for thirty shillings a year, about thirteen or fourteen years later William rented another house in Curland, for which he paid two guineas a year, his landlord was Thomas Murless. About seven years ago William also rented a meadow from Murless, the rent he paid, which included the house and garden, was five guineas a year.

Six years ago Robert Manning sold to his son William, for the sum of £10.0s.0d., a leasehold cottage and garden together with a plot of ground or orchard containing one and a half acres, all being situated in Buckland St Mary. Robert had continued to occupy the house and garden, whilst William had occupied "the orchard or plot of ground with the common appurtenant thereto" [right to use of a common]. This had been valued at £5.0s.0d.

William and his wife have seven children, William aged eleven years, Ann nine years, Maria seven years, Mary five years, Rebecca three years, Robert eighteen months and John aged three months.

The family are now chargeable to the parish of Curland.

[*Signed.*]

The above recites an examination taken on 27 November 1800. At that date the justices requested Mr Bartlett (position unclear) to give a valuation on Manning's estate in Buckland St Mary.

20 December 1800.

Mr Bartlett replies that he values the estate, including the right of common, at £5 per annum.

Postscript:

"I state this under the idea that he has a right to stock a greater number of cattle than the premises will keep in the winter."

30 July 1801.

Counsel's opinion has been requested from Mr Serjeant Lens:

"It is agreed between the parishes of Curland and Buckland St Mary that if the law will not admit the right of stocking the common appurtenant with more cattle than the acre and a half will winter, that then the value of the acre and a half and right of common appurtenant occupied by the pauper, and the renting of [the plot of ground] at five guineas a year will not be occupying [a tenement worth] £10 a year while he resided in Curland, but if the unlimited right of common can be supported for more than the acre and a half will winter then that it will be occupying £10 a year or upwards, and a settlement will be gained in Curland. Your opinion is therefore desired whether or not this is an occupation of £10 a year, the parishes having agreed to abide by your decision."

Opinion.

"I am of the opinion that by the common law the right of common annexed to any land or tenements as appurtenant or appendant must be measured as to its extent by the number of cattle which the premises is capable of maintaining at other periods of the year. As this case is by agreement stated to depend on that matter of law it is not material to consider what the reputed annual value of these premises, together with the right of common such as it was deemed to be, might amount to. I am therefore of opinion that under these circumstances and the effect of this agreement, this is not an occupying to the amount of £10 a year."

Signed John Lens, Lincolns Inn. 1 July 1801.

[S.R.O., settlement examination D/PS/ILM. 6/45.11 & 12.]

For references to staymaking see M Dorothy George, *England in transition* [Penguin 1953] p.38 &p.72. Also Elizabeth Ewings, *Everyday dress 1650-1900* [Batsford 1984].

[Case 100] **17 November 1801. Martha Fear.**

Before H. Hippesley and James Tooker; sworn at 'Old Down Inn'.

Martha Fear, a widow residing at **Stratton-on-Foss**, states that she is thirty-seven years old and was born in the parish of Stratton. Martha further states that she was there delivered of twin children, born bastards.

John Fear, a coalminer lodging in Stratton, was the father. He was apprehended to answer the complaint of the overseers respecting the said bastards.

On 15 October 1785 Martha was lawfully married to John Fear, in Stratton church, but her husband went away immediately after the marriage ceremony, and she has not seen him since.

Martha has heard, from his brother, that John Fear is dead, and that they had attended his funeral.

[*Mark*.]

[S.R.O., settlement examination D/P/Stratton-on-Foss 13/3/4.62.]

[Case 101] **2 May 1803. James Dix.**

Before William Bingham and Thomas S. Jolliffe.

James Dix, residing at **High Littleton**, states that he is now aged thirty-eight years, and that he was born in **Emborough**, in which parish his father, William

Dix, was legally settled. Sixteen years ago he hired himself to Thomas Webb, of **Binegar**, serving four years, during which time he slept in Webb's house. Seven or eight years ago James rented a house from Mr James Brodribb, deceased, at the rent of thirty-two shillings a year. He also rented two acres of ground, for a potato crop, from farmer George Kingman, at eight guineas yearly.

It appears that James was unable to pay the full amount, so he underlet part of the ground, the under tenants paid the money themselves into George Kingman's hands.

Four years ago James rented a house from Mr T. Brodribb at the rent of two guineas a year. At Lady Day in 1801 James took a plough paddock, belonging to Mr William Bath, for a crop of potatoes, the paddock being about one and a half acres. They could not agree about the rent, Mr Bath asked more than James was prepared to give, finally it was decided that James should pay Mr Bath in potatoes, and that he would give him twenty sacks.

There was a bad crop of potatoes that year, and the price rose to twelve shillings a sack, in consequence of which Mr Bath accepted fourteen sacks only, which amounted to eight guineas.

Fifteen years ago James married Ann Gulliver, they have six children – William aged fourteen years, George ten, Elizabeth eight, Thomas four, James three and Samuel two years old.

[S.R.O., settlement examination D/P/High Littleton 13/3/7.40a.]

[Case 102] **31 May 1803. John Silverthorne.**

Before W. Phelips and John Strode.

John Silverthorne, residing at **Bruton** (Brewton), states that he is now aged sixty-nine years. He was born in the parish of **South Brewham**, where his father was legally settled.

At the age of seventeen he was hired as a yearly servant to the Earl of Ilchester, to serve as an under-groom; his wages were to be £6 per annum.

John had been hired at **Redlynch**, in the parish of Bruton, but he followed the family to **Melbury House, near Evershot**, and His Lordship's other seat at **Abbotsbury**, on the Dorset coast. After the groom died John succeeded him, and his wages were raised to £10. John served the Earl until he died, and continued in the service of the Countess at **Discove** (Redlynch) and Melbury.

The Dowager Countess died at **Melbury Osmond**, Dorset, and it was in that parish that John served for the last year and a half of Lady Ilchester's life.

After John had been in Lord Ilchester's service for four years he married Elizabeth Chapman (his wife died about one and a half years before Lady Ilchester's death). While his wife was alive John sometimes lodged with her at Evershot, Dorset.

After Lady Ilchester's death John went to work for Mr John Field at **Melbury Sampford**. He stayed for one and a half years, lodging at a farmhouse near Mr Field, but boarding with his master.

When John left Mr Field he hired himself to Andrew Baine Esq. at **West Coker**. His wages were seven shillings a week. After two years John returned to Redlynch, where he worked for the Earl of Ilchester as a day labourer, up to the time of the Earl's death; since which time he has lived in Bruton, without employment and receiving relief from the parish.

[*Signed.*]

[S.R.O., settlement examination D/P/Bruton 13/3/8.69.]

11 June 1803.

John Silverthorne to be removed to **Melbury Sampford**, Dorset, from Bruton.

[S.R.O., D/P/Bruton 13/3/1. 175.]

[Case 103] **23 February 1805. Thomas Simmons.**

Before James Bernard.

Thomas Simmons, residing at **Stogumber**, states that he served an apprenticeship until the age of twenty-four at **Escott** in the parish of Stogumber. Half a year after the expiration of his apprenticeship he went and lived as a servant with William Hook in the tithing of **Halsway**, also in the parish of Stogumber, for four and three quarter years. He then lived with Robert Withers for one year, again in Halsway.

Thomas then married, and about three years later, in February 1803, he was chosen by ballot to serve in the militia. Thomas was able to provide Joseph Hurford as his substitute, having received £5 from the parish officers of Stogumber to enable him to do so as Thomas and his wife already had one child, and his wife was pregnant of a second child.

Thomas further states that he has never resided in any parish other than Stogumber since he was bound apprentice at the age of seven years.

[*Mark.*]

[S.R.O., settlement examination D/P/Crowcombe 13/3/1.20.]

[Case 104] **5 December 1806. Benjamin Danger.**

Before Thomas Hobbs, clerk.

Benjamin Danger states that he is aged twenty-eight, he was born in **Pawlett**, where he lived with his mother until he was twelve years old. At that age he was bound apprentice by his trustees to Isaac Danger of **Charlinch**, carpenter. The apprenticeship was to be for seven years; Benjamin served his time and then served one year more.

He then went to **Puriton** where he worked as a journeyman with Samuel Summers, carpenter, Benjamin was paid eight shillings a week; he worked in Puriton for one year and three months.

Six years ago Benjamin went to **Huntspill** where he worked with John Burge, carpenter, as a journeyman, being paid nine shillings a week, and worked two years at the same wages. Benjamin then agreed with Burge to work for a year, wages to be ten shillings. Benjamin served that year, since then he has continued to live with Burge at the same wages, when his health permitted him to work.

[*Mark.*]

[S.R.O., settlement examination D/P/Huntspill 13/3/6.16.]

[Case 105] **24 January 1807. William Clarke.**
Before W.H. Colston.
William Clarke, residing at **Evercreech**, states that he was born at **Lamyatt**. At the age of seventeen he was apprenticed to Thomas Raishley of **Bruton**. Four years ago William was married to Ann, by whom he has two children, William three years old and James one year.

[*Signed.*]

[S.R.O., settlement examination D/P/Evercreech 13/3/4.15.]

30 March 1807.
William Clarke's case was sent for counsel's opinion, this being given by H. Hobhouse of Brunswick Square.
William Clarke, whose settlement was in **Lamyatt**, "was placed as an apprentice under an agreement, written upon a six shilling stamp, to Thomas Raishley in the parish of Bruton".
The apprenticeship was to be for three years, William to be paid three shillings a week the first year, three shillings and sixpence the second year, and four shillings the third year, although no money was paid to Thomas Raishley as a consideration.
The apprenticeship conditions follow:
5 June 1797. Articles of agreement between Thomas Raishley of Bruton, cordwainer, and William Clarke the younger of the parish of Lamyatt.
Thomas Raishley binds himself to teach or cause to be taught William Clarke "the full art and mistery of the trade of cordwaining as he himself knoweth and behave to and use the said William Clarke in a fatherly tender manner and to pay the said William Clarke for three years " (as above).
William Clarke on his part binds himself to "his master faithfully to serve his secrets keep his lawful commands everywhere gladly do, he shall do no damage to his said master, nor see it done of others but to his power shall let or forthwith give notice to his said master of the same he shall not waste his

said master's goods nor lend them unlawfully to any he shall not absent himself from his said master's service day or night unlawfully but in all things as a faithful servant he shall behave himself towards his said master and all during the said term. And the said William Clarke to provide himself with meat drink washing lodging and wearing apparel in sickness and in health."

The service was in Bruton and William Clarke usually slept there, except for Saturday and Sunday nights when he returned to Lamyatt and slept at his father's house, it is certain that he never slept in either parish for forty successive nights. Clarke is now residing in Evercreech and is likely to become chargeable, the opinion of counsel is requested as to which parish should be considered to be his parish of settlement, Bruton or Lamyatt?

Counsel decrees that the contract of apprenticeship should have been under seal to make it valid (on the grounds that the act of 31 Geo. 11.c11 [1757-58] only did away with the necessity of the contract being indented). This contract being defective as a contract of apprenticeship it could not confer settlement as a hired servant, the opinion given is that William Clarke's settlement is in Lamyatt.

[*Signed by H.Hobhouse.*]

[S.R.O., counsel's opinion D/P/Evercreech 13/3/6.5.]

[Case 106] **11 February 1807. Charlotte Mason.**

Before [indistinct] Palmer.

Charlotte Mason states that she is now about fifty-six years of age, and believes that she was born in the parish of **St John**, in the province of **New York, America**. About twenty-nine years ago she was married to Thomas Mason at St John's church, in America, in which country they lived until about twenty-four years ago, and then removed to **Guernsey**, where they lived for five years. Two years ago Charlotte and her husband went to **Douglas**, in the **Isle of Man**, and it was there fourteen months ago that her husband died.

Charlotte was returning to Guernsey on the dispatch *Captain Rose*, when she was wrecked upon the coast of **Wales**. From thence she was landed at **Uphill**, in the Axe estuary, and came from there to **North Cadbury**.

Charlotte Mason further states that she has heard her husband and his mother, Mary Mason, say that he was born in North Cadbury, an illegitimate son of Mary Mason, and that he and his mother were removed from North Cadbury as soon as possible after the birth. Thomas was educated in **London** until he was about fifteen years old, at which time he went to America.

[*Mark.*]

[S.R.O., settlement examination DD/X/PR.36. (Penrose collection, North Cadbury.)]

[Case 107] **27 January 1808. George Capron.**

Before W. Hanning.

George Capron, apprehended in the parish of **Merriott** as a rogue and vagabond, states that he was born in **Towcester, Northamptonshire**. On 17 February 1806 he was married to Ann Blair at **Coventry, Warwickshire**. Since then he has gained his living by gathering 'viol' [vial] bottles [for medicines] and selling articles made by him and his wife. He does not have a hawker's licence.

George has pretended to be a castaway seaman, but he never was, although he and his wife have begged the country as such.

[*Signed.*]

Hawkers' licences were issued by the Justices at Quarter Sessions. A genuine castaway seaman would have been able to claim relief from the churchwardens of the parishes through which he passed.

[S.R.O., settlement examination D/PS/ILM. 6/48.1. (Ilminster petty sessions).]

[Case 108] **15 February 1808. Thomas Newton.**

Before Jeffrys Allen and [? illegible initials] Allen.

Thomas Newton, a balloted militiaman serving as a private in the 2nd Somerset Regiment of Militia, for the parish of **Huntspill** where he has a wife and one child. His family are now chargeable to the parish of Huntspill. Thomas states that he was born in the parish of **Wiveliscombe**, in which parish his parents were legally settled.

Fourteen or fifteen years ago he hired himself for a year to Richard Pain, who then kept the 'Fox and Goose' in **Brent Knoll** (South Brent). Thomas served Pain for two years at wages of one shilling a week.

Thomas then worked as follows:

Hired himself to William Champenny of **Burnham** for one year.

Hired himself to Charles Kirle of **Huntspill** for two years, at wages of five guineas a year.

Hired himself to Edward Chapple of Brent Knoll for two years, at wages of £7.10s.0d. a year.

Has done no other act to gain a settlement.

[*Signed.*]

[S.R.O., settlement examination D/P/Hunstspill 13/3/6.19.]

7 October 1808. Betty Newton, widow of Thomas Newton.

Betty Newton, who is living in and is chargeable to the parish of Huntspill, states that she is aged about thirty-two or thirty-three years, she was born in the parish of **Puriton**. Some seven years ago Betty lived with Edward Chapple of Brent Knoll (South Brent) where her late husband Thomas was employed as a yearly servant. Betty is unable to say what wages he received.

Betty and her late husband lived together for two years, after which Thomas went to **Berrow** for a short period, but later returned to the parish of Huntspill where he worked at the canal for about a year. Thomas then went to **Bristol** where he also worked at the canal for about a year. Upon his return to Huntspill he was married to Betty.

Betty Newton further states that she often saw her late husband from the time he left her at Brent Knoll until her marriage with him, which was about three years ago. Betty has two children by her husband, William aged two and a quarter years, and Fanny aged five months.

About twelve months since her husband was drawn into the 2nd Somerset Militia as a private for the parish of Huntspill.

Immediately he was drawn he marched and was quartered at **Salisbury**, where he died about sixteen or seventeen weeks since. Thomas had done no other act to gain a settlement.

[*Mark.*]

[S.R.O., settlement examination D/P/Huntspill 13/3/6.18.]

1808.

Betty Newton and family removed from Huntspill to Brent Knoll.

[S.R.O. D/P/ Brent Knoll 13/3/2.30.]

[Case 109] **16 February 1808. Thomas Charlton.**

No Justices named.

Thomas Charlton, a linenbleacher, residing at **Horsington**, states that he is aged sixty years, and was born at **Eccles, Lancashire**, where his father occupied a farm at the rent of £35 per annum. At the age of sixteen Thomas was bound apprentice by his father, for five years, to Joseph Andrews of **Manchester**, linenbleacher.

Andrews was to find Thomas in board and lodging, and to pay him £8 towards providing him with clothes. Thomas has lost the indenture; he had served the term of the apprenticeship then had served Andrews a further five years as a yearly servant.

After serving Andrews, Thomas went as a yearly servant to Richard Ainsworth of **Saltsford Township**, and served a year. Thomas then worked nineteen years for John Phillips and Co., of **Chailey, Staffordshire.**

Two years after he started working for Phillips he was married, at **Cheadle**, Lancashire, to Elizabeth Cope.

Thomas and Elizabeth had had several children. It was during this service that his wife had died.

Thomas next served George Smith at **Grytch**, near **Matlock**, Derbyshire, and stayed three quarters of a year.

He then served four years with Charles Smith at **Northampton**.

Next to **Bitton, Gloucestershire**, taking his children with him, and where both Thomas and two of his sons worked as weekly servants for Messrs Watts, Harris and Co., here they were employed in assisting the construction of workshops, buckinghouse and boiling house for the manufacture of calicoes [items of white cotton cloth].

Thomas then made an agreement with Watts and Co., to take the dwelling house, workshops and implements of trade, as well as a close of pasture of about an acre, at the rent of £30 per annum. Thomas would bleach their calicoes at 10d a piece [28 yards] and their cotton yarn at 2½d per pound.

Thomas worked under this agreement for two years, during which time he bleached what was required of him by Watts and Co., and bleached linen for several other persons. The work that he did for Watts and Co. was done at a lower rate than he would have worked for, for any other person.

Harris and Co. (sic) took the grass which grew on the close, after it had been mown by Thomas from time to time, it being necessary to keep it in a proper state for use as a bleaching ground.

The agreement, which had been in writing, was kept by Watts and Co.

Thomas further states that he has done no other act to gain a settlement; he has lately been married to Margaret King of **Horsington**.

[*Signed*.]

[S.R.O., settlement examination D/P/Horsington 13/3/6.11.]

[Case 110] **6 May 1808. John Curry.**

Before Thomas Hobbs and G.H. Templer.

John Curry, residing **Huntspill**, states that he was born in the parish of **Berrow**, and that he is now aged nineteen years. At the age of seven years he was bound out by the parish officers of Berrow to John Smithfield of **East Brent**, yeoman, in respect of his land in Berrow.

John was to serve until he was aged twenty-one years.

After John had resided with Smithfield for more that a year he was turned over to John Puddy of **Voale** in the parish of **Mark**, cordwainer. John served Puddy for seven years, which service consisted of two years in Mark and five years in **Blackford**, in the parish of **Wedmore**.

When John's apprenticeship was completed he returned to Berrow and worked as a journeyman in his trade for seven weeks, then worked as a journeyman with William Chubb, cordwainer, in Huntspill for about fifteen months. After this he had worked with Thomas Heale for eight weeks and then with Thomas Hardacre for two years.

John Curry further states that John Smithfield died about four years ago.

[*Mark*.]

[S.R.O., settlement examination D/P/Huntspill 13/3/6.17a.]

6 May 1808.

John Curry, removal order Huntspill to Wedmore.

[S.R.O., D/P/Huntspill 13/3/6.17.]

[Case 111] **30 September 1809. Robert Bennett, otherwise Trivett and Susannah Trivett.**

Before W. Hanning and W. Palmer.

Susannah Trivett, a single woman residing at **Allowenshay**, [near **Ilminster**] states that Robert Bennett,. otherwise Trivett, is her son and was born a bastard in the parish of **Knowle St Giles**.

[*Mark.*]

Robert Bennett, otherwise Trivett, a labourer residing **Chard** parish, states that he never lived a yearly servant out of the parish of Knowle St Giles. He was never bound an apprentice or occupied a tenement rated at £10 a year. In fact he had never done any act to gain a settlement.

Robert also states that he and his wife Sarah, their children Nancy aged five and a half years, Frances four and a half and William one and a half years old, are all resident in and chargeable to the parish of Chard.

On 4 June 1800 Robert was admitted and has ever since been a member of a Friendly Society, established in Chard, the rules of which were exhibited, confirmed and filed at the general quarter session for the county of Somerset on 30 April 1794, "pursuant to the statute in that case made and provided".

Robert had resided in Chard since 7 August last "under and by virtue of the said act".

[*Mark.*]

[S.R.O., settlement examination D/P/ILM. 6/49.16. (Ilminster petty sessions.)]

[Case 112] **27 December 1809. Charles Meech.**

The justices are not named.

Charles Meech, labourer, residing in Whitelackington, states that he is the son of John Meech, who had formerly rented **Silvenge Mill** in the parish of Whitelackington, for which he paid £13 in rent.

At the age of fifteen Charles agreed to serve Mr James Wheller of **Puckington**, for six months only, receiving eighteen pence a week.

Charles afterwards enlisted as a soldier, and was promoted to Lance Sergeant in Earl Poulett's Fencible Cavalry [a defence unit, not liable for overseas service] and was stationed at **Reading** in the recruiting service.

At Reading banns of marriage to Mary Grantham were twice published. Mary was a servant, but Charles did not know to whom, neither did he know the name of her mother, who was dead, nor the name of her father, who was alive, or her father's business.

Charles then had to march to **London**, where he met up with Mary who had travelled there by coach. In London they were married by licence, and according to the rites and ceremonies of the Church of England. Charles did not know in which church they had been married. Neither does he know where or by whom the licence was issued, although he paid two guineas for it and fetched it himself.

Some men from the regiment, namely Mark Cudmore and his wife, George Hutchings and Thomas Watt and his wife were present at the marriage.

Charles later obtained a certificate from the parson, which he has lost. This marriage had taken place fourteen years ago.

Charles and Mary have five children, John aged twelve years, born at **Bridlington, Yorkshire**, Thomas ten years, born **Kelvedon, Essex**, Jane six years, William two and a half years and James one year old, all born at Whitelackington.

[*Signed.*]

27 December 1809. Mary Meech.

Mary Meech, residing in Whitelackington, states that she is now aged thirty-two, and was born at Reading in Berkshire. After her mother died she went to live there with her aunt and uncle Thomas and Mary Grantham. When she was ten years old her aunt put her to service with a butcher, but Mary does not recollect his name. When she was aged twenty-two she hired herself for a year, her wages to be £3, and a month's warning or wages, but Mary does not remember the name of her master.

During this time she became acquainted with Charles Meech, who was then a corporal in Lord Paulett's Fencible Cavalry, banns of marriage between them were twice published, but then Charles had to march to London. Mary also went to London, and they were married in a parish church by a parson, who read the ceremony with his gown on.

[*No mark or signature.*]

[S.R.O., settlement examination D/PS/ILM. 6/49.29. Ilminster petty sessions.]

[Case 113] 22 February 1811. Jane Hatch.

Before Thomas Williams and T.S. Horner.

Jane Hatch, residing in **Mells**, states that she is twenty-eight years of age. She does not know where she was born. Her father, William Hatch, was legally settled in **Leigh-on-Mendip**. Three and a half years ago she bargained with William Wilton, gentleman, of **Frome** (Frome Selwood) to serve him for a year at the yearly wages of five guineas, and her meat, drink and lodging. Jane served Mr Wilton over two years.

In 1809 she was married to John Read, a labourer employed by Mr Fussell of

Mells, edgetoolmaker. John earned occasionally ten shillings and sixpence to twenty-five shillings a week when supplied with water, but at other times, when water was scarce, he worked as a husbandman when he could get employment.

Jane further states that after she was married to John Read for about a year, she heard that John had a former wife living, and that she had been seen in the parish of Mells.

Although Jane no longer considered herself to be a married woman, she and John decided to continue to live together, so she hired herself to him as a servant for a year, her wages to be £5.15.0d. a year and "received a shilling in earnest".

Jane is now with child, which child is likely to be born a bastard and to become chargeable to the parish of Mells.

[*Mark.*]

[S.R.O., settlement examination D/P/Mells 13/3/3.47.]

22 February 1811.

Jane Hatch, who is with child, which child is likely to be born a bastard, is to be removed from Mells to Frome Selwood.

[S.R.O., removal order D/P/Mells 13/3/1.92.]

[Case 114] **15 April 1812. William Slade.**

Notice "to the constables, tythingmen and others, His Majesty's peace officers of **Combe St Nicholas**. Notice summoning James Wyatt, overseer of the poor, to appear before the Justices of the Peace, at the 'George Inn', **Ilminster**, on Wednesday 29 April, at ten in the forenoon, to answer the complaint of William Slade for refusing him relief in sickness".

[*Signed W. Palmer.*]

Note from W. Palmer to Mr Wyatt:

"The income of a man or woman and three small children in health, according to the price of bread now, must be twelve shillings and three pence a week, in sickness more is required.

"Take care that from this day William Slade's family have that sum per week at least, until the return of this summons."

[*Signed W. Palmer.*]

(This is an example of the Speenhamland system in operation, the amount of relief being related to the current price of bread.)

[S.R.O.,Miscellaneous D/PS/ILM. 6/51.17.

(Ilminster petty sessions).]

[Case 105] **29 April 1812. John Budd.**

Before W. Palmer and W. Hanning.

John Budd, a labourer, residing in **Fivehead**, states that he is aged eighty years, and was born in the parish of **West Hatch**. At the age of seven years he was bound apprentice to Mr Joseph Orchard of **Chilworthy** in the parish of **Ilminster**, by reason of an estate that Mr Orchard occupied in West Hatch. John completed his apprenticeship, and afterwards served Mr Orchard for two years as a yearly servant. Since then John has done no act to gain a settlement. He married Joan his present wife about fifty years ago at **Beercrocombe** [the register there shows that John Budd married Joan Hunibun on 26 October 1762]. They are now chargeable to Fivehead.

    [*Mark.*]

    [S.R.O.,settlement examination D/PS/ILM. 6/51.17. (Ilminster petty sessions.)]

    [S.R.O.,D/P/Beercrocombe 2/1/4. (Marriage register)]

[Case 116] **14 March 1813. William and Nathaniel Watts.**
Before W.H. Festing and W. Palmer.
William Watts, residing in **Broadway**, states that eight years previously, while living with his father at **Curry Mallet**, he agreed with Thomas Channing to be a partner with him in a crop of potatoes; these were to be planted in two and a half acres of land in **Isle Abbots**. Thomas Channing was to provide the land, manure it and prepare it for the crop – William Watts was to plant and manage the crop, find the seed and dig the crop. The produce was to be equally divided between them.
About midsummer of that year, William went to **Clayhanger** in the parish of **Whitelackington**, and worked for Channing as a labourer, and resided with him until the following Michaelmas, at which time William took a house at **Ashill**, at the yearly rent of two and a half guineas.
On 21 October 1804 William was married, at **Whitelackington** church, to his present wife Martha (nee Channing). Immediately afterwards they went to live in the house at Ashill.
About six weeks after Michaelmas William began to plough out the crop of potatoes, this took about a week, the crop was then divided between himself and Channing. At the time of putting in the crop the land was worth £9 per acre, amounting to £22.10s.0d. in the whole for the growth of the crop.
William and Martha have five children: Sarah seven years old, Harriet five years, Susannah four years, Matthew two years and Grace aged four months.

    [*Mark.*]

Nathaniel Watts, father of William Watts, states that William lived with him as part of his family until the time that he took the potato ground. William's settlement is in the parish of Curry Mallet, which settlement he gained by serving Mr Robert Scott, in Curry Mallet, as a yearly servant for four years prior to his marriage.

[*Mark.*]

A further settlement examination presents the agreement in a different way.

Thomas Channing was to find all plough labour, fetching the seed and manuring the land, and getting it ready to receive the crop, William Watts was to plant, weed and take care of the crop, which was then to be divided between them. William does not know if manure was put on the ground at the time of the agreement.

[S.R.O., settlement examination D/PS/ILM. 6/52.13 & 14. (Ilminster petty sessions.)]

[Case 117] **30 June 1813. James Tucker.**

Before J.C. Hippsley and T. Williams.

James Tucker states that he is aged forty-two years, he was born at **High Littleton**, where his father James Tucker, engineer and blacksmith, was legally settled.

James lived with his father in **Midsomer Norton** until he was eleven years old, when his father died. James the elder had received parish relief and charitable gifts from the parish of High Littleton.

James junior worked at **Grove Coal Works** for five or six years, then at **Radstock** and other places. At the age of twenty-one James enlisted as a soldier in 115th Regiment of Foot, in which he served for two years. He was then in Northumberland, where he was discharged with a bad leg.

James next went tunnel driving at **Newent, Gloucestershire** for nine months; worked at the coal mines in **Staffordshire** and **Derbyshire** for two or three years; then went into **Lancashire, Northumberland** and **Yorkshire** for nearly twelve months. James then returned to Derbyshire, where he worked for thirteen or fourteen years.

Eighteen years ago James was married at **Gloucester** to Eleanor Bonner, they have five children: William aged seventeen years, Anna sixteen, James twelve, Richard ten and John seven years old.

James has done no act to gain a settlement for himself.

Seven years ago James was impressed in the sea town of **Liverpool**, he served on board the *Cowes* frigate for five years, at the end of this time he was discharged on account of a back injury which he had sustained by being bruised between some timber.

Ten or eleven years ago James had rented a lodging room with bed and some furniture in it, at **Mesham** near **Ashby** in Derbyshire; (sic) he paid two shillings a week, finding his own board. His landlord and family lived in another part of the house.

Later James got a chaff bed or two, and a little furniture of his own. The door of his room which communicated with the landlord's part of the house was walled up. James then paid only one shilling and twopence for the room, in which his family lived for three years while he was at sea.

[*Mark.*]

[S.R.O., settlement examination D/P/High Littleton 13/3/7.47.]

[Case 118] **1815. Ann Fussell.**

Date and names of justices not given.

Ann Fussell of **Bruton** was born a bastard in **East Pennard**. Six years ago when she was the age of thirteen years, she was hired by her mother, Mary Coles, to Mr James Hoddinott of **Evercreech**, silkthrowster, as a servant for three years.

Mr Hoddinott was to find her in meat, drink, clothes, washing and lodging; Ann was not to leave the premises without permission. The agreement was entered in a book and signed by Ann, her mother, Mr Hoddinott and his servant Henry Holloway, the book was left with Mr Hoddinott.

Ann served for three years. She slept in a cottage next to her master's house with several other girls and took her meals with the girls, Ann was mostly employed in the silk business, but occasionally helped in the kitchen or ran errands. At the end of the three years she hired herself to her master again for one year, and was to receive one shilling and sixpence a week.

During the three years that Ann worked for Mr Hoddinott he employed over one hundred girls who called themselves apprentices.

The working hours in the mill were 5 a.m. to 6 p.m. in the summer, and 7 a.m. to 8 p.m. in the winter. They had an hour for breakfast and an hour for dinner, and after 6 p.m. in the summer and 8 p.m. in the winter their time was their own to do as they pleased, but they could only go off the premises by the superintendent's leave.

Evidence was given by Henry Holloway, late servant to Mr Hoddinott, about the drawing up and signing of the agreement:

The agreement was similar to the agreement entered into by the other employees in the silk throwsters business, Holloway further states that he has not seen the agreement since it was signed. Mr Hoddinott resided in **London**, and only resided at his silk factory a month in a year. The girls were left in the care of a woman who was to see that they were properly looked after, and that they were given two pence a week for pocket money.

As Ann Fussell was now living in Bruton and was with child, this examination was sent for counsel's opinion as to whether Ann's settlement should be considered to be in East Pennard or in Evercreech.

3 March 1815.

"I am of the opinion that the pauper gained a settlement in Evercreech."

[*Signed* J. Topping, Lincoln's Inn.]

[S.R.O., settlement examination and counsel's opinion. D/P/Evercreech 13/3/4. 46]

For a description of silk throwing see M. Dorothy George, *London life in the eighteenth century*. [Penguin reprint, 1976].

6 May 1815. On 7 April 1815 Ann Fussell, single woman, was delivered of a male bastard child, in the parish of Evercreech.

John White the younger, of the parish of Bruton, tiler and plasterer, is the reputed father. He is to pay fifteen shillings, and then two shillings each week to the overseers. Ann is to pay one shilling a week to the overseers.

[S.R.O., bastardy order. D/P/Evercreech 13/5/2. 61.]

[Case 119] **24 December 1816. Elizabeth Newton.**

No justices are named.

Elizabeth Newton, aged sixty-seven, residing in **Crowcombe**, states that she was born at **Huntsham, Devonshire**. She married her late husband John Newton, at **Bridgwater**, and they lived many years in Crowcombe, where John rented a farm at forty guineas a year, and where he was legally settled.

Her husband died in 1805, and by his will left her a freehold house, and a leasehold house in Crowcombe for life, and after her death both properties to be divided between her three youngest sons, Bernard, George and Abraham.

George and Abraham had been living with their mother and father as part of their family, George left home three months after his father's death, and had acquired a settlement by service. Abraham left after about eighteen months, and lived as a yearly servant in **Bawdrip**, and obtained a settlement there.

Elizabeth continued to live in the freehold house for five or six months, after which she hired herself to various persons, viz:

The Reverend Mr Humphries in Crowcombe, served seven or eight months.

Mr Tucker in **Spaxton**, served one year and five weeks. then served ten weeks in Bridgwater.

Henry Palmer, in **Huntspill**, served him as a weekly servant.

John Jennings, in Huntspill, served six months.

At Lady Day in 1809 she hired herself to Benjamin Giblet of **Pawlett** for a year, at the wages of nine guineas per annum, and served him for three years, during the fourth year her master died, but Elizabeth remained in the same parish and served Mr John Lennard for a year and two months.

As her sons had acquired settlements in their own right, none of her children were dependent upon her, and had received no assistance from her during her two years in Pawlett, but during the third year she paid for half a year's schooling for Abraham.

Elizabeth lived at various places for a year, then came to Crowcombe and lodged with George Nation; who rented her freehold house at the yearly rent of eight pounds. She paid him a shilling a week for her lodging and firing, but she found her own bed and food. After about two months, with the consent of her three youngest sons, she sold the freehold house and leasehold house for the sum of £255.

Since her husband's death she had received the rent of both houses, which amounted to £12 a year. Elizabeth further states that she has done no act since whereby she could have obtained a settlement, and that she is now chargeable to Crowcombe.

[*Signed*.]

[S.R.O., settlement examination D/P/Crowcombe 13/3/1.23.]

[Case 120] **10 June 1817. John Munckton and family.**

He and his wife, Jemima, and their children, John aged seven years, Grace six years and Solomon aged three years, are to be removed from **Curry Rivel** to **St Anne's, Westminster.**

2 July 1817. Notice of appeal.

Lodged by **St Anne's, Soho** , to be heard at **Bridgwater** sessions.

It appears that Jemima and the children had been removed to St Anne's without John, the father.

11 July 1817.

Letter from Mr Allen, **Carlisle Street, Soho Square**, complaining that no answer had been received requesting a copy of the settlement examination. It was now accepted that by serving a year in the parish of St Anne's, John Munckton had gained a settlement there.

It will be seen from the settlement examination that John is now aged ten years and Hannah (who has not previously been noted) is aged six years. Grace and Solomon are not mentioned.

[S.R.O., D/P/Curry Rivel 13/3/2. 36-36b.]

3 February 1821. John Munckton.

Before Webb Stone and M. Blake.

John Munckton, a butcher aged fifty-five, now residing at **Taunton St Mary**, states that he was born in the parish of Curry Rivel, he was never an apprentice but learnt his trade from his father. Thirty years ago, being unmarried, he agreed with Mr Samuel Hinton of No. 3 **Gerrard Street, Soho, London,** to serve him as a porter at sixteen guineas a year and his board and lodging. He served Samuel Hinton more than a year and quarter under this agreement.

Since then he has never agreed for service by the year, has never possessed any tenement of his own and has never served any parochial office.

Between twenty and thirty years ago he married Sarah Stone in Westminster, and has by her one daughter aged twenty, now in service at **Long Sutton**.

After the death of his first wife he married Jemima Hutchings at Ruishton twelve or thirteen years ago, and has by her two children; John aged ten years and Hannah six years old. Both children are at the workhouse at **St Gunes** (sic), Soho.

[*Signed.*]

[S.R.O., settlement examination D/P/Taunton St Mary 13/3/5. 120.]

[Case 121] **6 June 1817. Richard Huntsmill.**

Summons to bring Richard Huntsfield (sic) before the magistrates to be examined.

20 June 1817.

Richard Huntsmill appears before D.Durbin.

Residing in **Easton-in-Gordano** (St George's), he states that he is aged forty. He does not know where he was born; his father was a stickmaker and travelled the county (sic).

At the age of seventeen years Richard went abroad, and remained there for seventeen years, except when the vessel called at **Pill**. At the end of that time he lived in **London**.

Eleven years ago Richard was married to Rosanna, by whom he has four children.

[S.R.O., settlement examination D/P/Easton-in-Gordano 13/3/2.54 & 54a.]

11 May 1819. Rosanna Huntsmill.

Wife of Richard Huntsmill, stickmaker. Who was on the bench is not recorded.

Rosanna Huntsmill, residing Easton-in-Gordano (St George's) states that she was born at **Yatton**. Her maiden name was Tailor. Twenty-five years ago she was married at **Clifton, Gloucestershire**, to Thomas Watkins of Easton-in-Gordano, mariner; Thomas had died eleven years since in a French prison.

Rosanna believes that Thomas's legal settlement was in the parish of **Westbury-on-Trym**, Gloucestershire.

Two years after the death of Thomas Watkins, Rosanna was married, at the parish church of St Philip, **Bristol**, to her present husband Richard Huntsmill, by whom she has four children. They are Betsy aged nine years and Richard aged seven years, both born **Whitechapel**, London; John, aged five years, born **Mile End New Town**, London; and Rosanna aged three years and born at

Bethnal Green, London.

Her husband left her last June and she does not know where he is, or where he was legally settled.

[*Signed*.]

[S.R.O., settlement examination D/P/Easton-in-Gordano 13/3/2.26.]

[Case 122] **24 September 1817. Caesar Jackson.**

Before Mr Combe and Mr Uttermere.

Caesar Jackson, residing at **Ashill**, states that he is aged twenty-three, and was born in the city of **Philadelphia**, in **North America**.

Six years ago he hired himself as a monthly servant to Mr Johnson at **New Orleans**. He came to England with Mr Johnson, and served him about eight months. He then hired himself for a year to Mr Charles H. Boyd, a comissary in the army [civil servant in the Commissariat department], wages to be twenty-five guineas. The same day that he was hired Caesar and Mr Boyd went to **France**, where after eight months Mr Boyd became insolvent, and Caesar had to leave his service.

However he hired himself immediately to Mr Guy Bryan Marshall, Caesar asked for the same wages as he had received from Mr Boyd, whereupon Mr Marshall replied: "I would rather give you more than less."

Mr Marshall and Caesar returned again to France after a short visit to England, then six weeks later they came again to England. Caesar lived with Mr Marshall, as his servant, in the parish of Ashill; this service was from May 1816 until he was discharged in March 1817. Mr Marshall then left England. Caesar had lived with Mr Marshall fourteen months, and had received sixteen pounds in wages. Caesar is now chargeable to the parish of Ashill.

[*Mark*.]

[S.R.O., settlement examination, D/PS/ILM. 6/56. 25. (Ilminster petty sessions.)]

[Case 123] **1818. Elizabeth Harper.**

The date and names of the justices are not given.

Elizabeth Harper, residing at **East Wells** in the **Out parish of St Cuthbert's, Wells**, states that she was born in the parish of **St John**, near the city of **Worcester**. Thirteen years ago she was married, at **St Martin in the Fields, Middlesex**, to Thomas Harper.

Her husband had lately been convicted of forgery, and transported "beyond the seas for the term of his natural life".

Elizabeth had heard that seven or eight years before they were married Thomas had hired himself as a coachman to Richard Cooper Esq., of **Stratton Hall** in the parish of **Pancras, Staffordshire**. While Thomas was in Mr Cooper's employ they moved to the parish of **Walcot**. After four months

Thomas was discharged, whereupon he hired himself to the Reverend Archdeacon Turner of the **Liberty of St Andrews, Wells**. Thomas and Elizabeth had been married between the two hirings.

Thomas served Archdeacon Turner for ten years. During the first eighteen months of his service he had stayed in his master's house during the day, but slept in East Wells, where Thomas had rented a house from Mr William George, at the yearly rent of £8. Elizabeth is still residing in that house.

Five years ago Thomas Harper purchased a dwelling house in East Wells from one James Carter, for £150. Only £100 was actually paid to Carter, and a conveyance was made out and executed to Thomas and his trustee.

Neither Thomas nor Elizabeth had ever lived in the house; neither did they receive any rent for it. Thomas had caused the house to be pulled down and rebuilt. Immediately afterwards it was sold for the benefit of his creditors. However while Thomas had been in possession of the house he had paid to the poor rate, and had received the produce of the garden which he had planted.

Elizabeth has two children by her husband – Elizabeth, aged ten, and Sarah, six years.

[S.R.O., settlement examination D/P/Wells St Cuthberts 13/3/17.240.]

Shepton Mallet Gaol Returns.
Under commitments.
Thomas Harper aged thirty-five.
Committed by Francis Drake Esq.; 16 September 1815.
Late residence, Wells.
Under charge or offence.
Charged on the oath of William James, on suspicion of having forged the name of the said William James, with the intent to defraud the Rev. John Turner of the sum of eight pounds, ten shillings, or some part thereof.

[S.R.O., Q/AGs. 13/2.]

[Case 124] **13 February 1818. Edith Scammell.**
Settlement examination, taken in **Middlesex**.
Edith states that about five years ago she was apprenticed to Mr Hoddinott [a silk throwster – see case 118] in the parish of **Evercreech**, and served her master there for four years.

19 February 1818.
Edith Scammell's vagrant's pass from **Whitechapel**, Middlesex, addressed to the contractor for removing vagrants in the county of Middlesex, signed by W.L. Rogers.
Edith Scammell was apprehended in the parish of St Mary, Whitechapel, on 13 February 1818. She had been "wandering abroad and lodging in the open

air".

She had been examined and convicted of being a rogue and vagabond. She was to be sent to the house of correction for seven days, and then sent to Evercreech, as this was her parish of settlement.

The contractor was directed to convey Edith to **Colnbrook**, Buckinghamshire, there he was to deliver her to the constable together with this pass and a duplicate of the examination. The contractor was to obtain a receipt. Edith was then to be conveyed on in like manner until the parish of Evercreech was reached.

[*Mark.*]

[S.R.O., vagrant's pass. D/P/Evercreech 13/3/5.2.]

[Case 125] **23 February 1819. Elizabeth Templer, otherwise Templeman.** Before W.H. Festing.

Elizabeth Templer, otherwise Templeman, states that she is aged eighty years, and was born in **Exeter**, she is the widow of Thomas Templer, otherwise Templeman.

They were married in 1755 at the parish church of **St Mary Major**, Exeter. Her husband belonged to that parish and they had been neighbours. Thomas had lived with his father, who was a brazier [brass worker].

Neither she nor Thomas, her husband, had done any act whereby they could have gained a settlement.

Her son Thomas and daughter Sarah had always lived with her. Elizabeth is now chargeable to the borough of **Chard**.

[*Mark.*]

24 February 1819. Thomas Templer, otherwise Templeman.
With Sarah Templer, otherwise Templeman, spinster, before W. Hanning and H.P. Collins.

Thomas Templer, otherwise Templeman, a clockmaker, residing in the Borough of Chard, states that he is now aged fifty, he was born in London and is the lawful son of Thomas Templer, otherwise Templeman, deceased, and Elizabeth his wife. His mother is now living in Chard. Thomas has never done any act whereby he could have gained a settlement.

[*Both made marks.*]

Richard Bragg Quier, overseer of the poor for the Borough of Chard, upon his oath states that Thomas Templer, otherwise Templeman, and Sarah Templer, otherwise Templeman, and their mother, Elizabeth Templer, otherwise Templeman, are all chargeable to the Borough of Chard.

Extract from the parish register of St Mary Major, Exeter:

Thomas Templer and Elizabeth Osborne, both of the parish of St Mary Major, were married by banns 24 December 1755.

Extract made 17 February 1819 by Wm. Stabback, Rector of **St Stephens**, Exeter for the Rev. Mr Colson, Rector of St Mary Major.

Extract from the parish register of **St Paul**, Exeter:

Sarah, daughter of Thomas and Elizabeth Templeman, baptised 26 October 1756.

Extract made 17 February 1819 by Richard Eastcott, off[iciating] minister.

Extract from the parish register of St Mary Major, Exeter: Thomas, son of John and Mary Templeman baptised 11 April 1736.

Extract made by W. Marwood Tucker, off[iciating] minister. No date.

Extract from the Register Book of Freemen of the City of Exeter: "1780, Templer, Thomas of **Barnstaple**, watchmaker by heirship."

Extract made 17 February 1819, by John Campion, clerk to the town clerk.

A certificate, dated 23 February 1819, from John Wheadon, member of the Royal College of Surgeons: "In consequence of advanced age and extreme debility,a removal from Chard to Exeter would endanger the life of Elizabeth Templer."

[S.R.O., settlement examination and other documents, D/PS/ILM. 6/58. 14. (Ilminster petty sessions.)]

24 February 1819.

Elizabeth Templer, otherwise Templeman, to be removed to St Mary Major, Exeter, from Chard Borough.

[*Endorsed*] Removal order suspended.

Sarah Templer, otherwise Templeman, and Thomas Templer, otherwise Templeman, watchmaker, to be removed to St Mary major, Exeter, from Chard Borough.

[S.R.O., D/PS/ILM. 6/10. nos 5, 6 & 8.]

[Case 126] **23 October 1819. Sarah Corp, widow.**

Formerly Sarah Millard, spinster. Statement taken by Mr Sherrin.

Sarah Corp, residing in the In parish of **St Cuthberts, Wells**, states that she is aged forty-two years, and was born at **Wedmore**.

At the age of fourteen she hired herself to Mr Mathew Tuck, of the Out parish of St Cuthberts, her pay to be £3 per annum, she served nine months.

Her further service was to Mr Court of Wedmore, £3 per annum, for one year.

Mr Tuck (as before) at £4 per annum, for one year.

Mr Carter of **Wensely Farm**, Wells at four guineas per annum, for three years.

During all this service Sarah had received meat, drink, washing and lodging.

When she went to live with Mr Carter her late husband William Corp also went to work for him. William was to receive eight guineas per annum, and his meat, drink, washing and lodging.

William served for three years, then hired himself to Mr Brookes of the Out parish of St Cuthberts. After William had been at Mr Brookes for seven months, he and Sarah were married at the church of St Cuthberts, this was about twenty-one years ago. They went to live in a house belonging to Mr Carter, staying there five months, but paid no rent.

William and Sarah then rented two rooms at **Dulcot**, belonging to William Hobbs, paying one shilling a week, and stayed there two years.

They then rented a house at Dulcot from William Ellis, and paid three guineas a year, and stayed two years.

They next rented another house at Dulcot from Mr Robert Cook, paying three guineas a year, they had stayed there five years when William died.

Sarah was left with two small children, and was allowed, for their support, four shillings a week, until the youngest child died, when the allowance was reduced to two shillings and sixpence. After two years Sarah gave up her pay. She further states that she has done no other act to gain a settlement, except as noted above.

[S.R.O., settlement examination D/P/Wells St Cuthberts 13/3/17. 225.]

[Case 127] **13 December 1819. James Willcox.**
Before Francis Drake and J.S. Phillotte.

James Willcox states that he is aged thirty years, and that he was born at **Godney**, in the parish of **Meare**. At the age of fifteen James went to live with his uncle, Mr Thomas Weare of **Wookey**. He lived with his uncle for five years, being employed in husbandry, but did not receive any wages.

After he had been with Mr Weare for a year or two, his master asked him if he would like to make a bargain with him, to which James replied "that he would trust Mr Weare's generosity", whereupon Mr Weare said that "James was no servant of his and he might go when he felt himself hurt".

At the end of five years James returned to his father for a year. About three months before he left his father he married Maria Bunn of **Wedmore**. They have four children – Fanny aged eight years, George four, Mary Ann two and a half and Joseph aged fifteen months.

[*Mark.*]
[S.R.O., settlement examination D/P/Meare 13/3/1.21.]

31 January 1820.
James Willcox and family removal order from Meare to Wookey.
[S.R.O., D/P/Meare 13/3/2.23.]

[Case 128] **19 January 1820. Elizabeth Purse.**
Before M. Blake.

Elizabeth Purse, aged twenty years, residing in **Taunton St Mary**, together with her son William Cornish, states that she was born in the parish of

Taunton St Mary. Three and a half years ago she married Daniel Purse, who afterwards enlisted in the 46th Foot. Elizabeth accompanied her husband to **New South Wales**, and then to **Madras**, where she left him.

Elizabeth had heard her husband say that he was born in **Chard**, and thus Chard was her legal parish of settlement. She also states that she has a child by her husband, named William, aged three and a half years, who was born in Taunton St Mary before she was married.

[*Mark*.]

The above has been checked, using the Regimental Location Lists at the National Army Museum. The 46th Foot were at Madras in 1818-19, and then, after further postings overseas, were back in Canterbury in 1834. Assistance from the above museum is gratefully acknowledged.

[S.R.O., settlement examination D/P/Taunton St Mary 13/3/5.93.]

[Case 129] **28 June 1820. John Rose, labourer.**

Before M. Blake and Webb Stone.

John Rose, residing in **Taunton St Mary**, now aged thirty years, states that he was born at **Lytchett Beacon** (Litcheat Bacon), in the parish of **Lytchett Minster**, Dorset. Ten years ago he agreed to serve as under ostler to John Lane, then an ostler at the 'Castle Inn', **Taunton**, his wages to be £14 per annum. John Rose served one year and agreed for a second year, of which he served nine months.

"During that time he slept in the ostlery at the 'Castle' which was situated over the drain which divides the parishes of Taunton St Mary Magdalen and **Bishops Hull** and the said drain divided this informant's bed longwise, and this informant is uncertain in which parish he may be considered to have slept."

John has done no other act to gain a settlement. He married Grace Perry eight years ago, they have two children, John aged seven years and William aged five years.

[*Signed*.]

[S.R.O., settlement examination D/P/Taunton St Mary 13/3/5.103.]

[Case 130] **26 July 1820. Sarah Miller.**

Before M. Blake and Webb Stone.

Sarah Miller, residing in **Taunton St James**, states that she is now about seventy years old and was born in **Bawdrip**, which was her father's parish. She has never been an apprentice. At the age of twenty she became housekeeper and cook to Mr Palmer of **Home Park, Sonning, Berkshire**. Her wages were twenty-five guineas a year, she served Mr Palmer between four and five years.

Sarah then took a place at Sir Evan Neapean's, **Admiralty, London**, where she stayed two to three months.

Sarah returned to Somerset, where she took a house and shop in Taunton St Mary, at £33 per annum, besides the rates and taxes, the shop belonged to Miss Foy, of Taunton St James. Sarah occupied the property for six and a half years. She then received £10 from Miss Norris to take over the lease for the last half year, Miss Foy being agreeable to this arrangement.

Sarah lodged in Taunton St Mary, after she had given up the lease, for which lodging she paid one shilling and sixpence a week.

After visiting her sister in Devonshire for three months, Sarah took a position as cook and housekeeper with Mrs Hilliar of **West Coker**, her wages to be £20 a year and an allowance of two guineas a year for tea. At the end of nine or ten months, finding the work too hard, she left Mrs Hilliar's service, receiving eighteen guineas which included her tea allowance.

After leaving West Coker Sarah went to London, where she took lodgings, first at some mews near Berkeley Square, for which she paid two shillings a week, then at Wigmore Street, where she lodged with a dressmaker by the name of Chattin, and where she paid three shillings a week.

After calling on one Elizabeth Nicholls, who was a servant at Lord Harcourt's house, it was suggested that Sarah should come and live in the house to keep Elizabeth company. Lady Harcourt agreed to this arrangement. Sarah stayed two years at Lord Harcourt's residence, but she did not perform any service there. When Lord Harcourt's family were at the house they had footmen, coachman, house maid and lady's maid with them but no cook or housekeeper. The porter's wife acted as cook, and the lady's maid as housekeeper.

During the time that Sarah resided at Lord Harcourt's house she maintained herself in clothes and provisions out of her own pocket.

At the end of two years Sarah was engaged as cook and housekeeper to Mr Dashwood of **Sidmouth**, Devonshire. Sarah had only been there three weeks when she was taken ill, and had to leave her post. Since then she has not been in service for a year, neither has she rented any property worth £10 per annum, but she has resided in Devonshire with members of her sister's family or has lodged in Taunton. Furthermore she has done no act whereby she could have gained a settlement.

[*Signed*.]

[S.R.O., settlement examination D/P/Taunton St Mary 13/3/5.121.]

[Case 131] **4 October 1820. Rebecca Rea.**

Before R. Combe and W. Hanning.

Rebecca Rea, residing in **Broadway**, states that in October 1815, she was married to William Dimmock at the parish church of **Stonehouse**, near

Plymouth. William was then a private in the 43rd Regiment of Foot. Rebecca was not present when the banns were published, and she does not recollect her name being mentioned at the time of the marriage; however she has been informed that the entry of her marriage in the parish register is by the name of Elizabeth Cornish. She further states that she was never known by that name.

At Lady Day 1818 Rebecca came to Broadway, where she agreed to serve Mr Goodland for a year, and she has served him over two years under that agreement. Rebecca is now with child.

[*Mark.*]

Attached to this document is an extract from the parish register of Stonehouse which shows the marriage of William Dimmick (sic) to Elizabeth Cornish, spinster. Dated 5 October 1815.

[S.R.O., settlement examination D/PS/ILM.6/59.17. (Ilminster petty sessions.)]

[Case 132] **13 December 1820. William Hare.**

Before M. Blake and Webb Stone.

William Hare aged twenty-eight years, residing at **Cheddon Fitzpaine**, states that he was born in the parish of **Taunton St Mary**. At the age of fifteen years he hired himself to Mr John Rowsell of **Holway**, and lived with him one year. Five years ago he hired himself to Mr Dandridge, a gentleman of independent fortune, at **Bath**, William's wages were to be sixteen guineas a year.

William served Mr Dandridge for twenty-three months, during this time they stayed at various watering places, **Bath, Lymington Spa**, near **Warwick**, and then went to **Clifton**, near **Bristol**, where they lived at Richmond Terrace. In May 1817 they moved to No. 22 Harford Street, Bath.

Three months after leaving Bath William quit Mr Dandridge's service and soon after that he married Agnes Wills of Cheddon Fitzpaine. They have one child called Edmund.

[*Mark.*]

[S.R.O., settlement examination D/P/.Taunton St Mary 13/3/5.113.]

2 March 1822.

A further examination of the above William Hare contains details not found in the first examination. Before M. Blake and Webb Stone:

William Hare, residing at Cheddon Fitzpaine, states that when he hired himself to Mr Dandridge his master was living at Camden Place, Bath. When they went from Bath to Lymington Spa they had made several short visits to families on the way.

After William had served his master for one year his wages were raised to twenty guineas a year. On their return to Bath Mr Dandridge took lodgings at 22 Harford or Alfred Street. Three weeks later they proceeded towards

London, making several short visits on the way, they lodged in London for three weeks, then went to **Harlow, Essex**.

During this time William's second year of service expired and he left Mr Dandridge's employment. William has never since been in service. He was married, to Agnes Wills of **Cheddon**, in London some three and a half years ago. They have two children, Edmund William aged two years and Louisa of the age of five weeks.

[*Mark.*]

[S.R.O., settlement examination D/P/Taunton St Mary 13/3/5.162.]

[Case 133] **31 January 1821. William Godfrey.**
No justice named.

William Godfrey, a shoemaker, residing at **Taunton St Mary Magdalen**, states that he was born in the parish of **St John** in **Worcester**, and is now aged thirty-eight years. He was never an apprentice or a servant, and never made any agreement to serve for a year, but worked as a travelling shoemaker from town to town.

Ten years ago William took lodgings in Grub Street, **Cripplegate** from John Greenaway, paying four shillings a week in rent, these lodgings he occupied for four months. Seven years ago William had rented lodgings from Mr Jackson of **Islington**, at the same rent, and where he stayed for four months. Apart from these two rentings he had never rented a property of the value of £10 a year, and has done no act to gain a settlement.

William understood, from his father Francis Godfrey, that the settlement of himself, his brother and sister was in **Taunton St Mary**. Francis Godfrey, who had died in 1799 at **Hockley** near Birmingham, possessed a book entitled *The Pilgrim's Progress* [by John Bunyan, first published 1678] in which book were entered the names of William and his brother and sister, also the parish. William Godfrey is unmarried.

William supposes the book, if still in existence, to be in the possession of his uncle John Sheldrake, Webb Street, Blackfriars Road, **London**.

[*No mark or signature.*]

[S.R.O., settlement examination D/P/Taunton St Mary 13/3/5.119.]

[Case 134] **29 March 1821. Lewis Page.**
The son of the late Thomas Page who had left **Winsham** in February 1800, and who had died in the workhouse.

Copy of a letter from W.H. Festing, as clergyman and magistrate, to the parish officers of **St Sidwell, Exeter**, requesting relief for Thomas Page's widow.

Attached to the above document is a page, torn from a *New Testament*, on the back of which is written the following information:

"John Page born October 5 1747; Mary Page born December 25 1749; Betty Page born January 14 1750; Thomas Page born November 2 1753; Marriah Page born November 4 1755; Simon Page born October 4 1759; Lewes Page born August 13 1763; Ann Page born February 8 1766. Thomas Page born February 2 1729 (died July 1800, at Exeter)."

Also attached is a copy which states:

"The above is a true copy of the births of the children of Thomas and Elizabeth Page of the parish of St Sidwell, Exeter, taken from the leaf of a new testament belonging to Mary [. . . illegible] daughter of Thomas and Elizabeth."

[S.R.O., D/P/ Winsham 13/3/4.31. (Misc: Settlement document).]

30 May 1821. Lewis Paige (sic).

Before R. Combe and R. Uttermare.

Lewis Paige, a clothweaver residing at **Winsham**. states that he was born in that parish, and is now aged fifty-eight years. He has always lived in Winsham and worked as a clothweaver, except for seven years when he resided in **Newfoundland**.

Lewis was married in Winsham to his present wife Elizabeth about eighteen years ago, they are now both chargeable to the parish of Winsham.

Lewis further states that twenty-one years ago his father, Thomas Paige (who was living in the parish of Winsham under a certificate dated 3 May 1757 from the parish of St Sidwells, Exeter), being no longer able to support himself, Thomas went to Exeter where he was settled, and where Lewis later saw him in the workhouse of the parish of St Sidwells. Thomas died in the month of July following.

Lewis says that his mother's name was Elizabeth, and that he has brothers and sisters, namely John, Mary, Elizabeth, Thomas and Maria.

[*Mark.*]

[S.R.O., settlement examination and removal order D/PS/ILM. 6/12. 18. (Ilminster petty sessions).]

[Case 135] **8 May 1821. Abraham Lane.**

No magistrate named.

Abraham Lane, a sloober [wool twister], residing at **Shepton Mallet**, states that he was born in Shepton Mallet but his parents were legally settled in the parish of **Frome**. He was never an apprentice, but when an unmarried man he hired himself as a sloober to Mr Broderip of Shepton Mallet, clothier, to serve him for a year. He was to have Sundays to himself, and his wages were to be ten shillings and ninepence a week.

Abraham was to sloob 240 pounds of wool a week. If he did not reach this target then there would be a reduction in his wages.

Abraham also states that he has done no further act to gain a settlement.

[*Mark*.]

Subscript. That his father belonged to Frome, he died in Frome parish workhouse, he had been supported by that parish for some time, he learned his trade of a scribbler from his father, married at twenty-four, hired himself for a year after his . . .

The above is in a diferent hand from the main document, and is not completed.

[S.R.O., settlement examination D/P/Shepton Mallet 13/3/3.95.]

[Case 136] [Blank] 1822. Hannah Hillyar.

Names of justices not given.

Hannah Hillyar, a single woman residing at **Taunton St Mary**, states that she is aged fifty-four years, she was born in **Kidderminster**. Hannah was never an apprentice or servant. When she was about one year old her father died. Two years later she and her mother together with another child were removed from Kidderminster to Taunton St Mary, in which parish they received relief.

When Hannah was nine years old she ran away from the workhouse and went to her grandfather at **Axminster**, but she soon returned to Taunton, where she went to work at quilling the silk [winding it on to the bobbins] at Mrs Thions in **East Reach**. Hannah lived at Mrs Thions's house, receiving from her fifteen pence a week and her lodging and breakfast, she lived six years under this agreement, and received her wages each week.

Hannah was then employed by Mary Porter, High Street, also at quilling and under the same terms, remaining there for two years. After she left Mary Porter, Hannah went to **Pawlett** begging for work. There Mr Carter asked her if she could make hay, to which she replied "that she knew nothing about it but was willing to learn anything they could set her about".

She worked as indoor servant [meaning to live-in] for Mr Carter until Michaelmas, receiving one shilling and her board and lodging.

At Michaelmas Hannah returned to Taunton and the quilling work, however she agreed with Mr Carter to return next year, which she did, returning about haymaking time until Michaelmas. Hannah continued in this way for about nine years, in the summer months with Mr Carter, and in the winter with Mrs Thions, usually working about five to six months in each place but never more.

Hannah continued at the quilling, working for Dame Tooze and living in her house for four or five years, afterwards she was asked by Mr Waterman if she would carry milk for him, for which he would give her two shillings a week. She carried milk for ten years under this agreement, sleeping at Mrs Tooze's house in **Taunton St James**, and working at the quilling during the day. She then left Mr Waterman's employ as he had an apprentice bound to him; however she continued at Mrs Tooze until two years ago, at which time the house was pulled down, since when Hannah has lived in Taunton St Mary. She has not hired herself for a year or 'otherwise'. She has never been married.

[*No mark or signature.*]

For a description of silk throwing see M. Dorothy George, *London Life in the Eighteenth Century*. [Penguin reprint, 1976.]

[S.R.O., settlement examination D/P/Taunton St Mary 13/3/5.184.]

[Case 137] 2 July 1822. James Clare.

Before W. Waldegrave and W.B. Barter.

James Clare, aged twenty-three, states that he was born at **Radstock**. He has done no act to gain a lawful settlement, having worked underground as a coal miner since he was seven years old. James is the son of George Clare, coal miner, whose settlement was in the parish of **Ashwick**.

Ten months ago James was married to Mary, they have one child, born before marriage, now aged one year and named James.

The family are now in need of relief, in consequence of want of work.

19 July 1822.

John Clare and wife removed to Ashwick.

[S.R.O., settlement examination D/P/High Littleton 13/3/7.79.]

[Case 138] 22 September 1822. Elizabeth and Christian Damon.

Elizabeth being the wife of Richard Damon; and Christian Damon, wife of John Damon. Heard before W. Hanning and W. Raben.

Elizabeth Damon, residing in **Crewkerne**, states that she was married at **Broadwindsor, Dorset**, three and a half years ago. Two and a half years ago her husband Richard, who had not gained any settlement, went to **Newfoundland**, and has not returned.

[*Mark.*]

Instructions for completion of Ann Cording's Military Pass, 1822.

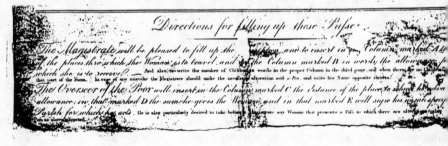

Christian Damon, residing in Broadwindsor, Dorset, who is the mother of Richard, states that about sixteen years ago when Richard was aged eleven years, she agreed with Robert Crocker of **Stoke Abbott, Dorset**, that her son should serve him for one year at the wages of one shilling a week. Richard served Crocker one and a half years, he then returned to his mother's house, and worked as a day labourer until his marriage.

[*Mark.*]

Elizabeth Damon to be removed from Stoke Abbott to **Crewkerne**.

[S.R.O., settlement examination D/PS/ILM. 6/13.24.]

[Case 139] **28 December 1822. Ann Cording.**

The wife of James Cording, with her two children.

The following abstract is from a pass given to the wife of a soldier.

A pass is given to wives and families of soldiers embarked for foreign service, and the widows, wives and families of soldiers dying or employed on foreign service are entitled to certain allowances from the overseers of the poor on their way to their places of residence or settlement [58 Geo.iii c92].

This pass gives the following details:

The husband: Name, James. Rank, private. Corps, 13th Light Infantry. Troop or company, Captain Burnside's. Where died or where serving, Chatham.

Description of the woman: Her age, thirty. Her height, four foot eleven inches. Colour of hair, brown. Colour of eyes, grey. Complexion, dark. Her dress, light pink gown and beaver bonnet.

Number of children: Boys, one aged eleven months. Girls, one aged three years.

The next part of the pass contains the route that Ann had to travel from Chatham to **St Decumans** [the combined parishes of **Watchet** and **Williton**.

The headings are:

Name of place through which the woman is to travel.

Rate per mile for the woman and her children (if any).

Distance of the place where relief is to be advanced to that where it is to be continued.

Sum paid by each overseer.

Signature of each overseer paying the woman.

Remarks.

Ann Cording's route was from **Chatham, Gravesend, Dartford, London, Brentford, Hounslow, Colnbrook, Staines, Bagshot, Hartley Row, Basingstoke, Andover, Salisbury, Hindon, Wincanton, Somerton, Langport, Taunton, Bridgwater** and then to St Decumans.

Ann was paid 3½d. per mile, she travelled between parishes three to twenty miles apart.

23 April 1823.

Letter from J.Halliday Esq. (Magistrate). Written from Chapel Cleeve.

"Sir, Ann Cording states that she is in great distress without anything more than the parish allows for her support and no bed to lie on. If this statement is correct, she must of course be provided with what is absolutely necessary, till the next meeting of the magistrates at **Yard** [a hamlet near Watchet]."

[S.R.O., DD/WY. Box 39 No 25. (Wyndham estate papers).]

[Case 140] 13 December 1823. Robert Cox.

Before W. Waldegrave.

Robert Cox, a papermaker, of **West Harptree**, states that he was married eleven years ago, "the Friday after old Christmas day [6 January being seen by many as the 'true' date of Christmas after the loss of eleven days in the change to the Gregorian calendar in 1752]. His wife is called Susannah, and they have six children – John aged nine years, Henry seven, Charlotte five, Eliza three and twins, Harriet and Elizabeth, now aged twenty-two months. The family are living at **Chew Magna**.

[*Mark.*]

Examination of Mr Charles Gumm, papermaker, who states that "the person lying in bed is Robert Cox, and on the 12th of December last he was at work in my paper mill, the lever of the press weight flew out and fractured the skull of Robert Cox".

Robert was stated to have been bound apprentice by the parish of **Banwell** to William Simmons, cooper, but later turned over to Mr Charles Gumm of Banwell, papermaker (father of the above Charles Gumm), and went with him to another paper mill in the city of **Wells**. Since Robert finished his apprenticeship he has worked for Mr Charles Gumm, senior, and his son, as a journeyman papermaker.

This examination was taken at the house of Mr Charles Gumm, of West Harptree.

[S.R.O., settlement examination D/P/Wells St Cuthberts 13/3/17.179.]

[Case 141] 16 August 1823. Elizabeth Palmer.

Before S.T. Wylde.

Elizabeth Palmer, a widow lately residing in the parish of **Whitwick**, in the county of **Leicestershire**, states that she is the widow of Robert Palmer whose legal parish of settlement was at **Thringstone**, Leicestershire, where he had served as an apprentice to Thomas Smith, a stocking weaver. Her husband died about three years after they were married, she had two children by her late husband.

Since the death of her husband Elizabeth has lived with a man by the name of William Huntshaw, as his wife. She has had three children by Huntshaw but two of the children are now dead. The survivor, whose name is Eliza, was born in **Congresbury** about three years and four months ago, as Elizabeth and Huntshaw were travelling through the parish with some hardware.

William Huntshaw died a year ago, before he died he told her that he had been married to another woman before he was married to her. Elizabeth made enquiries and found that William and his previous wife had been married at **St Peter and Paul, Aston**, in **Warwickshire**, on 6 May 1816, and that his wife is now living at **Birmingham**.

[*Mark.*]

[S.R.O., settlement examination D/P/Congresbury 13/3/1.35.]

5 January 1824.

Elizabeth Palmer, widow, residing in Congresbury, states that in 1810 she was married to Robert Palmer, who lived at **Ashby de la Zouch**. They went to Thringstone, but after six months there they moved to Birmingham, where Robert died some months later; they had one child, Mary Ann, now aged eight years and living with her mother at Congresbury.

Elizabeth and her child had been removed from Birmingham to Thringstone where she had received relief as and when needed.

[*Mark.*]

[S.R.O., settlement examination D/P/Congresbury 13/3/1.1.]

5 January 1824.

Elizabeth Palmer and her child Mary Ann are to be removed from Congresbury to Thringstone.

[S.R.O., removal order. D/P/Congresbury 13/3/3.29.]

[Case 142] 1825. John Standerwick.

Names of justices not given, nor the date.

John Standerwick, an out-pensioner from the Royal Hospital, **Chelsea**, who is in receipt of 1s.8½d. a day pension, states that he was born in the parish of **Taunton St Mary**, he was never an apprentice neither had he been in service.

John had lived with his mother in Taunton until he was aged nine years, then his mother died and he went to **London** and joined his father who lived at Little Bell Alley. John lived there with his father for three or four years, and then went to sea, he continued in the seafaring line ten or twelve years, during this time he occasionally stayed with his father, who had a large house in Great Winchester Street, London Wall, and who kept servants.

John stayed there when he was discharged from Indiamen or other merchant ships. John had resided with his father several times before he was aged twenty-one years.

He considered that he was entitled to several houses in North Street, Taunton, which were his mother's jointure.

[*Blank*.]

Chelsea hospital was opened in 1692. Out-pensioners were men who had been discharged from the army, yeomanry, militia and the Honourable East India Company, and who were receiving a pension with which they could support themselves in the community.

[S.R.O., settlement examination D/P/Taunton St Mary 13/3/5.209.]

[Case 143] 26 January 1825. Grace Vagg.

Before J.B.Uttermare and W. Hanning.

Grace Vagg, a widow residing in **South Petherton**, states that she was born at **Buckfastleigh, Devonshire**. She was married on 1 December 1820 at **St Peter Port** church, **Guernsey**, to Richard Vagg, now deceased. She has two children by her late husband, Mary aged three years and five months and Ellen aged two. Her late husband had done no act to gain a settlment since their marriage.

[*Signed*.]

Examination of John Vagg the younger, yeoman of South Petherton, as to the settlement of Grace Vagg, widow of his brother Richard Vagg. Richard had been bound apprentice by indenture to Samuel Dean of **Yeovil**, blacksmith, to serve him for seven years. Richard had served over six years when he became ill, and returned to his father's house at South Petherton for two or three months, he then returned to Dean and served out his apprenticeship, after which he worked as a journeyman.

[*Signed*.

26 January 1825.

Removal order: Grace Vagg and her two children from South Petherton to Yeovil.

[S.R.O., settlement examination D/PS/ILM. 6/16.34. (Ilminster petty sessions).]

[Case 144] 14 June 1825. John Ford.

Before Arthur Chichester and William George Clark.

John Ford, a labourer, residing in **Creech St Michael**, states that he was born at **Great Torrington, Devonshire**, and is now aged forty-five years. At the age of sixteen he hired himself, as a servant, to John Thorne of Torrington, whom he served for two years and received his wages at £2 per annum.

When aged eighteen John enlisted as a private in the North Devon Militia and served seven years, the regiment was disembodied "on the conclusion of peace in 1801" [the Treaty of Amiens, 1802; preliminary articles signed in London on 1 October 1801].

John then returned to Torrington with his wife and family, he stayed there for

130

twelve years working as a labourer, during this time his wife died.

John then hired himself to Mr John Nicholls, a merchant of Dartmouth, whom he served for two and a half years, his wages being £12 the first year and £20 the last year. John travelled with Mr Nicholls to **Newfoundland**.

On his return to England John Ford worked as a labourer at different places until last September, at which time he came to Creech St Michael.

[*No mark or signature.*]

[S.R.O., settlement examination D/P/Creech St Michael 13/3/7.34.]

[Case 145] **25 September 1826. Charles Maggs.**

Before John Purnell and Thomas R. Jolliffe.

Charles Maggs, residing at **Stratton on the Fosse**, states that he is aged sixty-two years. He was born at **Midsomer Norton**, in which parish his parents were settled.

Thirty-nine years ago he bargained with Mr George Savage of Stratton to serve him for a year; Charles's wages were to be £5 and his master's old clothes. He was also to receive his meat, drink and lodging at his master's premises. Charles served for that year, and two years afterwards.

Nineteen years ago Charles took thirteen cows, of Reuban Carter of **Holcombe**, for one year at the rent of £136.10s.0d. (during that year he resided in a house at Stratton).

The following year Charles took twelve cows of Carter, for which he paid rent of £126. Charles remained at Stratton for a quarter of a year. He then removed into the parish of Holcombe, where he lived in part of Carter's farm house for the remainder of the year, and paid the rent according to agreement.

Charles has done no other act to gain a settlement. Thirty-six years ago he was married to Maria, at Midsomer Norton.

[*Mark.*]

S.R.O., settlement examination D/P/ Stratton on the Fosse 13/3/4.19.]

25 September 1826.

Charles Maggs and his wife Maria to be removed from Stratton on the Fosse to Holcombe.

[S.R.O., D/P Stratton on the Fosse 13/3/2.14.]

[Case 146] **31 January 1827. John Sibley.**

Before W. Hanning, Vincent Stuckey and J.S.H. Lee.

John Sibley, residing at **Curry Rivel** (Curry Rivell), states that he is aged forty-two, and that he was born at **Mosterton, Dorset**. He was married, nine years ago, to Sarah, by whom he has three children – Mary, seven years old, James five and Rhoda aged one and a half years.

Twenty-five years ago John hired himself to John Wilment, a dairyman in

Broadwindsor, at the wages of £3.10s.0d. a year; John served Wilment one year and three to four months.

Ten years ago he came to live in Curry Rivel and worked as a day labourer. About four years ago William White, who had been chosen at the Court Leet to serve as tithingman [constable or deputy constable] desired John Sibley to serve for him. John and another man who had been chosen at the same time were both sworn before a magistrate to serve the office of tithingman.

[*Mark*.]

John Sibley and family to be removed to Broadwindsor from Curry Rivel.

A Court Leet was a manorial or hundred court which elected minor officials to enforce the bye laws.

[S.R.O., settlement examination D/PS/ILM.6/18.3. (Ilminster petty sessions.)]

[Case 147] **14 April 1827 William Nash.**

Counsel's opinion given by Mr Henry Jeremy of **Taunton**.

The case set out:

William Nash and his family, paupers chargeable to the parish of **Puxton**, were removed to **Congresbury** where William Nash was legally settled, unless a settlement was gained in Puxton by renting a property. The ground plan of this property is given below together with garden attached.

The property belongs to William Welsh. It is divided into two tenements which are occupied by William Nash who pays £10 per annum, the landlord paying all rates and taxes, and Robert Morgan who pays £6 per annum.

The entrance, back shed and privy are used by both tenants. The outer door is locked at night but the key is left in it for the convenience of both.

Each tenant has a lock and key for the door leading to his own room on the ground floor. The pauper has two bedrooms and a lumber room on the upper floor reached by a staircase from the room marked A. Robert Morgan has two bedrooms reached by a ladder from the entrance, marked B. There is no communication between the two tenants' bedrooms.

The rhine, a ditch dividing the parishes of Puxton and Congresbury and now filled up, used to run behind the house, part of it is beneath the wall of the back shed and part is included in the ground occupied by William Nash.

The pauper had occupied the tenement more than a year before the act of Geo. IV. and it is worth more than £10 per annum. The opinion requested is whether the tenement rented by William Nash is a separate and distinct dwelling house or building within the statutes of 59 Geo.III c50 and 6 Geo. IV c57 52. so as with the ground held, is sufficient to confer a settlement in Puxton [see appendices].

The landlord seems to have encroached on the parish of Congresbury in occupying the whole of the rhine with the back wall and fences, but it is presumed that so trifling a deviation would not preclude a settlement in Puxton under the statutes noted above.

The counsel's opinion given was that the tenement occupied by the pauper could not be considered a distinct dwellinghouse sufficient to confer a settlement, and in any case where the premises or tenement be in two or more parishes the parish of settlement is determined as to where the part in which the pauper sleeps is situated.

[*Signed by Henry Jeremy.*]

[S.R.O., settlement paper D/P/Congresbury 13/3/4.1.]

[Case 148] **22 July 1829. James Phillis.**

Justices not named.

James Phillis, a broadcloth weaver, residing in **Shepton Mallet**, states that he is about seventy-three years old, he was born in the city of **Canterbury**, at the age of nine years he was apprenticed to Thomas Richmond of Shepton Mallet, broadcloth weaver. James served his apprenticeship for nearly nine years, he then paid Richmond two guineas to "be given out of his time". When James was twenty years old he married Hannah, his first wife, at Shepton Mallet, they had seven children who were all born at Shepton Mallet, these children were:

Joseph who died at sea about three years ago.

Eleanor, married to a man at Paulton.

James, a soldier who died at **Seringapatam, India,** about twenty-five years ago.

Hannah and Sarah, twins. Hannah married a soldier and died in **London** about six years ago.

Sarah married a seafaring man of **Hull.**

Thomas, now or lately an artillery soldier.

John who is still residing at Shepton Mallet.

James and Hannah also lived at Shepton Mallet until about twenty years ago, at which time they went to London, they lodged at various places and James worked for different persons for five or six years. James then took two unfurnished rooms at No.8 Fisher Street, Red Lion Square, which is in the parish of **St George the Martyr, Middlesex**. The rent of the rooms was four shillings and sixpence a week, which was paid to Mr Mills, who lived in the same street.

They occupied these rooms for a year and a quarter, during which time Hannah died. After this, which was about twelve years ago, James came to **Frome,** here he worked as a journeyman weaver for half a year, and occupied a small house at one shilling a week. Whilst in Frome James married his present wife Elizabeth. (James had done no act by which he could have gained a settlement in Frome.)

They then returned to London, where James worked for different persons and they lodged at various places, about four years ago he took a house at **Brixton**, paying four shillings and sixpence a week, after living there for three-quarters of a year James was employed to reside in, and take care of, a house under repair, this house was situated near the General Post Office. James lived there for a year, but his wife still resided at Brixton. James then took lodgings in the parish of **St George's, Southwark**. He has done no act to gain a settlement.

James arrived back in Shepton Mallet two weeks ago, to which parish he is now chargeable.

[*Blank.*]

[S.R.O., settlement examination D/P/Shepton Mallet 13/3/3.101.]

[Case 149] 30 December 1829. Hannah Cook.

Before Thomas B. Uttermare and J.S.H. Lee.

Hannah Cook, wife of John Cook, late of **Ilminster**, labourer, states that she was married to him at **Somerton** five years ago.

John Cook is now at **Plymouth**, under sentence of transportation for felony. Hannah has received a letter from him dated "His Majesty's ship *Captivity*".

Her husband was a native of **Hemyock, Devon** (Hemmiock), and she has received relief from the overseers of Hemyock for eleven months, that is to say until nine weeks ago. She has two children by her husband, Susan aged four years and Ann one year and nine months old.

Hannah is now chargeable to Ilminster.

30 December 1829.

Examination of William Cook of Wambrook regarding the settlement of his son John Cook.

William Cook states that he is legally settled in **Wambrook** [transferred from **Dorset** to **Somerset** in 1896], in right of an estate that he occupied there, and which was of the yearly value of over twenty pounds. His son John was born in **Thorncombe, Devon** [transferred to Dorset in 1844], but had lived with his father in Hemyock until he was fifteen years old, and he has not gained a settlement elsewhere.

[*Mark.*]

Hannah Cook, wife of John Cook, and her family, to be removed to Hemyock, Devon, from Ilminster.

[S.R.O., settlement examination and removal order D/PS/ILM. 6/20.56.]

31 October 1832.

Hannah Cook, wife of John. Before Thomas B. Uttermare and R. Combe.

Hannah Cook, now residing in Ilminster, states that about 4 January 1830 she and her children Susan and Ann were removed from Ilminster to Hemyock. After she was there about a week Mr Fry, one of the overseers, told her she could go where she liked. Hannah then returned to Ilminster and has resided there ever since, and has been relieved by the parish of Hemyock until the last fortnight, when the overseer of Hemyock told her that they would not relieve her in future.

Three years ago last March her husband was sentenced to be transported for seven years, he is still a prisoner on board the *Captivity* hulk at **Devonport**.

During 1831 Hannah visited her husband twice; and on 30 April last was delivered of a son, called Samuel [baptised 28 October 1832], who is now living with her, together with her daughters Susan, seven years old, and Ann, four years and five months old. [Despite being on the hulk, John is given as Samuel's father.]

Hannah and her children are now chargeable to the parish of Ilminster.

[*Mark*.]

Hannah Cook, wife of John Cook, and Susan, Ann and Samuel, the children of herself and her husband, to be removed to Hemyock from Ilminster.

John Cook, aged twenty-eight, had been committed to **Wilton** gaol; his crime was stealing a horse and saddle, the property of William Stanton. Tried on 28 March 1829. Found guilty and sentenced to seven years transportation.

20 April 1829: removed to *Captivity* hulk at Devonport.

[S.R.O., Q/AGi. 14/4. Felons register of Ilchester gaol.]

[S.R.O., Baptismal Register D/P/ILM. 2/1/8.]

[S.R.O., Settlement examination and removal order. D/PS/ILM. 6/23.21. (Ilminster petty sessions.)]

[Case 150] **18 January 1830. James Tapley**.

The justices are not named.

Settlement examination taken at James Tapley's lodgings in **Cripplegate Without, London**. James states that he was born in the parish of **Bishops Hull**, Somerset. At the age of thirteen years he was bound apprentice to John Chilcott, shoemaker, who lived in North Street, **Taunton**. James did not serve out his apprenticeship. Instead he went to **Bristol** and on his return Chilcott would not take him again; he was then apprenticed to Thomas Warren, but he again went to Bristol before his time was completed.

James then returned to Taunton at the time of the contested election between Hammett, Popham, Halliday and Morland [1790]. James then came to London, where he was married to Jane, by whom he had eleven children.

James further states that he has never rented any property worth £10 a year, and although once chosen to serve as beadle he was not elected as he did not belong to the parish. James's two eldest sons are in the East India Company's service.

[*Mark.*]

[S.R.O., settlement examination D/P/Taunton St Mary 13/3/5.443.]

James Tapley, son of Joseph Tapley. of **Taunton St Mary Magdalen**, victualler and baker, did apprentice himself with the consent of his father, to John Chilcott, [shoe and bootmaker; James was not apprenticed by the parish], the sum of £6 was paid by Joseph Tapley to Chilcott. James's apprenticeship to be for seven years.

This indenture is dated 5 June 1775.

[*Endorsed.*]

24 November 1779.

Thomas Warren agrees to take over the apprenticeship.

[S.R.O., D/P/Taunton St Mary 13/3/16.11.]

[Case 151] **24 February 1830. William Edwards and others.**

Sarah Edwards and John Sparkes, otherwise John Edwards.

Before Thomas B. Uttermare and W. Hanning.

William Edwards, residing at **Hawkchurch, Dorset** [transferred to Devon in 1844], states that he is aged sixty-eight, and was born in **Wootton Fitzpaine**, Dorset. Between thirty and forty years ago he married Sarah, and about thirty-five years ago he left her and went into the navy. After about twenty-six years he returned from the **West Indies**, and found his wife married to another man.

[*Mark.*]

Sarah Edwards, wife of William, residing in **Donyatt**, states that soon after her husband left her she went to Wootton Fitzpaine, in which parish her daughter was born, she and her child were removed back to Hawkchurch. When the child was six or eight months old she was left with William's mother, in Wootton Fitzpaine, while Sarah went into service in Donyatt. There Sarah co-habited with Edmond Sparkes. Six months after her husband returned she was delivered of a son named John, who is now twenty-seven years old.

[*Mark.*]

John Sparkes, otherwise John Edwards, residing Donyatt, aged twenty-seven years, states that he went to work with Edward Dinham, to be taught the trade of a potter. He was to be paid for the first year three shillings a week, the second year three shillings and sixpence and the third year four shillings.

John had continued to work for Dinham for eight years. He then went and worked as a labourer. About six years ago John married Mary, by whom he has three children, James aged five years, John three years old and Charlotte about eight or nine months.

John senior is now chargeable to the parish of Donyatt.

[*Signed*.]

[S.R.O., settlement examination D/PS/ILM. 6/21.18. (Ilminster petty sessions.)]

[Case 152] 4 March 1830. William Cook, otherwise Dudley.

He is aged about five years and five months, being the base born child of Margaret Matilda Dudley, now the wife of Thomas Cook. To be removed to **Walcot** from the In parish of **St Cuthbert's, Wells**.

[S.R.O., DD/FS box 75 bundle 1 no. 38.]

10 March 1830.

The information of Margaret Matilda Cook, wife of Thomas Cook, of the City of Wells, labourer.

Before Robert Welsh and Edward Spencer.

Margaret Cook states that her maiden name was Margaret Matilda Dudley, she was a native of Bristol; she professes the Roman Catholic faith, and was brought up in that religion. On 5 September 1823 she was married at the Roman Catholic chapel in the city of **Bath**, by Rev. Dr Cooper, a Roman Catholic priest.

On 8 October 1824 she was delivered of a male child, who was christened at the parish church of Walcot, by the name of William Cook.

On 20 November 1826 she was again married to Thomas Cook. This marriage was according to the rites and ceremonies of the Church of England. The marriage took place at the parish church of Walcot. Since then Margaret has had two more children – James three years of age, and Ann, who was born on 26 January 1830.

[*Signed Margaret*.] Note subscribed: "The above is the mark and writing of Margaret Matilda Cook."

[*Endorsed*.]

Examination of Margaret Matilda wife of Thomas Cook as to a bastard child.

From the date of Harwicke's Marriage Act in 1754 [26 George II, c33] until civil registration was introduced in 1837, marriages were only legal if performed by a minister of the Church of England. There were, however, two exceptions, for the marriages of Jews and Quakers.

From this we see that William Cook, aged six years, was considered to be illegitimate.

[S.R.O., settlement examination DD/FS box 23 bundle 3. no.24. (Foster of Wells).]

[Case 153] 30 June 1830. Ann French.

Before Thomas B. Uttermare and J.B. Coles.

Ann French, a spinster, residing at **Curry Rivel**, states that she is aged seventeen years, and was born in Curry Rivel, also that she has done no act to gain a settlement. She further states that she is now with child.

Her sister Mary French, also a spinster, residing **Stocklinch Magdalen**, states that her mother Elizabeth French, who died at Curry Rivel last November, was the widow of Joseph French, who had been a soldier and was killed at the Battle of Waterloo. Elizabeth had lived many years in Curry Rivel, and had frequently been relieved as a parishioner of **Middlezoy**, in which parish Joseph had been legally settled. Mary had often been to Middlezoy for her mother to receive pay from the parish officers.

[*Signed.*]

Ann French to be removed to Middlezoy from Curry Rivel.

[S.R.O., settlement examination D/PS/ILM. 6/21.41. (Ilminster petty sessions).]

[Case 154] **23 December 1830. Elizabeth Chilcott.**

This single woman, now pregnant with a bastard child, is chargeable to the parish of **Dulverton**, and is to be removed to the parish of **Taunton St Mary**.

[S.R.O., D/P/Taunton St Mary 13.3.2. 221.]

12 April 1831.

Letter from Jos. Williams, assistant overseer of Dulverton, to Mr Bale, assistant overseer of Taunton St Mary Magdalen:

"Sir, I beg to acquaint you that Elizabeth Chilcott is now at Dulverton laughing at the imposition that she has practized of being with child. I am desired by Robert Brewer to write to you that he expects the twenty shillings paid into your hands for her lying in will be repaid him as she has had no child you can have no legal claim on him."

A receipt from Rob[ert] Brewer that he has received £1 from Mr Bale. Dated 6 July.

[S.R.O., Miscellaneous. Settlement document. D/P/Taunton St Mary 13/3/13.75.]

[Case 155] **26 January 1831. George Lawrence and family.**

Before Thomas B. Uttermare and W. Hanning.

George Lawrence, now residing in **Chard**, states that he is aged thirty-six years and was born in the parish of **Stocklinch Ottersay**. He was married at Chard to Mercy seven years ago. They have three children – Charlotte six years old, Eliza three years and George about one year. George senior has not gained a settlement of his own, and he and his family are now chargeable to the parish of Chard.

Elizabeth Hosgood, the wife of Peter Hosgood of **Crediton**, states that George Lawrence is her brother. She is now aged over fifty years and was present at her brother's birth; this had taken place in that part of the poor house which belongs to Stocklinch Ottersay, which was the parish in which her father was settled.

[*Mark of George Lawrence.*]

[*Mark of Elizabeth Hosgood.*]

Here is an inquiry as to the place of birth. The small village of Stocklinch was divided into two parishes, each with its own church. George had been born in the poor house, part of which belonged to **Stocklinch Magdalen** and part to Stocklinch Ottersay, as George's father was settled in the latter parish and George had not acquired a settlement of his own. It was to Stocklinch Ottersay that he and his family were removed from Chard.

George Lawrence and family to be removed to Stocklinch Ottersay from Chard.

[S.R.O., settlement examination and removal order D/PS/ILM. 6/22.9. (Ilminster petty sessions).]

[Case 156] **1 March 1831. Giles Foster, also known as Thomas Foster.**
Before G.T. Scobell and John Parish.

Giles Foster, residing **High Littleton**, states that he is aged fifty-four years. He was born at **North Curry**, the son of George and Sarah Foster. George and Sarah (whose maiden name was Coombs) were married at North Curry. George rented a farm of about £60 a year.

Giles lived with his father until he was nearly fifteen years old, at which age he went to live with his uncle, Charles Smey, who was a farmer at **Aller**. Giles lived with his uncle for two years as an indoor servant, he then hired himself to his uncle for a year (Lady Day to Lady Day) at the wages of £5 per annum.

Giles then worked as follows:

Farmer John Jeffery at **Huish Episcopi** (Hewish Episcopi) as a yearly servant, wages £5 per annum, the next year with Jeffery wages were £5.10s.6d., during the third year Giles only served six months.

Then went harvesting for Mr Bidsee and others at Wick St Lawrence for one month.

Next, to Mrs Chappel as indoor servant at **Worle** for six months.

Next, to Mr Hillier at **Nempett** for six months.

Then to Mr Samuel Thomas, grazier, at **Wick St Lawrence**, with whom an agreement was made for a year at wages of £12, at the end of the year a further agreement was made, but Giles only stayed until harvest time.

He then worked for Farmer Weaver, as a day labourer, at **Chew Magna**, wages nine shillings a week, Giles paying his own board and lodging, at one shilling per week. He rented half an acre of potato ground from Farmer

Weaver for £5.

He was next asked by Farmer Gredley, of **Knapp, North Curry,** to go and take care of a farm for him at **Brislington**. Giles was to be paid ten shillings a week, and to have his lodging and beer.

After Gredley and his family came to live at the farm Giles continued in his employ at the same wages (although these were increased at harvest time). Giles stayed four years, until Farmer Gredley moved to **Saltford**. Giles went with him and served him for four to five years, but made no agreement, Giles then gave a week's notice and went as a hind or bailiff to Dr Scohele.

He worked for Dr Scohele, in High Littleton, for two years, at the wages of ten shillings a week, paying his own board and lodging.

He then worked as a day labourer for J.Hill, Esq. at **Paulton** for two years.

During the time that Giles worked for Mr Hill, he was married to Jane, they have one child, baptised at High Littleton, and named Henry, who is now eight years old. Giles is now chargeable to the parish of High Littleton.

[*Mark.*]

Giles must have been very ill as by 18 October 1831 Jane is a widow. Jane had taken her husband's examination to Wick St Lawrence where she saw a Mr Day, who told her that her husband's settlement was in Wick St Lawrence. Giles would have had four legal settlements during his life, by birth in North Curry, being hired by his uncle for a year at Aller, by serving Farmer Jeffery for a year, lastly by serving for one year in Wick St Lawrence.

[S.R.O., settlement examination D/P/High Littleton 13/3/3.13b.]

[Case 157] **20 July 1831. William Needs and family.**

Before H. Sainsbury and George Rous.

William Needs junior, residing in the parish of **Frome** (Frome Selwood), states that he is forty-three years of age, and was born in the parish of Frome. His parents William and Mary Needs were legal parishioners of **Mells**; they were removed to Mells in 1801, together with their four children, William junior was one of those children, he can remember being taken there by one of the Frome overseers. The family returned to Frome on the same day.

In 1814 William Needs, the father, died, and soon afterwards his son William took the same house at the yearly rent of £9.14s.0d. and the use of a loom. William occupied the premises until 1820. He had also rented two pieces of ground for which he paid the sums of five shillings and sixpence, and six shillings. William's wife Sarah had died five years ago, leaving six children, of whom five are alive.

William further states that his father paid eight guineas for the house, with an additional sum after the loom was put into the house, the loom was not "let into the wall or fixed to the house". William considers the value of the loom to be sixpence a week.

Edward Millard, who lived near the house in question, states that William Needs the father considered that the house was worth £8 a year rent and the loom five shillings a quarter.

[*Signed.*]

[S.R.O., settlement examination. D/P/ Mells 13/3/3.127.]

13 June 1801.

William Needs senior [the father of the above], his wife Mary, Priscilla aged 15 years, William aged 10, Sarah aged 8 and Lydia aged 4 years, their children, are to be removed from Frome to Mells.

[D/P/Mells 13/3/.2. 137.]

[Case 158] **28 May 1832. Benjamin Bulgin.**

Before W. Hanning and R. Combe.

Benjamin Bulgin, residing in **Dowlish Wake**, states that he is aged about seventy-three years, and was born in that parish. In May 1785 he purchased a cottage from the Rev. William Speke, Lord of the manor of **East Dowlish**, the lease of which was for ninety-nine years, determinable on his and his son's life – and which is now determinable upon the death of him, Benjamin Bulgin.

Eight or nine years ago he rented a dairy of cows in Dowlish Wake, from Mr Joseph Pitt, for £60. At Candlemas [2 February] 1820 he took a dairy of fourteen cows from Mr Darby of **Dinnington** at £140 (being £10 a cow). He then took thirteen cows at £9 a cow.

During the time that he rented Mr Darby's cows he lived in Dinnington in a house belonging to Mr Darby. At Christmas in 1821 Mr Darby took away the cows, but Benjamin continued to reside in Mr Darby's house at Dinnington. On 8 November 1822 he, being involved in a lawsuit, about the dairy, with Mr Darby, sold his cottage in Dowlish to his son-in-law John Rowe of Netherhay [a hamlet in **Broadwindsor** parish], Dorset, for £15.

During the time that he lived at Dinnington and rented the cows he always slept there, although he retained his house at Dowlish Wake, where he kept a bed and goods, and where he occasionally slept after Mr Darby took away the cows. The house at Dinnington was not worth more than one shilling a week; and his own cottage at Dowlish was worth about £3 a year. He is now chargeable to the parish of Dowlish Wake.

[*Signed.*]

Benjamin Bulgin and Mary his wife to be removed to Dinnington from

Dowlish Wake.

[S.R.O., settlement examination D/PS/ILM.6/14.18. (Ilminster petty sessions).]

[Case 159] 1 September 1832. Thomas Brown.

Before J. Wickham, taken and sworn at the House of Correction in **Shepton Mallet**.

Thomas Brown, lately residing at Taunton, but now a prisoner in the House of Correction at Shepton Mallet, states that he is now aged thirty-nine, and was born at **Tring** in **Hertfordshire**. His father was born near **Coventry**, and worked as a navigator at Tring, then at **Bristol**, where he lodged at **Bedminster** at the 'Royal Oak' and after that at the 'Wheat Sheaf'. Thomas did not know what rent his father paid.

They stayed at Bristol for two years, then his father went to **Dartmoor** and worked at the prison. He next worked for Lord Bonington at **Saltash**, and from thence he worked at different places as a navigator.

Thomas worked with his father until he was about sixteen years old, he then went to **Tiverton** and worked on the Grand Western Canal as a day labourer, then to **Witheridge** and worked for Mr Wyndham. Next he worked on the Grand Surrey Canal for six months. Whilst in **Surrey**, Thomas married Anna, his late wife, at the parish church of **Wonersh**. Together they went to a place near **Boston** in **Lincolnshire**. After five months they returned to Surrey, and then went to **Bearwood** in **Berkshire**, where they stayed nine or ten months. Thomas then worked about the country until he came to **Taunton**.

Thomas Brown's mother is living at 21 Howards Green, City Road, **London**. She is aged seventy and is a washerwoman. His wife died four years ago last July, at which time Thomas was working at **Buckland** in **Devonshire**. Thomas has five children by his wife – Harriet aged fifteen; Mary Ann, at Wellington, aged twelve years; John Henry aged eight years; Susan six years; and Charles five. Thomas does not know where he was baptised.

[*Mark.*]

[S.R.O., settlement examination. D/P.Taunton St Mary 13/3/5.505.]

[Case 160] 26 September 1832. Elizabeth Flood and family.

She is the wife of Simeon Flood, and there is evidence from James Flood, of **Staple Fitzpaine**, the father of Simeon Flood. Before Thomas B. Uttermare and Vincent Stuckey.

Elizabeth Flood states that she was married to Simeon Flood in the parish of **Bishopstone, Wiltshire**. At the time she married Simeon Flood he went by the name of Solomon William Penning Fountain. She did not discover that his real name was Simeon Flood until she came to Staple Fitzpaine. Elizabeth has three children by her husband, Frederick William aged six years, Edwin

George three years old, and Eliza Ann aged two.

James Flood states that in 1793 he was hired as a yearly servant by Mr James Selway of Bickenhall. He served one whole year and received his wages of five and a half guineas, having entered Mr Selway's service on Lady Day and quitted the following Lady Day.

Simeon Flood – who has absconded – is his son and lived at home until about ten years ago. Simeon had not gained a settlement of his own as he had always lived with examinant and his uncle.

[*Mark of Elizabeth Flood.*]

[*Signature of James Flood.*]

Confusion reigns! In the document Simeon is several times referred to as Charles Flood; however this has been corrected thrice to Simeon.

Elizabeth Flood and family to be removed to Bickenhall from Staple Fitzpaine.

[S.R.O., settlement examination D/PS/ILM. 6/23.3. (Ilminster petty sessions).]

27 March 1826.

At Bishopstone, South Wiltshire:

Solomon William Penning Fountain, of Kidderminster, Worcestershire, was married to Elizabeth Street.

[W.R.O., Denning index of marriages.]

14 May 1826.

At Bishopstone: Frederick William, son of Solomon William and Elizabeth Fountain, was baptised. Father's occupation given as tailor, his abode Kidderminster.

[W.R.O., 577/8.]

1851 census.

At West Hatch, Somerset: Frederick Flood, aged 26, born Bishopstone, Wiltshire, with Mary his wife and three children.

[HO. 107/1922.]

[Case 161] **28 September 1832. Eliza Woodland.**

Before Thomas B. Uttermare and W. Hanning.

Eliza Woodland, residing at **Ilton**, states that she was born in **Puckington**, and is now aged nineteen. She has done no act to gain a settlement, she is now with child, and the child is likely to be born a bastard. She is chargeable to Ilton.

[*Mark.*]

5 October 1832.

Examination of Ann Woodland regarding the settlement of her daughter Eliza. Ann states that Eliza was born in the parish of Puckington.

[Mark.]

5 October 1832. Robert Woodland.

Robert Woodland, residing in Ilton, states that he he was born in Puckington and is aged fifty-five years. About 1808 he was removed from **Bridport** to Puckington, where his daughter Eliza was born after he was removed; Robert has done no act to gain a settlement in Puckington.

[Blank.]

The information of William Jones [?acting] overseer:

Robert Woodland rented half an acre of ground for potatoes from Mr Hugh Bindon in the year 1814, which was before Mr Bindon's daughter was married to Mr Born, which is seventeen years ago; at that time Robert Woodland's house rent was only £3.10s.0d. a year, and Puckington parish paid part of the rent.

The next ground that he rented was from Mr Samuel Adams, who does not keep any book account, however when the rent for the grounds was paid, the renters had a supper from their landlord, two women who were employed in cooking it were Elizabeth Mico and Honora Ray, the latter was taken in labour that very night and was delivered of a child before daylight on Christmas day the following morning, and if the child had lived it would have been ten years old on 25 December, as appears from the register of baptisms in the parish church; which proves that Robert Woodland rented the ground in question in the year 1822, and that the ground rented by him from Mr John Bond [no further information about him] was subsequent to that rented from Mr Samuel Adams.

[Signed.]

[Endorsed.]

19 July 1822.

Thomas Churchill let Robert Woodland the house, garden and withy bed at £9.14s.0d. a year for ten years.

Eliza Woodland to be removed to Puckington from Ilton.

[S.R.O., settlement examination D/PS/ILM. 6/23.20. (Ilminster petty sessions).]

[Case 162] 2 August 1833. Joseph Slade.

Before John Lax, mayor, and J.Nicholls.

Joseph Slade, residing in the **In parish of St Cuthbert's Wells**, states that he was born at Wells twenty-three years ago. He was the son of Joseph and Elizabeth Slade.

At the age of ten years he went to work for William Mayger, a rasterer [plasterer] as a mortar boy, he worked by the day and received wages every Saturday night. Joseph worked for Mayger for six years.

He then worked for Robert Edgill, a rasterer, for twelve months, and for Samuel Richards for nearly twelve months. No agreements had been made with any of these persons.

Four years ago Joseph went to the 'Red Lion' in Wells, and worked for Mrs Wilkins, who later became Mrs Hood. Joseph did not receive any wages but had the yard, which was the benefit of the stables. After a few months his master and he had a few words and he was told to go.

Joseph went to **Somerton**, but the next day he went with Mr Badman and his mother and asked Mr Hood to take him back, which he did, and Joseph remained there for seven months.

Joseph then worked at the 'Queen's Head' in **Glastonbury** for six months, followed by six months at the 'Star' in Wells. He further states that he has never done any act to gain a settlement. Seventeen months ago Joseph's father was ill, and the parish officers had an order of removal to send him to **Malmesbury, Wiltshire**. His father died and his mother was removed to Malmesbury.

Joseph is now very ill and unable to be removed.

[*Mark*.]

[S.R.O., settlement examination. DD/WM. 67. p28. (Wells Museum deposit).]

[Case 163] **27 May 1834. George Nations.**

Before G.H. Carew.

George Nations states that he was born in the parish of **Bishops Lydeard**, in which parish his parents had settlement. At the age of fourteen years he started hiring himself as a servant, and he served the following masters:

As a yearly servant in husbandry to Mr Pratt at **Staplegrove**, served two years.

As a servant to John Collard Esq. at **Wiveliscombe** for one and a half years.

As a servant in husbandry to Mr Hawkings at **Kingstone** for three years.

As an indoor servant to Dr Woodford at **Taunton** for five years. During this time George married his present wife.

As a servant to Mr Witch at **Milverton** for four years.

As a servant to Mr Bedford in **London** for two years.

As a servant to Dr Woodford again, at Taunton for two years.

As a servant to Dr Lyddon at Taunton for four years.

As an indoor servant to John Cook Esq. at Taunton for three years.

As a servant to the Rev. Daniel Campbell at **Crowcombe** for two years.

George further states that he has done no other act to gain a settlement.

[*Signed*.]

[S.R.O., settlement examination D/P/Taunton St Mary 13/3/5.521.]

[Case 164] **12 June 1834. Mary Crump and family.**

This case is from a solicitor's deposit.

Mary Crump states that her maiden name was Mary Bennett, she was born in **Gloucestershire**. Her maiden settlement was in the parish of **St James, Westminster**, which she gained by hiring and service.

Afterwards she went to **Edmonstone**, and worked as a servant to Dr Fox who was proprietor of a private asylum.

Mary met James Crump there, he worked as a gardener and keeper. She left Crump there, but after a week he came and joined her. They cohabited for a few months, but were later married at **Gillingham, Kent**, about 13 May 1824.

Clump then entered as a landsman on board the *Ramillies* man of war. Mary came to London and was admitted to St Luke's Lying In Hospital, where she was delivered of a son on 28 July 1824, named James.

After Crump left the *Ramillies* they lived for several years at Chatham; their son Thomas was born there on 28 May 1829. They then went to **Reading** where two more children were born – Charlotte, on 4 December 1831, and a child born last year called Eliza, but not yet baptised.

In 1834 Crump and his family came to reside in the **In Parish of St Cuthbert's, Wells**. After three months Crump absconded and left his family chargeable to the parish.

Mary knew nothing about her husband except what he had told her – that he had been born in **Birmingham**, he had been apprenticed and was a widower; also that his mother lived at No.2 Dudley Street, Birmingham.

The parish officers then gave Mary money to go to Birmingham, supposing that Crump had gone there. However Crump's mother told Mary that his real name was James Boughton, he had been married before, his former wife was living and together with her children was chargeable to and supported by the parish of Birmingham.

7 June 1834.

Birmingham Workhouse. Letter from Vestry Clerk to the parish officers of Wells and Bristol:

"I regret exceedingly you have sent this family in an illegal manner and I return them to you that they may be provided for according to law."

[*Signed W.W. Bynner.*]

4 July 1834.

Letter from Robert Davies, solicitor for the In Parish of St Cuthbert's, Wells to Henry Rice Esq., solicitor for the churchwardens and overseers of St James, Westminster:

"Mary is now to be sent to St James, Westminster, together with her son James. The three younger children are within the age of nurture [under seven years old, by 22 George iii c83] and cannot be separated from their mother. It

146

will be necessary for the parish of St James to call upon Chatham (birthplace of Thomas) and Reading (birthplace of Charlotte and Eliza) for their maintenance."

[S.R.O., settlement examination DD/FS Box 75, bundle 3.]

23 June 1834.

Mary Crump, wife of James Crump, who has deserted her, and her four children, James aged ten years, who has not gained a settlement in his own right, Thomas five years of age, Charlotte three and Eliza one year.

Removal order from In Parish of St Cuthbert's Wells to the parish of St James, Westminster.

Note in margin: Mary Bennett and James her son.

[S.R.O., DD/FS. Box 75. Bundle 11. p29. (Foster of Wells).]

[Case 165] **24 February 1835. Ann Bishop.**

Before J. Williams and W.C. James.

Ann Bishop, wife of John Bishop, mason, who had gone from her, states that her maiden name was Attwood. She was married to John at **Chewton Mendip** in 1823.

Ann had four children by her husband, all born in wedlock, Mary Ann aged eleven years, John five years, James William two and three quarters of a year old and Worthy Alexander of the age of nine months. Ann and the children are all chargeable to **Timsbury**, where they are residing.

Ann had heard her husband say that he was legally settled in **Priddy**. for six or seven years past he had received "second poor money" from Priddy while they were living out of the parish, and they were treated as belonging to the parish of Priddy, where John's mother and several brothers and sisters were living.

John had last received "Second poor money" at Christmas time.

[? *Signed, document a copy*]

[S.R.O., settlement examination D/P/Priddy 13/3/2.4.]

"Second poor money" would have been received by those of the poor who were not being relieved by the parish. In this case it is probable that the money had come from trustees of the John Plummer charity.

John Plummer, of West Harptree, by his will dated 1729 left a messuage and land from which the clear yearly profits were to be divided between the parishes of West Harptree and Priddy, and then distributed to those in need.

[S.R.O., D/P/Priddy. 18/1/1. Copy of will made in 1786.]

[Case 166] **23 March 1835. Thomas Cook and family.**

Concerning the settlement of his daughter Mary Ann Cook. Before Robert Brooks and Francis Besly.

Thomas Cook, residing in the **In Parish of St Cuthbert's, Wells,** states that he is aged sixty-two years. He was married on 5 April 1801 to Amy Andrews, in the parish church of **Pilton**. Mary Ann Cook, his daughter, is now aged twenty-two.

Before he was married, Thomas hired himself to James Pike of Pilton, farmer, at the wages of five guineas a year and board and lodging.He served one whole year and immediately afterwards he was married.

After twelve months Thomas enlisted into the marines. He served two years. During his service his wife and child were supported by Pilton parish.

Thomas came to Wells about twenty-four years ago. He had been crippled during the time that he left the marines and came to Wells.

Two of his children died at Wells, and the parish of Pilton paid for their burial; Thomas has received regular relief from the parish of Pilton.

[*Mark*.]

[S.R.O., settlement examination DD/WM. 67. p53. (Wells Museum deposit).]

23 March 1835.

Mary Ann Cook, before Robert Brooks and Francis Besley.

Mary Ann Cook states that she is the daughter of Thomas Cook, she will be twenty-two on 22 May next; she is not married, but has one bastard child called John Robert, who was born 8 January last. She has always lived at home, she receives relief from the In Parish of St Cuthbert's, Wells.

[*Mark*.]

[S.R.O., settlement examination DD/WM. 67. p54.]

23 March 1835.

Mary Ann Cook and John Robert her child, to be removed from the In parish of St Cuthberts, Wells to Pilton.

[S.R.O., DD/FS. Box 75. Bundle 11. p35.]

1835. George Cook.

Before Robert Brooks and Francis Besley; undated.

George Cook, residing in the In Parish of St Cuthbert's, Wells, states that he is the son of Thomas and Amy Cook. He was born at Pilton, and is now aged thirty-four.

George lived with his father until the year 1818, at that date he went to the Island of **Antigua** as a plough boy on Mr Tudway's estates, where he remained for eleven years. He then returned to England because of illness.

George is living in Wells with his father. When he came home he applied to the overseer of the parish of Pilton, who gave him relief of two shillings and sixpence a week, for nearly a twelvemonth. The overseers of Pilton have relieved him several times since then.

George further states that he has never done any act to gain a settlement in his own right, he is now chargeable to the In Parish of St Cuthbert's, he has received seven shillings relief from the overseers.

[*No mark or signature.*]

[S.R.O., settlement examination DD/FS Box75. bundle 10.162. (Foster of Wells).]

1835. George Cook's settlement judged to be in Pilton on his examination and that of his father Thomas Cook.

[S.R.O., Miscellaneous DD/FS Box. 75. Bundle 11. p37.]

The Tudway family of Wells owned plantations on Antigua, in the **Caribbean**. Many interesting records of these estates are deposited in the Somerset record office; from the plantation pay lists we see that George Cook's salary for the year 1822 was £100.

[S.R.O., DD/TD Box 53.]

28 December 1837. George Cook.

Before John Lax and Joseph Giles.

George Cook, still residing in the In Parish of St Cuthberts, Wells, states that at the age of thirteen he hired himself to Mr William Pulsford of the **Out Parish of St Cuthbert's, Wells**. His wages were one shilling a week, victuals, lodging and clothes. He worked one and a half years for Mr Pulsford, then worked as a day labourer until he went to Antigua.

[*Signed.*]

[S.R.O., settlement examination DD/WM. 67. p85.]

28 December 1837.

George Cook to be removed from the In Parish of St Cuthbert's, Wells to the Out Parish.

Endorsed 1 January 1838. Delivered a duplicate of this order together with notice of order of removal and settlement examination.

[S.R.O., Miscellaneous DD/FS Box 75. Bundle 11. p52.]

Letter from William Pulsford, 11 Darlington Street, **Bath**.

Dated 5 December 1837.

"My dear Sir, At so long a distance of time I cannot take upon myself to speak correctly without reference to my memorandums which I now cannot lay my hands upon, or having some communication with the pauper himself.

"But as it stands at present I am strongly inclined to think that he lived with me under a hiring for a year, giving him a suit of drab livery, breeches and boots, also a stable dress. Such an agreement I had at the time I was constantly visiting hunting and shooting in Dorsetshire. I perfectly recollect that I lodged as well as boarded him.

"As it is parish business I will trouble you in future to pay postages of any further communi[cation]."

[S.R.O., DD/FS. Box 73. Bundle 11. no. 13.]

[Case 167] **5 May 1835. John Clatworthy.**

Before Bennett Michell

John Clatworthy, confined to bed by sickness, states that he was born at **Winsford**. He lived with his parents until he was nine years old, at which age he went to live with Mr Lyddon, of **Edbrook** in the parish of Winsford, where he remained for six months. Following this John lived with Robert Lyddon, of **Morebath, Devonshire**, for eleven months; and then returned to his parents, as he had a dislocated arm.

John Clatworthy then served as follows:

Mr Jones of the 'Feathers Inn' at **Minehead** for four years, wages two guineas a year.

Rev. Mr Bradley of Minehead for six months, agreement was for six pounds a year and a suit of clothes.

Returned to his parents.

Mr Bouchier, attorney, at **Wiveliscombe**, stayed four years and six months, wages nine guineas a year.

Mr Bucknell of **Crowcombe**, stayed six months, agreement was for fifteen guineas a year.

Employed at **Bristol** as an under butler at different places, for eighteen months, did not make any agreements.

Mr Stone of **Exton**, wages to be twenty guineas a year.

Rev. Philip Wilson at Exton, wages to be twelve guineas a year, stayed six months.

Returned to his father whom he agreed to serve for a year, wages to be two shillings a week and board and lodging, he had received his wages partly in pocket money and partly in clothes.

John further states that he has done no other act to gain a settlement.

[*Signed.*]

[S.R.O., settlement examination D/P/Winsford 13/3/21.]

[Case 168] **18 June 1838. Samuel Day.**

Before D.S. Moncrieffe.

Samuel Day, residing at **Mark**, states that he was born in Chedzoy, and is now aged thirty years.

When he was seventeen years old he bargained with Mr George Gatcombe of **Huntspill**, to serve him for a year, Lady Day [25 March] to Lady Day, at the wages of £5.

Samuel lived a whole year with Mr Gatcombe, then under yearly hirings he worked another three and a half years for him. Samuel then worked as a day

150

labourer for several weeks, after which he bargained with Mr John Gatcombe, also of Huntspill, to serve him for a year at the wages of £8.

The contract was renewed for a further year at the same wages. At the end of the second year, Samuel bargained with Mr Robert Sully of Mark to serve him for a year, his wages to be £9. He then served Mr Sully another year and received his wages as before.

Samuel further states that he has done no other act to gain a settlement. His wife is named Eliza, their children are Martha aged one year and eight months, and Mary aged eight months.

[*Signed.*]

[S.R.O., settlement examination D/P/Mark 13/3/4.94.]

[Case 169] **10 September 1840. Elizabeth Foster and family.**
To be removed from the Out Parish of **St Cuthbert's, Wells**, to **High Littleton**, because Elizabeth's husband, Henry, is a prisoner in **Ilchester** gaol.
29 May 1848.
Elizabeth Foster and James, John and Eliza her children to be removed from the In Parish of St Cuthbert's, Wells to High Littleton. [16a.]
29 May 1848.
Elizabeth Foster, single woman, to be removed from the In Parish of St Cuthbert's, Wells to High Littleton. Same reference. 16f.
1 June 1848.
Appeal notice against removal. 16g.
20 June 1848.
Opinion given that appeal will not succeed. 16h.
26 June 1848.
Appeal withdrawn. [16.i.]

[S.R.O., D/P High Littleton 13/3/4. 16b.]

29 May 1848. Elizabeth Foster.
The daughter of Henry and Elizabeth Foster. Evidence given by the mother regarding her daughter's settlement. Before Henry Barnard and Joseph Giles.

Henry and Elizabeth Foster were married at Wells twenty-one years ago.

At the assizes in 1840 Henry was tried for housebreaking and sentenced to be transported for ten years. Also in 1840 Elizabeth and her four children were removed to **Clutton** workhouse; they were taken from Wells to the house of the overseer of High Littleton, who took them to Clutton. High Littleton accepted them as parishioners, and gave them relief while they lived at Clutton, **Farrington Gurney** and Wells.

After they had lived in the workhouse for four months Elizabeth (the mother) had applied for out door relief, this was allowed at the rate of six shillings a week, so that she and the children were able to leave the workhouse. The other children were named Robert, James, John and Eliza.

Elizabeth, the daughter, a single woman aged twenty years, had lived with her mother until two years ago. She now resided at Wells, from which parish she received relief of one shilling a week and a loaf of bread.

    [S.R.O., settlement examination D/P/High Littleton 13/3/4.16.]

Henry Foster appears in the *Description book of Ilchester gaol*:

14 August 1840. Henry Foster, aged 33, height five foot, seven and a quarter inches.

Person, stout; complexion, dark; visage, oval; hair dark; eyes, hazel; born, Wells; marks, scar on tip of nose; trade, labourer; last abode, Wells; married with five children; read and write, imp: [probably means imperfectly].

Remarks, transportation for ten years.

    [S.R.O., Q/AGi. 15/4.]

From the Felons Register of Ilchester gaol:

8 August 1840. Wells summer assizes.

Henry Foster, aged 33, charged with John Porter, aged 21. Offence, breaking the dwelling house of Joseph Allard, and stealing twelve pounds, nine shillings in money, and other articles.

Foster found guilty and sentenced to ten years transportation.

Previous conviction, one month for assault, but acquitted of stealing fish from a pond.

Porter found guilty and sentenced to fifteen years transportation. Porter had previous convictions for felony and poaching.

3 September 1840, both prisoners removed to the *Stirling Castle* hulk at Devonport.

    [S.R.O., Q/AGi. 14/6.]

Extract from John Smith's Removal Order, 1841.

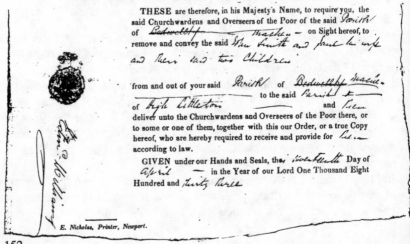

THESE are therefore, in his Majesty's Name, to require you, the said Churchwardens and Overseers of the Poor of the said *Parish* of *Bedwellty ———— Machen —* on Sight hereof, to remove and convey the said *John Smith and Jane his wife and their said two Children*

from and out of your said *Parish* of *Bedwellty Machen* ———— to the said *Parish of ———* of *High Littleton ————* and *them* deliver unto the Churchwardens and Overseers of the Poor there, or to some or one of them, together with this our Order, or a true Copy hereof, who are hereby required to receive and provide for *them* according to law.

    GIVEN under our Hands and Seals, the *nineteenth* Day of *April ———* in the Year of our Lord One Thousand Eight Hundred and *Thirty Three.*

    E. Nicholas, Printer, Newport.

[Case 170] **19 April 1841. John Smith.**
Before R.W.P. Davies and John Andsell. Examination taken at **Llangynider**, Brecon, Wales.John Smith, a miner residing in Llangynider, states that he was born at **High Littleton**, he is now thirty-eight years of age. His father was also born at High Littleton and died there. John had worked with his father at Paulton until he was aged nineteen years, he then went to Wales and was employed in the Iron Works at **Risca** for twelve months, then at **Varleg** Iron Works for two years, then at **Beaufort** Iron Works.

Eleven years ago John married Jane Flook at **Monyddysloyne**. they had five children, four of whom are living, Silas aged ten years, Charlotte seven years, Ann five years and Martha eighteen months old.

John has not gained a settlement, about eight years ago he and his wife were removed [order dates below] from **Bedwelty, Monmouthshire**, to High Littleton. John is now unable through illness to provide for himself and his family, and is chargeable to the parish of Llangynider in the union of **Crickhowell**.

[*Signed*.]

[S.R.O., settlement examination D/P/High Littleton 13/3/2.44. 17 April 1833. Removal order D/P/High Littleton 13/3/2.30. 19 April 1841. Removal order D/P/High Littleton 13/3/2.44 John Smith and family from Llangynider to High Littleton.]

7 May 1841.
Note to say that John Smith is unable to follow his occupation as a miner owing to asthma. Signed by Frank Irwin, surgeon, **Ebbw Vale** Iron Works.

[S.R.O., D/P/High Littleton 13/3/2.44a.]

[Case 171] **7 January 1842. James Rayner.**
Names of justices not given.
James Rayner, residing in the workhouse of **Wells** union, states that he is aged twenty-nine, and is the son of John and Rosena Rayner. He has no knowledge of his parents' settlement.

In 1826 James was apprenticed for seven years to Mr James Keke Coles [probably James Keate Coles] of Wells, papermaker. James received seven shillings a week for the first three and a half years, and the same for the second three and a half years, with the addition of one shilling and sixpence a day for 'overwork'. James also received three suits of clothes during his apprenticeship.

[*Signed*.]

Examination witnessed and signed by George Thorn.

[S.R.O., settlement examination D/P/Wells St Cuthbert's 13/3/17. 149.]

[Case 172] **21 January 1842. George Taylor.**

Before C.A. Elton and William Henry Gore Langton.

George Taylor, "now an inmate of the **Bedminster** Union Workhouse in the parish of **Long Ashton**", states that he is aged between fifty and sixty years, and was born in the parish of **Mark**, where his father is still living.

At the age of seventeen George enlisted as a soldier, and served until March 1818, he then went to the **Cape of Good Hope**, where he worked for the government for five years.

George then returned to England and found employment as a weekly labourer in Bedminster. A week ago he came to Mark, where his father was receiving parochial relief, however the Relieving Officer refused to give George any relief unless he was sent home by an order.

[*Mark.*]

[S.R.O., settlement examination D/P/Mark 13/3/4.95.]

[Case 173] **7 March 1842. Edmund Day.**

Before G.B. Northcote and H.J. Addington.

Edmund Day, residing at **Brent Knoll** (South Brent) states that he was born at **Stock** in the parish of **Churchill**, and is now aged forty-four.

When he was of the age of nineteen and was single, he bargained with Mr John Howell Cook of the parish of **Lympsham**, to serve him for a year at the wages of £15 and clothes. Immediately afterwards Mr Cook went to **London**, "as he was walking the hospitals", and Edmund went with him. They remained in London about three months.

Cook then went to live in Brent Knoll where he stayed for about two years, Edmund remained in his service. They then removed to **Bridgwater**, where Cook lived in lodgings, and Edmund continued in Cook's service under a proper yearly agreement.

After about four to five months Cook again moved, and went to **Martock**, Edmund accompanied him, but left after seven months. The whole of Edmund's service with Cook was four years.

Edmund then went to **Bristol**, where after spending three months in service, he got married. He is now a widower, and states that he has done no act to gain a settlement since he left Cook's service.

[*Signed.*]

[S.R.O., settlement examination D/P/Brent Knoll 13/3/4.15.]

[Case 174] **6 October 1842. William Silverthorne.**

Before J. Clarke and E.S.Drewe.

William Silverthorne, residing in Wellington, states that he is aged thirty-five. He was born at **Westbury Leigh, Wiltshire**. However, when still a child, he removed with his parents to **Melksham**, Wiltshire, which was their parish of settlement.

Last winter, while residing at **Kingswood**, Wiltshire, with his wife and their children (Elizabeth aged twelve years, Louisa ten years, George eight and Frederick two years old) William and his family were removed to **Melksham** where they were supported by the parish. They did not stay at Melksham long as the parish gave William £2 in money to get employment elsewhere. William has done no act to gain a settlement.

For the last five months they have lived in **Wellington**, where William had been employed on the railway [see below] and where his wife had been delivered of another daughter, now aged two and a half weeks and not yet baptised. The family are now chargeable to Wellington.

[*Mark.*]

The Great Western Railway Line from Bristol to Exeter was opened in 1844. It runs north of Wellington. In 1843 this stretch of line, westwards from Taunton, terminated at Beam Bridge. Just after Beam Bridge is the White Ball Tunnel. Work on this major undertaking commenced in 1842, and was finished in 1844. Details from E.T. Macdermot, *The History of the Great Western Railway.*

[S.R.O., D/G/W.47.no.36. Wellington Board of Guardians.]

[Case 175] **8 May 1843. Elizabeth Carter.**

Regarding the settlement of her late husband, John Carter. No justices are named.

Elizabeth Carter, residing at **Holcome Rogus, Devon** [see below] states that she is aged thirty [sic, but an error]. She married her late husband John Carter at **Bath** twenty-two years ago, they had ten children, of whom six are alive, although only five are living with Elizabeth in the parish of Holcombe.

The family came to Holcombe about a year ago. John had worked on the railway in the parish of **Burlescombe** until last January when he died. The family are now chargeable.

John had told his wife that he was from the parish of **Lyncombe** and **Widcombe**, where his father had belonged. Ten or twelve years ago the family had been in distress, as John was afflicted with an abscess in his back, and was sent to Bath hospital for two weeks, the family were then relieved by the parish of Lyncombe and Widcombe.

The children living with Elizabeth are Eliza ten years old, John eight, Sophia five, Selina two, and Ann six weeks old.

[*No mark or signature.*]

Some Devonshire parishes were included in the **Wellington** Union, viz: Burlescombe, **Clayhidon, Culmstock, Hemyock** and Holcombe Rogus.

[S.R.O., settlement examination, Wellington Board of Guardians records, D/G/W. 47. no. 59.]

[Case 176] **28 July 1843. John Brine.**

The justices are not named.

John Brine, residing at **East Wells**, states that he is aged thirty-one years, and that he was born at **Sparkford**, in which parish his parents, John and Ann Brine, were legally settled. Thirteen years ago John junior hired himself for a year to Mr W. Grist, confectioner of East Wells, his wages to be fifty-two shillings and his board and lodging: "My work was to go about selling cakes, upon the sale of which I got a profit of about two pence on a shilling for myself, independent of my wages."

John stayed with Mr Grist for two years, since which time he has done no act to gain a settlement. In 1834 he was married at **Shepton Mallet** church to Isabella. They have three children – Elizabeth seven years old, George four years and Robert two years.

"I am ready to swear to the truth of the above statement." Witnessed by George Thorn.

[*Mark*.]

[S.R.O., settlement examination D/P/Wells St Cuthbert's 13/3/17. 156.]

[Case 177] **14 November 1844. Ann Hitchcock.**

Concerning the settlement of her son William Coleman. Before Rev John Clarke and Rev William Burridge.

Ann Hitchcock, a widow residing at Broadway, states that she is aged sixty-eight years. When she was aged twenty-three she was married to Samuel Coleman at **Bickenhall** and had five children, of whom three are living. William Coleman is one of those children.

Samuel Coleman lived for ten and a half years after they were married. He had received relief from the parish of **North Curry** for nine months before he died.

Ann used to go with her husband to the overseers at the vestry room. The overseers would ask Samuel a few questions and then pay him some money. He had received as much as seven shillings a week.

Ann used to fetch the money herself once a month, except when the weather prevented her going. On such occasions Mrs Andrews, shopkeeper, of North Curry used to "take it up".

When Ann was able to go herself she used to go to the pay table in the vestry room and receive it from Mr Woodman, who was clerk to the parish.

After Samuel died, Ann applied to the parish of North Curry for relief for herself and the children, of whom three were living – Elizabeth aged six years, Charles three and William eighteen months. They were relieved by one shilling and sixpence a week for each of them until they became nine years old.

Ann used to fetch the money herself, but continued to live in Bickenhall for three years after Samuel died.

Ann then married Job Hitchcock, and removed with him from Bickenhall to **West Buckland** with her two younger children, for whom she continued to receive relief. Elizabeth had been apprenticed by the parish of North Curry when she was nine years old.

When William was of the age of nine years his father-in-law [step-father] Job Hitchcock, who worked for Mr Bryant, butcher, of West Buckland, agreed with his master that William should also work for Mr Bryant, and that he would receive wages of three pence a day which would be paid to his father-in-law. During the time that William worked for Mr Bryant he had meat, drink, washing and lodging at his father-in-law's house.

William Coleman recites details given in Ann Hitchcock's examination, he then states that he worked for Mr Bryant for four or five years, after which he served several different masters. His wages varied from fifteen pence to one shilling and sixpence a week. He also received his meat, drink, washing and lodging.

William further states that he is now aged thirty-five years. When he was twenty-two years old he married Mary Cross, daughter of Joseph Cross. They have five children – Elizabeth, twelve years old, Mary Ann eleven, Charlotte eight, James four and Sarah nine months.

William continues his statement saying that he receives relief from North Curry because of his illness. After his marriage he lived with his wife's father Joseph Cross, who died about six years ago, since when he continued to live in the same house, paying rent of £1 a year. Joseph Cross had six children, of whom Mary is the youngest. Joseph died without making a will, and neither William nor his wife have taken out letters of administration.

[*Mark of Ann Hitchcock.*]

Notice of chargeability.

Thomas Braddick Westlake Blackmore, one of the relieving officers of the poor law union of Wellington, gives evidence that: "William Coleman, his wife Mary and their children Elizabeth, Mary Ann, Charlotte, James and Sarah are chargeable to the parish of West Buckland, and are receiving weekly relief of four loaves of bread, value one shilling and seven pence."

[S.R.O., settlement examinations D/G/W.47. no.72. (Wellington board of guardians records).]

[Case 178] **1845. Sampson Chivers.**

No magistrate named nor date given.

Sampson Chivers, a coalminer residing at **High Littleton**, states that he is aged sixty-three, he was born and baptised at **Camerton**.

Sampson's grandfather was John Chivers, who it was said came from the South. He had been employed as the Bailiff of **Highgrove Coal Works** at High Littleton, and was killed there. John Chivers had married Elizabeth Carter of **Clutton**, she had been buried at High Littleton over thirty years ago. John and Elizabeth had several children (that were known to Sampson).

These children were:

Thomas.

Samuel, who used to be called "the doctor" [the seventh son of a daughterless family; superstitiously believed to have healing qualities]. Samuel's children were Thomas, the present postman of **Timsbury**, and James, the present parish clerk of High Littleton.

Josiah, whose daughter Jane married Sampson Chivers.

Ann, now Ann Rogers.

Robert, Sampson's father, who married Sarah Brookes of Compton Martin. Robert and Sarah had three sons and four daughters, Sampson was the sixth child.

Sampson had married his cousin Jane at **Bath, St James**, over forty years ago, they had six children who were:

Ann, now the wife of Thomas Burt of **London**.

Elizabeth, now in service in London.

Fanny, now the wife of John Stockey of **Clevedon**.

Hester, now in service in Bristol.

Mercy, aged eighteen. She is unwell, and is living with her father.

Mary Ann, aged sixteen, also living with her father.

All the children were born in High Littleton. Jane, Sampson's wife, died two years ago and was buried in High Littleton.

Sampson's father Robert and his wife did not live together for at least fourteen years before Robert died, except for short periods. Sampson's mother was a cripple. She lived with her daughter Betty Henton at **Paulton**, in which parish she died and was buried.

Robert had been a collier. He had left his wife and family at High Littleton when he went out of the neighbourhood, and had done no act to gain a settlement.

Sampson Chivers further states that he lived with his mother in High Littleton until he was married. After marriage he lived for ten years in a house belonging to Henry Tucker at the yearly rent of £6. He then rented a cottage and garden from Mr Joseph Harris at the same rent.

Sampson next went to **Farmborough** where he rented a house from Mr Rush, at the rent of £4 for a year.

Returning to High Littleton, Sampson rented a house belonging to John Wilkins, also for £4, and lived there until it was burnt down.

Sampson then took his present house in High Littleton, renting it from Mr Thomas Miles, the steward of William Jones Burdett Esq. Again the rent was £4 per annum, and where he has lived for the last fourteen or fifteen years.

Sampson goes on to say that he has done no act to gain a settlement except as stated above. He has never served in a parish office, has never lived as a covenant servant for a year, nor has he owned any property. Furthermore he has never been relieved by any parish except during the last week, when he received five shillings in money, and bread. His daughter Mercy has done no act to gain a settlement for herself.

The following information is also contained in the examination.

While living in Harris's house, Sampson took, of farmer James Boulter of High Littleton, half an acre of land to grow a potato crop, at the rate of £8 an acre. The ground was "fresh broken up".

Sampson and his son Joseph (sic) planted the whole ground and dug the potatoes, some of which they sold to John Tucker. Sampson's brother John had some of the same field at the same time. Sampson paid rent of £4 for his part of the field and he never underlet any part of his half acre. Neither had he ever rented any potato land before or since, although at the same time he had about twenty lugs [120 yards] of ground at Haygrove in Farmborough parish, which he grubbed up by permission of Mr William Adams, steward for General Popham, and which he had planted with potatoes. This land he had held for three or four years but had paid no rent for it.

[S.R.O., settlement examination D/P/High Littleton 13/3/5.2.]

See S.R.O., D/P/High Littleton 13/3/5 for documents numbered 1 to 24, regarding other members of the Chivers family, including a family tree.

[Case 179] [Blank] **1845. Stephen Plummer Slade**

Examined regarding the settlement of Joyce Slade, wife of his son William Slade. The justices are not named. No date is given.

Stephen Plummer Slade, engineer and smith, residing at **High Littleton**, states that he is aged sixty-six years, and was born at **Stanton Drew**. He was the third child of John and Mary Slade.

When Stephen was five years old his mother died, about a year afterwards John Slade and his family went to live at **Paulton**.

John died in 1791, and was buried at Paulton. While the family lived there they occupied a freehold property which John Slade had inherited from his uncle Stephen Plummer. John Slade had made a will, and had appointed Mr Simon Hill and Mr Joseph Hill of Paulton to be guardians to his son Stephen Plummer Slade. Stephen lived with his elder sister until she died in 1792. In February 1793 Stephen was bound by his guardians to be an apprentice for seven years to Thomas Palmer of **St George**, in the county of Gloucester, engineer and smith. He was bound by indenture.

Stephen served his apprenticeship until the latter part of January 1797, living in his master's house at St George, except for some nights that he slept at **Bitton**, Gloucestershire, while working the engine at the spelter [zinc] works there. this was before October 1796.

In 1797 Stephen went with his master to erect an engine at **Smallcombe Coal Works** at **Midsomer Norton**. He was still employed as an apprentice. He lodged at the house of John Hurton at **Radstock**. In the afternoon of Saturday 21 October 1797, after work, Stephen went to his master's house at St George and slept there that night. On the Sunday afternoon, on his way back to Radstock, he met with a return chaise, and went to the 'Golden Hart Inn' at **Clutton**, and slept there on the Sunday night. The next day he went to Stanton Drew and slept in the public house at Stanton Wick on the Monday night. On Tuesday 24 October 1797 he went to Bristol and "entered as a sailor in the Royal Navy".

He slept that night at [blank] house on the quay. The next day, Wednesday, Stephen went on board the [blank] and sailed the day after.

He remained at sea until 1802, at which date he was discharged at Plymouth.

His master, who had not known of Stephen's intention to go to sea, had died during the time Stephen had been away. On his return to St George Stephen asked Thomas Palmer's widow for his indenture, which she gave him. Stephen had offerd half a guinea for it, the other half of the indenture was with his guardians.

Stephen now lodged at Paulton and received his share from the sale of his father's property. He further states that he had done no other act to gain a settlement. He was married in September 1803 to Sarah Sperring, at **St Mary Redcliffe, Bristol**; they have had nine children.

William Slade, the husband of the pauper Joyce Slade, was the eighth child. He was born at Farmborough in November 1818, and was baptised there.

[S.R.O., settlement examination D/P/High Littleton 13/3/6.38.]

[Case 180] 3 March 1845. Charles Filer.

Before William Perkins and Joseph Giles.

Charles Filer, residing in the **In Parish of St Cuthbert's, Wells**, states that he was married in March 1834, at **Poole, Dorset**, to Elizabeth Bird. They have three children – Charles aged nine, Elizabeth eight, and Mary Ann five years. The family are now chargeable to St Cuthbert's. Charles states that he has received relief, from 25 February last, of three shillings and four loaves of bread.

In 1821, when he was fifteen years old, Charles was bound apprentice for seven years to Samuell Culverwell of **Bedminster**, brushmaker. The indentures were signed by both parties opposite a seal, the premium paid was £30.

Charles served his master for a year in Bedminster, Culverwell then moved to **Swansea** and Charles went with him, and served his master for five years, during which time Charles lived in his master's house, including the last forty days of his service.

In 1828 Culverwell did not have enough work to keep Charles on, he was then aged twenty-one years, and he and his master put an end to the apprenticeship. His indentures were given up to him.

Charles then went to **Bristol** for several months, and then to **London**, carrying his indentures with him, and worked as a journeyman in his trade for three years.

In 1831 Charles Filer left London to go on the 'tramp' [see below] to work in his trade. Immediately before he had left London he had lodged in the house of William Strutt, a carpenter, in Russell Court, Great Dover Road, **Southwark**.When he left to go on the 'tramp' he left with Strutt his box containing his clothes and his indenture of apprenticeship.

Charles returned to London after four years, and went to Russell Court to get his box, but Strutt was gone from there, and the person who lived there knew nothing about the box, or the whereabouts of Strutt.

Charles has never done any act whereby he could have gained a settlement, except as stated above. He is now very ill, and believes that his life would be in danger if he was removed to Swanseas in his present state of health.

[*Signed.*]
3 March 1845.

Robert Thorley, relieving officer of the Wells Union, gives evidence that Charles Filer is too ill to be removed, he has received three shillings in money and four loaves of bread as relief.

[S.R.O., settlement examination DD/WM. 67. pp 259-262 (Wells Museum deposit).]
'Tramps':

From the early eighteenth century to the middle of the nineteenth century skilled workers could be found travelling from town to town in search of employment; these men were artisans who belonged to the craft clubs; forerunners of trade unions. They received support from their clubs while on the 'tramp'. See E.J.Hobsbawm on "The Tramping Artisan" in *Labouring Men.*

[Case 181] **7 February 1846. Robert Hawkins and family.**
They are to become chargeable to the parish of **St James**, in the **Bath** Union.
11 February 1846.

Meeting of the Board of Guardians certifies that Robert Hawkins and family became chargeable on 7 February.

Signed by Charles Balsford, chairman, and C.Brown, clerk.

16 February 1846.

Examination of Robert Hawkins (taken at No. 4 Philip Street, Bath) by Henry Gordon, acting out of petty sessions because Robert was too ill to attend in person.

Robert Hawkins states that he was married to Mary in the parish church of Bathwick. They have three children, Richard seven years old, Edward six years and Jane one year old.

[*Signed.*]

16 February 1846.

Elizabeth Hawkins, regarding the settlement of her son Robert Hawkins, porter. Before Henry Gordon and Philip Sheppard, J.P.s, and Richard Mills, assistant overseer of the parish of St James, Bath.

Elizabeth Hawkins, residing at **Glastonbury**, states that she was married at **Evercreech** forty years ago to Thomas Hawkins, now deceased. Robert Hawkins, their son, was born at Evercreech on 7 September 1815. Thomas had been apprenticed to Mr Allen of Evercreech, a plumber and glazier.

Elizabeth knows that her husband slept in his master's house for forty nights before his apprenticeship was completed. Elizabeth produced his indenture of apprenticeship, dated 30 October 1797. The indenture had been legally stamped.

Thomas had died about two years ago, since which time Elizabeth had been allowed two shillings and sixpence weekly from the overseers. In February 1845 she went to the Rev Mr Napier, one of the guardians, and Mr Backhouse, the relieving officer, and asked their permission to go and live with her daughter in Glastonbury. Permission was given, and they said "your money shall be sent through the post".

Elizabeth had received her relief in that way ever since. Robert Hawkins, her son, had not acquired a settlement of his own.

[*Signed.*]

20 February 1846.

Henry Gordon, as examining justice, reports to Phillip Sheppard, J.P., regarding the above examination of Robert Hawkins.

[S.R.O., settlement examination D/P/Evercreech 13/3/4.45.]

21 February 1846.

Robert Hawkins, his wife Mary and their children Richard, Edward and Jane are chargeable to the parish of Bath St James. An order has been obtained for their removal to Evercreech.

[S.R.O., D/P/Evercreech 13/3/6.1.]

[Case 182] **1846-47. Abraham Criddle and family.**

They are his wife Harriet (nee Reed) and their five children – John, nine years, James six, Sarah Jane four, Mary Ann two, and Honor aged three months.

1 October 1846.

This family has become chargeable to the parish of **Ash Priors**.

27 January 1847.

Notice of chargeabilty issued.

1 February 1847.

Order of removal from Ash Priors to **Brompton Ralph**, and appeal against such removal.

Before Francis Popham and Rev Cecil Smith.

29 June 1847.

Appeal heard at **Bridgwater** quarter sessions. These documents are contained in a solicitor's deposit. The case had involved much legal work, and is a case of boring complexity, which hinges upon the question (unresolved) of whether Abraham Criddle's illness is such as will produce permanent disability or not; it will, however, suffice if we confine ourselves to recounting the background.

Abraham Criddle states that he has been subject to a skin complaint for four years (urticaria or nettlerash): "Large red itching spots on different parts of my body and sometimes my legs and feet swell very bad. Then I get very weak and cannot work. It used to go clean off when I had it first up to the last twelve months, but since then never so. My complaint came on in the winter time in the cold weather and as the weather gets warmer I get better. We never had any flesh [to eat].

"I work for Mr Saunders a farmer at **West Leigh** in **Ash Priors**. I do anything, put in potatoes or such things, he gives me tenpence a day, and now since the last fortnight or three weeks three pints of cider daily, and out of that I allow him one shilling and eight pence a week for rent. When at Brompton Ralph I had six shillings a week and liquor, and half a bushel of wheat weekly at six shillings a bushel Ash Priors parish have given me four shillings a week and six loaves weekly relief, this for myself and wife and five children to subsist on, and out of which I paid one shilling and eight pence weekly for house rent."

21 June 1847.

The overseers of Brompton Ralph took Abraham to **Wiveliscombe**. He walked there and was examined by Mr Edwards the surgeon, Mr Norman, and a third gentleman.

22 June 1847.

Abraham went to **Bishops Lydeard** and was examined by Mr Mortimer and another surgeon.

23 June 1847.

Abraham walked to **Nettlecombe** and back, sixteen miles.

24 June 1847.

Abraham walked to Brompton Ralph, **Stogumber** and back, seventeen miles. To eat Abraham had only bread, and a little barley and water to drink.

The surgeons say that the urticaria should only prevent a man from working a few days at a time, and should not cause permanent disability, but he needs good nourishment and a little physic. The disease could be made worse by bad diet.

We now come to the quarter sessions, and the hearing of the appeal, during which the justices declare:

"The truth of the matter is that the man has been starving, with his wife and five children, none of whom are earning, on four shillings and six loaves weekly, out of which he pays one shilling and eight pence weekly for house rent."

[S.R.O., DD/CCH j. Box 2. Bundle 5. (Couch of Stogumber).]

(Several years later we find from the 1851 census, that the Criddle family are back in Brompton Ralph: Abraham Criddle, aged 48, farm labourer, also in receipt of parish relief. Harriet Criddle, his wife, aged 38. John Reed, son-in-law [step-son] aged ? 14, farm labourer's son. Sarah J. Criddle, aged 8. Mary A. Criddle, aged 6. Honor Criddle, aged 2. Anne Criddle aged one month.

All the children except Honor were born at Brompton Ralph.

James Criddle, aged ten, and described as farm labourer, is found in the household of farmer Robert Dibble, at High House, Brompton Ralph. H.O. 109/1920. fo. 715 & 716.

[Case 183] **2 March 1848. Eliza Rapps**

To be removed from **Kilmersdon** to **High Littleton**.

9 March 1848.

Eliza Rapps. Before T.R. Jolliffe and William F. Knatchbull.

This examination concerns Eliza Rapps, aged thirteen and residing in Kilmersdon. Eliza spent two years in **Clutton** workhouse. About four years ago she was allowed by the guardians to live with her aunt, Elizabeth Ford, in Kilmersdon, and there she received one shilling and sixpence a week outdoor relief, on the account of the parish of High Littleton.

[S.R.O., settlement examination and removal order, D/P/High Littleton 13/3/4. 17a. and 17b.]

[Case 184] **16 July 1849. Emma Flower.**

Before T.R. Jolliffe and J.T. Jolliffe.

Concerning Emma Flower and her two children, Benjamin and Sarah, who reside in **Radstock**. She is the widow of Samuel Flower.

Samuel Flower, who died aged twenty-seven, took his settlement from his father Charles Flower, which he gained by serving an apprenticeship in **High Littleton**, to one Harding, a blacksmith.The apprenticeship was for seven years. The apprenticeship indenture was signed by Charles Flower's father, also called Charles.

The son Charles had married Tamar Crew at **Publow** twenty-nine years ago.

Emma received relief of one shilling and ninepence weekly, also three large loaves and one small loaf each week.

[S.R.O., settlement examination D/P/High Littleton 13/3/4.21.]

[Case 185] **5 December 1848. John Gregory and family.**

The magistrates are not named.

John Gregory, aged sixty, was the base born son of Phebe Gregory, deceased. While residing at **Paulton**, John became insane,and was removed to Dr Fox's asylum at **Brislington** [see below].This was twenty-three years ago, and High Littleton paid the expenses.

John was at Brislington for eighteen weeks. In 1838 John was removed to Dr Langworthy's asylum at **Box**, where he stayed until 1839. In 1847 John again became insane and was sent to Box until April 1848, at which date he was sent to **Wells Asylum** [more details below].

Whilst residing at Paulton the family had received bedding, bread and money, of various amounts, from the parish of High Littleton, all the time that they resided at Paulton.

John Gregory and family are to be removed from Paulton to High Littleton.

[S.R.O., settlement examination and removal order D/P/ High Littleton 13/3/4. 20 and 20b.]

Mentally disordered paupers who required treatment or confinement could be sent to a private asylum, the expenses incurred being paid by the parish to which the pauper belonged.

In Somerset, **Brislington House** was a private asylum founded by Dr Edward Long Fox, a member of the Society of Friends. In 1799 he bought land in Brislington and started building; the asylum opened in 1804. There was a separate room for each patient, public sitting rooms, a chapel and airing courts. In 1815 there were seventy patients and twenty-eight servants.

As well as those admitted privately, the asylum received pauper patients who could be employed in the work of the house.

Dr Fox, said to be "one of the kindest and most affectionate of men", was one of the first to introduce humane treatment of the insane.

[S.R.O., T/PH/FX. 1-6 (Copy provided by Bristol Record Office).]

John Gregory's admission to Wells Asylum is documented. He was the nineteenth patient to be admitted, entering the asylum on 1 April 1848. From his history notes we find that he was an illegitimate child, and knew nothing of his parents. He had been married at the age of twenty-three and had two children. He was unable to read or write, and had never attended any place of worship.

Notes on his condition follow which give his conduct as quiet.

In June John was noted as having become very stout. His weight on admission was one hundred and forty-seven pounds. On 1 July he was discharged in good health and spirits, leaving the asylum in the care of the parish officer, probably to the workhouse.

[S.R.O., D/H/Men. 17/1/1. case 19. page 73. (Case book Wells Asylum).]

[Case 186] 23 January 1852. Edwin and Sabina Cattle.

Edwin and Sabina Cattle are chargeable to the parish of **Langport Eastover**. They are to be removed to the parish of **Curry Rivel**, which is their legal parish of settlement.

The settlements to be relied upon are:

James Cattle, grandfather of Edwin, was settled in Curry Rivel by estate. George Cattle, James's son, was settled in Curry Rivel by birth. He also derived a settlement in Curry Rivel from his father's settlement by estate.

Elizabeth Cattle, the lawful wife of George Cattle, was settled in Curry Rivel by marriage.

Sabina Cattle is the illegitimate child of Elizabeth Cattle (born after the death of her husband George). Sabina is under sixteen years of age, and thus takes her mother's settlement.

Signed by overseers and churchwardens.

Notification that Langport intended to remove the Cattle children, unless the removal is appealed against.

[S.R.O., settlement examination D/P/Curry Rivel 13/3/1. 54a.]

[Case 187] 4 May 1855. Harriett Their.

Before William Hunt Esq., mayor, and Henry Bridges Smith Esq.; examination taken at **Bath**.

Harriett Their is the wife of James who is undergoing sentence of transportation. Harriett and her three children are now inmates of Bath Union workhouse.

Harriett states that when she was Harriett Bidwell she married James Their, at **Huntspill** on 27 August 1847. She was a farm servant and neither she nor her husband owned any property. After they were married James rented lodgings at sixpence a week, where they remained until the summer of 1848.

In the autumn of that year James went to work at **Stretchill**, near **Bridgwater**, for Mr Sanders and rented a cottage from him at £4 a year. Here they stayed a year, and then in 1849 returned to Huntspill, where James worked for different masters for two and a half years, again paying £4 rent for a cottage.

In 1852 they went to Bath and took lodgings at the weekly rent of one shilling and three pence, they stayed there until 6 March 1853, at which date James received sentence of transportation for ten years.

[*Mark.*]

Robert Their, a labourer, of Hunstspill, states that he is the brother of Joseph Their, and that Joseph is the father of James Their.

Joseph Their is aged sixty-three. When he was twelve years old he was hired by Mrs Carver at **Sand** (Zon)in the parish of **Wedmore**, Joseph served her one whole year, which included the last forty days of his service. He slept and had his victuals at the house of his mistress.

Shortly afterwards Joseph was hired for a year by Mr Joseph Brown, who lived near Mrs Carver. During his service, and including the last forty days, he slept and had his victuals at Mr Brown's house.

Twenty-eight years ago Joseph and his family became chargeable to a parish near **London**. They were removed to and received by the parish of Wedmore.

Eighteen to twenty years ago, when James was living with his father and his uncle Robert, he behaved so badly that they were obliged to turn him adrift.

James then applied to the Wedmore overseers, who apprenticed him to Mr Clement Champney of **Theale**. James served three or four years of his apprenticeship, during which he resided in Mr Champney's house, but his apprenticeship was then ended and James went away.

[*Mark.*]

10 May 1855.

Notice of removal from the parish of **Walcot** to Wedmore.

Harriett Their, a pauper, and her two legitimate children, Eliza aged seven years and Ann aged five years, and her illegitimate child, Charlotte aged two months.

28 May 1855.

Further information regarding the family.

James Their received sentence of transportation on 6 March 1853: "After transportation the wife entirely desered her two children, who have been inmates in the Bath Union for two years, at the expense of the common fund.

"During this period the wife has been living the life of a loose vagabond, and becoming pregnant, was (about two months ago) received into the Bath Union, and now has an illegitimate child."

167

From the receiving book of **Wilton** prison, near **Taunton**.
"James Thair (sic), aged thirty-two, committed from Bath at 9.30 p.m. on 7 March 1853.
Tried for housebreaking at the assizes.
Sentenced to be transported for a term of ten years."
[S.R.O., Q/AG/W. 16/2. 373.]

From the Bath Chronicle. Thursday 10 March 1853.
"A suspected wholesale burglar apprehended.
"In the months of December and January last, several burglaries and robberies were perpetrated in the neighbourhood of **Highbridge** and **Burnham**, and considerable property carried off. One of the sufferers in these instances was Mr Feare, a general shopkeeper, in the parish of **St Mark**, from whose premises a quantity of drapery and other articles were stolen. Means were taken for discovering the robbers, and a reward was advertised for information leading to their apprehension and conviction.
"It was ascertained that a man named James Thayer (sic), living at Hunstford (sic), a convicted thief, and but lately out of prison, had been seen near the premises on the night of the 3rd of January, the morning following which the burglary was discovered.
"It happened that Thayer's wife had occasion afterwards to visit a relative at St Mark, and inadvertently, on her departure, had left a handkerchief behind. On the appearance of the placard offering the reward, the party in whose possession the handkerchief had been left, took it to Mr Feare, who identified it by his private mark, as part of the property stolen from his shop.
"A warrant was obtained for the apprehension of Thayer, who had left the neighbourhood, and had taken up his abode, as it was supposed, in or about Bath. Inspector Ringland, of our police force, having had the warrant sent to him, succeeded in apprehending Thayer, at a house where he was lodging in **Holloway**, and found in his possession a quantity of goods of various kinds, which answered the description of those stolen from Mr Feare. Among them was a tin kettle which he identified by his private mark.
"The prisoner was conveyed to Highbridge on Monday, where he underwent a partial examination before the County Magistrates; but as several other charges are likely to be brought against him, he was remanded for a week.
"Since then his wife has been apprehended as an accessory, as she was observed by Mr Ringland, when he was looking out for Thayer, to go to the water-closet with something, and after she left it search was made, and two large bunches of keys of all descriptions were found concealed between the

rafters and the roof.

"One of the burglaries in which Thayer is supposed to have been concerned was perpetrated on the night of the 21st December last, at the dwelling house of Mr Baggs, a shopkeeper of Burnham, from which much valuable property, in ready made clothing and other goods, were stolen.

"On the prisoner being searched, some papers were found on him, from which it would appear that he and his wife were about to emigrate to **Australia** by a **Liverpool** ship, a printed form as a receipt for £3.3s. as passage money having been one of the documents.

"Thayer's personal appearance is that of a labourer, tall in stature and formidable in his physical contour."

[Case 188] 26 January 1859. Jane Linnell and daughter.

The justices' names are not recorded.

Jane Elizabeth Baker Linnell, otherwise Barrett, commonly called Jane Linnell and Sarah Ann aged two months, her bastard child, are chargeable to **Taunton St Mary**. An order of removal to **Berkeley, Gloucestershire** has been made, the grounds for which are as follows:

Jane and her child have not resided in Taunton St Mary for five years before the application for the order of removal.

Jane has not become irremovable, and has not gained a settlement in Taunton St Mary.

Jane has not produced any certificate acknowledging her to be settled elsewhere.

Jane and her child are now receiving relief from Taunton St Mary, which relief has not become necessary by reason of sickness or accident.

Jane was born in Berkeley on 6 July 1826, and has not gained a settlement in her own right.

In an order of removal dated 14 January 1840 Jane Linnell, described as Jane Elizabeth Barrett, a bastard aged about fifteen years, was removed from **Bedminster** to the workhouse of the **Thornbury** union, and was maintained there as a parishioner of Berkeley.

[*Blank*.]

[*Endorsed*] **29 January 1859.**

Original copies of the examination were returned to Mr Pritchard to be sent away, the time being up, if no appeal,about 19 February.

[S.R.O., settlement examination D/P/Taunton St Mary 13/3/1.437.]

[Case 189] 1 September 1859. Mary Honiball.

This document is an appeal by the parish officers of **Nether Stowey** against receiving the pauper Mary Honiball from **Crowcombe**.

The grounds of the appeal are that Mary Honiball was not legally settled in

Nether Stowey, and that the grounds of removal sent by Nether Stowey to Crowcombe are defective, viz:

It was not stated that the pauper was chargeable to Nether Stowey when the order was made out.

It was not stated when and where she had been hired by Mrs Jane Price.

It was not stated that Mary was childless and unmarried when she was hired, entered or during her service.

It was not [stated] that Mary was hired for a year at the wages of £4. Also Mrs Price and Mary had not resided in Nether Stowey for a whole year.

At some stage, when is not clear, Mary had entered the service of Mr Thomas Govier, and again the order of removal had not stated when and where, and if she was unmarried, etc.

The document ends by instructing the parish officers of Crowcombe to produce the pauper at the trial of the appeal.

[*Signed by John K. Fathing, John Northcott and James Palmer. A majority of churchwardens and overseers of the poor of the parish of Nether Stowey.*]

1 September 1859.

Mary Honiball to be removed from Crowcombe to Nether Stowey.

1 September 1859.

Appeal notice against her removal.

7 October 1859.

Removal order abandoned.

Bill of costs in this case £7.15s.2d.

[S.R.O., grounds of appeal against receiving a pauper. D/P/Crowcombe 13/3/4.14 to 17.]

[Case 190] **6 August 1862. William Elmes and family.**

To be removed from **Aberystruth** to **High Littleton.**.

[S.R.O., D/P/High Littleton 13/3/4. 32.]

8 August 1862.

Letter from Thomas Morgan, assistant overseer of **Blaina**, near **Tredegar, Monmouthshire,** to the overseer of High Littleton:

"William Elmes has become chargeable in consequence of having had an accident at the coal works, whereby he had his foot amputated. He had his arm amputated twenty years ago so it is evident that he cannot support himself and family. He hopes that you will relieve him to the amount of six shillings weekly. He hopes to get a donkey and cart and sell a little greengrocery, but that of course must be for your board [of guardians] to decide."

12 August 1862.

Thomas Morgan awaits a reply from the High Littleton vestry concerning

William Elms.

Statement of William Elms: He was married to Mary Ann Lovell at the registry office in **Newport**, Monmouthshire on 5 December 1859. They have one child, Fanny, aged two and a half years. William also has three children by a former wife – William aged fifteen, Charles twelve and Emily seven and a half years old.

William had his arm amputated about twenty years ago; and on 6 May last he met with an accident at the coal works and had his leg amputated also.

William's settlement would appear to be in High Littleton in respect of his birth, to which parish Morgan wishes to remove Thomas. Morgan goes on to ask Mr Cousin, the overseer of High Littleton, to let him know if the vestry will accept Elmes; and adds that if he writes on Thursday the letter should reach Blaina by Friday [!], in which case Morgan can start his journey on Saturday.

[S.R.O., miscellaneous D/P/High Littleton 13/3/4.30g and 30h.]

Examination of Stanford Birch, 1715 [case 12].

Appendix I

Select Bibliography
(* Starred books are mainly concerned with the West Country).

The Poor Law

Archbold Settlement Law. Vol.III London 1845.

Beier, A.L., *The problem of the poor in Tudor and Early Stuart England*, Methuen 1983.

Checkland, S.G. & E.O.A. (eds.), *The poor law report of 1834*, Pelican Classic 1974.

Digby, A., *The poor law in nineteenth century England*, Historical Association 1985.

Oxley, G.W., *Poor relief in England and Wales 1601 – 1834*, David and Charles 1974.

Vulliamy, A.F., *The law of settlement and removal*, London 1906.

Webb, S. & B., *English poor law history*, Part One: *The old poor law*; Part

Two: *The new poor law*, Frank Cass, 1963.

Poor law administration

* Anstruther, I., *The scandal of the Andover workhouse.* Geoffrey Bles, 1973 (reprinted Alan Sutton 1977).

* Crittall, E. (ed.) *The notebook of William Hunt, 1744 – 1749*, Wiltshire Record Society, vol.xxxvii, Devizes 1982.

In 1743-44 William Hunt was authorised to act as Justice of the Peace in the county of Wiltshire. His notebook gives a fascinating account as to how the judicial process was conducted by the Magistrates, much of whose work was concerned with the settlement and removal of paupers.

* Hurley, J., *Rattle his bones*, Exmoor Press, 1974. Concerns the setting up and administration of the Dulverton and Williton workhouses.

* Hembry, P. (ed.), *Bradford settlement examinations.* Wiltshire record society, vol xlvi, 1990. Examinations from the parish of Bradford-on-Avon.

Horn, P. (ed.), *Oxfordshire village life, the diaries of George James Dew (1846 – 1928), relieving officer.* Beacon Publications, 1983.

Social studies

* Ayres, J. (ed.), *Paupers and pig killers* (the diary of William Holland, Vicar of Over Stowey, Somerset, 1799 – 1818). Alan Sutton, 1984.

* Bettey, J.H., *Rural life in Wessex.* Moonraker Press, 1977.

Burnett, J. (ed.), *Useful toil* (autobiographies of working people, 1820 – 1920). Pelican Books, 1974.

* Coombs, H. & P. (eds.), *Journal of a Somerset Rector, 1803 – 1834 (John Skinner, Rector of Camerton),* Oxford University Press, 1984.

George, M.D., *England in transition,* Penguin Books, 1953.

George, M.D., *London life in the eighteenth century,* Penguin Reprint, 1976.

Hammond, J.L. & B., *The village labourer, 1760 – 1832,* Reprint, Alan Sutton, 1987.

Hobsbawn, E.J., *Labouring men,* Weidenfeld & Nicholson, 1964.

Horn, P., *Labouring life in the Victorian countryside,* Alan Sutton, 1987.

* Hudson, W.H., *The shepherd's life,* illustrated edition, The Bodley Head, London, 1987.(The stories of Wiltshire country people in the nineteenth century).

Mingay, G.E., *Rural life in Victorian England,* illustrated edition, Alan Sutton, 1990.

Plumb, J. H., *England in the eighteenth century,* Penguin Books, 1951 (vol. vii of the Pelican history of England).

Books used for reference

Bartholemew, J., *Survey gazetteer of the British Isles,* 8th edition, 1932.

* Brown, M., *Australia bound,* Ex Libris Press, 1988 (Emigration and transportation to Australia).

Cheney, C.R., *Handbook of dates for students of English history,* Royal Historical Society, 1970.

Fitzhugh, T.V.H., *The dictionary of genealogy,* Alphabooks, Sherborne,

1988.

* Fuller, M.D., *West Country friendly societies*, University of Reading, 1964.

Hawkings, D.T., *Bound for Australia* (Transportation), Phillimore,1987.

Higgs, E., *Making sense of the census*, HM Stationery Office, 1989.

Kerr, W.J.W., *Records of the 1st. Somerset Militia* (3rd. Battalion Somerset Light Infantry), Gale and Polden, Aldershot (nd).

Macdermot, E.T., *The history of the Great Western Railway*, 1931.

Richardson, J., *The local historian's encyclopaedia*, Historical Publications Ltd., 1981.

* Rogers, K.H., *Warp and weft* (Somerset and Wiltshire woollen industry), Barracuda Books, 1986.

Tate, W.E., *The parish chest*, Cambridge University Press, 1969 (now published by Phillimore, 1983).

* Walker, M., *Old Somerset fairs*, Glastonbury (nd).

Wigfield, W.McD., *The Monmouth rebellion*, Moonraker Press, 1980.

* Wigfield, W.McD., *The Monmouth rebels*, Alan Sutton, 1985 (vol lxxix, Somerset record series).

Statutes of the Realm

14 Elizabeth C5 (1572).

Previous statutes of 22 Henry VIII C12, 3 & 4, Edward VI C16, and 5
0Elizabeth i C3 to be void.

All persons found begging and wandering over the age of fourteen years
may be committed to the County Gaol, charges to be levied on the parish
where the beggar was taken. Punishment may be avoided if some honest
householder takes the offender into his service for one year (a bond of £5 is
required), for a second offence a bond of £10 is required and the offender
must serve two years.

Licences, to pass to their homes, may be issued by the Justices to soldiers
and sailors, harvest workers and serving men who have lost their
employment.

A register to be made of aged and impotent poor, parish officers to find
convenient places for them to live; the parish officers are also required to
assess and tax all inhabitants towards poor relief. Overseers of the poor to be
appointed.

Every month all lame, impotent and aged poor, except those bedridden or
leprous persons, to be sought out, and if not born in the parish, nor resided
there for three years, are to be conveyed, in a cart or on horseback, to the next
constable and so on until they reach the place where they were born. The
overseers are to set to work those paupers who are able to do so, and if they
refuse to work they are to be punished, this also applies to rogues and
vagabonds. The children of beggars over the age of five years and under the
age of fourteen may be taken into service, and shall be bound until the age of
twenty-four for men and eighteen for women (The age for women was raised
to twenty-one in 1601).

43 Elizabeth i C2 (1601).

Overseers to provide dwellings for paupers, which are not to be used for
any other purpose.

Families are to maintain their poor relations.

Substantial householders are to be nominated overseers.

Funds for the relief of the poor to be provided by taxation.

(This was a temporary statute, made permanent in 1640).

14 Charles ii. C12 (1662).

The poor relief act, which introduces the law of settlement and removal. This act ensured that it was possible to remove, within forty days, anyone coming into a parish with intent to settle, unless such persons occupied a house or tenement of the yearly value of £10.

These strangers could be returned to the parish where they were last legally settled, either as a native, householder, sojourner, apprentice or servant.

Persons could be removed if it was thought that they might become chargeable, however temporary workers could stay provided they brought an indemnity certificate from their parish of settlement.

3 William and Mary. Cll (1691).

From this date there were four more ways in which settlement could be claimed: by serving a parish office for a year, paying towards parish rate, being hired as a servant for a year, and by apprenticeship.

Any person coming into the parish who intends to gain settlement by forty days residence is required to notify the overseers or churchwardens, giving the whereabouts of his dwelling and the number of his family; this information is to be written into a register.

8 and 9 William iii. C30 (1696-97).

Any person bringing a properly made out indemnity certificate from parish 'A' to parish 'B' is to be allowed to work and only if they become actually chargeable are they to be removed.

2 and 3 Anne. C6 (1703).

Poor boys over the age of ten years may be apprenticed to the sea service until they become twenty-one; the churchwardens and overseers are to provide clothing.

Vagabonds and sturdy beggars may also be conveyed into the Queen's service.

5 George. i C8 (1718-19).

Overseers and churchwardens may apply to the Justices for a warrant to seize the goods and chattels belonging to a man who has absconded and left his family; any monies so raised shall be used for the maintenance of such families.

9 George. i C7 (1722-23).

Deals with payment of relief, registers of such payments to be kept.

17 George II. C5 (1744).

Concerns rogues and vagabonds and other disorderly persons. Regulations for passing vagrants to Scotland, Ireland, Isle of Man, Guernsey, Jersey and the Isles of Scilly.

Soldiers and sailors to have lawful pass from their commanding officer.

Those to be removed outside England and to overseas are to be sent by ship, under a warrant from the Justices; the full rate to be paid, to the master of the vessel, by the person serving the warrant.

17 George. ii. C38 (1744).

Overseers and churchwardens to keep accounts.

31 George. ii. C11 (1757-58).

This amends the 1691 statute regarding the settlement of apprentices.
(See section on apprenticeship in the introduction).

59 George iii. C12 (1819).

Select vestries to be formed, to order the relief of the poor, and to oversee the collection of the poor rate. Any parish that is unable to provide a workhouse or poor house, in their parish, may rent or purchase a dwelling in a neighbouring parish.

Relatives of paupers to provide relief.

Justices were empowered to conduct settlement examinations of persons in gaol or house of correction.

Pensioners of the army, navy, marines or ordnance may apply for relief from the parish, which they are to repay from their next allowance or pension payment.

Paupers born in Scotland, Ireland, Isle of Man, Guernsey and Jersey may be removed if they become chargeable. (Previously paupers could only be so removed if they committed an act of vagrancy.)

59 George iii. C50 (1819).

To gain a settlement the forty day residence was increased to a period of one year. The value of the tenement was to be £10 or over; and the rent had to be paid for one year.

4 and 5 William iv. C76 (1834) Poor Law Amendment Act.

Poor law commissioners to be appointed, they are to record their proceedings, and are to make yearly reports to the Secretary of State. To issue such regulations as may be necessary; copies of such regulations are to be sent to the overseers of the poor.

Magistrates are allowed to order out door relief to any adult person who is too old or too ill to work, without requiring them to enter the workhouse; the Magistrates are to satisfy themselves that the person is really in need of relief. United parishes are to be counted as one parish in cases of settlement, also for rating.

No lunatic or insane person may be detained in the workhouse for more than fourteen days.

Husbands, after marriage, are liable to support children, whether legitimate or illegitimate, as part of their family. Ratepayers may raise money on security for the purpose of emigration.

After passing of this act no settlement shall be acquired by hiring and service, or by residence under the same; or by serving an office.

No settlement that is incomplete under hiring and service is to be completed.

No settlement to be acquired by occupying a tenement unless the occupant has been assessed to the poor rate, and shall have paid the same for one year.

No settlement acquired by being apprenticed in the sea service; or to a householder exercising his trade as a fisherman.

Every child born a bastard after 1834 shall take the settlement of mother until the age of sixteen years, or until such child shall have gained a settlement in their own right.

No person is to be removed until a notice of chargeability has been sent to the receiving parish.

Cost of relief to be paid by the parish of settlement. Masters of workhouses are not to ill treat the inmates etc.; also that the two clauses dealing with the treatment of those in the workhouse are to be displayed therein.

(Much of this act deals with the rules and regulations regarding the workhouse; and the appointment and conduct of the master.)

7 and 8 Victoria. C101 (1844).

The duty of householders to receive poor children as apprentices was abolished; the Guardians were to bind poor children as apprentices instead of the overseers.

9 and 10 Victoria. C66 (1846).

Any person residing in a parish for five years before claiming relief may not be removed; but such person does not gain a settlement. (Irremovability.)

10 and 11 Victoria. C110 (1847).

Out relief, cost of the workhouses and salaries of union officers are to be paid out of union funds, and not directly from the parishes.

11 and 12 Victoria. C110 (1848).

Questions of dispute between parishes could now be referred to the Poor Law Board instead of to Counsel.

24 and 25 Victoria. C55 (1861).

Irremovability now reduced to a period of three years residence.

28 and 29 Victoria. C79 (1865).

Unions now responsible for rating and charges instead of the parishes.
Irremovability now reduced to one years residence. (This was to come into effect after 25 March 1866.)

39 and 40 Victoria. C61 (1876).

Guardians may now apply for orders of removal instead of the overseers (if authorised to do so by the local government board).
Guardians may apply to the parish to recover costs.
If a person has become irremovable, and has resided in a parish for three years, such person may now claim settlement in that parish.
Derivative settlements abolished, that is to say that nobody could now derive a settlement from anyone else, except a wife from her husband, and a child, if under the age of sixteen years, from a parent.
Husbands and wives, if over the age of sixty years, could now live together in the workhouse.

56 and 57 Victoria. C73 (1894).

Local Government Act. This act created Parish Councils.

19 and 20 George v. C17 (1929).

Poor law unions abolished. Functions of the Guardians passed to public assistance committees set up by county and county borough councils in 1930.

11 and12 George vi. C29 (1948)

National Assistance Act. This instituted the present system of assistance to the sick and those in need. This was now a statutory right, financed by the contributions paid by the working population.

(Ernest Bevin, born in Somerset at Winsford, who in 1948 was Foreign Secretary in the Government, is quoted as saying: "At last we have buried the poor law.")

A Digby *The Poor Law in Nineteenth Century England.*

Wife Selling

The article that follows, by Thelma Munckton, is reproduced from the journal Somerset and Dorset Notes and Queries (Volume XXXII, Part 328, September 1988). Originally titled "Sold For Two Sovereigns", it was inspired by Thomas Hardy's novel **The Mayor of Casterbridge**, *which was published in 1886.*

A note in the June 1937 issue (SDNQ, XXII, 141) refers to the custom of wife selling and cites an obituary in the *Somerset County Gazette* of 30 January 1937 of a 98 year old lady who claimed to recall such an incident in the **Kingsdon** area of Somerset from her childhood; if her recollection was sound, this must have taken place in the late 1840s. Hardy, too, must have read or known something of the custom to have Michael Henchard as a young man sell his wife, an episode which he sets in the late 1820s.

Actual evidence of such dubious transactions is, understandably, not easily found, but the writer has recently discovered an example in Somerset from the period of the Henchard sale. The information is contained in a group of five settlement papers produced some 20 years later in 1849 and now among the records of the **Ilminster** Petty Sessions Division in the Somerset Record Office.[1] As always with this class of record fullest details are to be found in the examinations and there follow those for the husband, Simon Mitchell, and his wife, Sarah:

County of Somerset.

The several examinations of Simon Mitchell of the parish of **Taunton Saint James** in the county of Somerset lathmaker and of Sarah Mitchell the wife of the said Simon Mitchell taken upon the complaint of the overseers of the poor of the parish of **Curry Rivel** in the said county by and before us two of Her Majesty's justices of the peace in and for the said county the 25th day of July 1849 who severally say, and first the said Simon Mitchell for himself said.

'I am, as I have heard and believe, about fifty three years old and was born in the parish of Thurloxton in this county. When I was about fourteen years old I was bound apprentice by indenture for seven years to John Mitchell of the said parish of Taunton Saint James, lathmaker. I served out such apprenticeship with the said John Mitchell in the said parish of Taunton Saint James, and have not since done any act to gain a settlement.

'The said John Mitchell, who is now dead, had the indentures, and I have heard that they were lost or destroyed. I have often asked for them but was told by the said John Mitchell that they were of no use and he could not find them. When I was about twenty two years old I was married at the parish of Taunton Saint Mary Magdalen in this county to the said Sarah Mitchell but I separated from her after living with her about seven years and have not had amy communication with her since and the the children which have since been born of her body are not mine.'

Simon Mitchell [*signature*]Sworn before us, Thos. B. Uttermare, William Speke.

The said Sarah Mitchell on her oath saith,

'I am the wife of the above named Simon Mitchell, about nineteen years ago he sold me for two sovereigns to James Larcombe of Curry Rivell in this county where I have lived with him ever since and have had ten children by him eight of whom are now living with me of the following names and ages James aged about fourteen years, Rosina thirteen, Charlotte eleven, Mary nine, Frederick seven, Edwin six, Herbert four, and Reuben aged about a year and a half. I and the said children are now chargeable to the said parish of Curry Rivel and are the same persons as are named in the certificate of chargeability of the Langport Union now produced and bearing date the twenty fourth day of July 1849.'

The mark of the said Sarah Mitchell.

Sworn before us William Speke & Thos. B. Uttermare.

The remaining papers consist of a certificate of chargeability from the Board of Guardians of the **Langport** Union, a notice from the parish officers Curry Rivel to those of Taunton St James setting out the grounds for the removal of Sarah and her family to the latter parish and the removal order itself. The Curry Rivel parish records contain a notice of intention to appeal by the parish officers of Taunton St James, dated 20 August 1849.[2] Attached to this is a removal order endorsed to the effect that the family had been delivered to the overseers of Taunton St James, except James Larcombe [*struck through*] who died before this order was carried out, dated 13 October 1849.[3]

Further research shows that Simon Mitchell was baptised at **Thurloxton** on 28 June 1796 as Simon Stone Mitchell, a base child, son of Tamasin Mitchel.[4] He married Sarah White at Taunton St Mary on 14 December 1823.[5] In the 1851 census of Taunton St Mary Simon is a lodger at 51 East

Reach; he gives his age as 47 and status as widower.

Back at Curry Rivel in 1841 the census shows James Larcombe, aged 50, shoemaker, living at Langport Westover with Sarah Mitchell, age given as 35, together with the following children, all named Mitchell: Edith 10,Harriott 7, James 6, Rosina 5, Charlotte 3, Mary 18 months, Frederick 4 months. Also living with this family is Henry Mitchell 14, shoemaker. Some of the children were baptised at Curry Rivel, all as Mitchell, children of Sarah Mitchell, 'separated wife', Langport Westover [in the last two entries the wording 'separated wife' has been omitted]: James William, baptised 8 February 1832, Harriette Eliza 27 May 1833, James William 8 June 1835, Rosina 8 May 1836, Charlotte Elizabeth 22 April 1838, Mary 7 June 1840, and Frederic Francis 12 September 1841.[6]

By 1851 James Larcombe is found still living at Langport Westover, but now he gives his age as 67, and is described as a pauper, formerly shoemaker; he also states that he is a widower. At the same time Sarah Mitchell is recorded as living at 50 High Street, Taunton, age 46, a washerwoman. The children remaining with her are Charlotte 11, Mary Jane 9, Frederick 8, and Reuben 2, the last three being given as scholars.

As for the children, only one marriage has been traced: Edith Caroline Mitchell, spinster, aged 21, was married to William Grant, widower, aged 40, occupation hairdresser at Taunton St Mary on 2 September 1852.[7] Although Sarah Mitchell had lived with James Larcombe for some nineteen years, and had eleven children by him, neither she nor the children were able to claim a settlement, by birth or residence, in Curry Rivel. Her husband Simon Mitchell's original settlement would have been by birth in Thurloxton, but he had gained a derivative settlement by completing his apprenticeship in Taunton St James. So as Sarah was still, legally, his wife she took her settlement from Simon, and her base born children took their settlement from her.

Thus real life provided a harsher twist in the tail than that which the novelist could ever have contemplated.

REFERENCES:
1. SRO ref. D/PS/ilm. 6/33 no. 19
2. Do. D/P/cur. r. 13/3/2 no. 81
3. Do. Do. 2/1/9; bur. 9 Oct. 1849, aged 14
4 Do. D/P/thu. 22/1/3.
5 Do. D/P/tau. m. 2/1/20.
6 Do. D/P/cur. r. 2/1/8, 9.
7 Do. D/P/tau. m 2/1/23.

12 November 1840. Sarah Larcombe buried at Langport, aged 52 years. Note by side of entry in burial register:

183

'Sister to Mr Walter Lock, landlord of the "White Lion" in North Street, where she died.

'She had been for some time previous to her decease in a deranged state of mind, her husband is now living with a female, Sarah Michell (sic), at Langport Westover, by whom she has several children, having deserted his wife some years ago.'

S.R.O., D/P/Langp. 2/1/5.

Since completing the above, I have discovered a further example of wife-selling, although the story is not as clear cut and the motives somewhat obscure. Like the previous example the evidence was found in a settlement examination in the Ilminster Petty Sessions records (ref. D/PS/ilm. 6/50 no. 34).

Basic details are that one Joseph Phelps otherwise Phillips married Elizabeth Christopher at **Chaffcombe** in January 1803, where a son, James, was born to them a year later. By the middle of 1804 Joseph had stripped the house of all its goods, abandoned her and moved to **Tatworth** in **Chard**, as she claimed in her examination. Six months later she went to live with Henry Morris in Furnham, another part of Chard, and a few months afterwards 'her husband with her own consent (having frequently been in her company in the mean while) sold her by publick auction with a rope round her waist in Chard market for half a crown' to the same Henry.

Subsequently she had two more children, one at Chard in 1806 and another at Chaffcombe in 1809, both registered as Joseph's children. It seems likely, however, that Henry was the father, although the mother could not give an unqualified answer. In fact she and others gave evidence that she continued to associate on a regular basis with her husband in Chard, generally on market days or at the Dolphin Inn 'on a club day', and also at Chaffcombe. She continued to receive a weekly allowance from him until 1808 and just prior to her examination had received two shillings by way of relief for herself and her eldest child from the parish of **Thorncombe** to which her husband had recently been removed. It is only by chance that her story came to light, for authority did not concern itself with her situation until she and her younger children became a burden on the parish of Chaffcombe as a consequence of Henry having been drawn to serve in the militia. Elizabeth would not have been entitled to the usual maintenance payable to a militiaman's family, but in the absence of the parallel series of removal orders at the crucial date it is not known if she and all or any of her children were also sent to Thorncombe.

Rodney Legg records another Somerset wife-sale in his *Literary Dorset*.

184

'One took place at **Stalbridge** market on a Tuesday in April 1814. The vendor was Thomas Tuffen of **Henstridge**, Somerset, who with his wife had been in the habit of attending local fairs and markets to sell gingerbread. On this occasion he contracted with Joseph Cains, a sawyer, for the sale of his wife, together with a basket and goods. Tuffen delivered her in a halter to Cains, who led her to his home.

'Nor was this the only Stalbridge custom that Hardy was to incorporate into *The Mayor of Casterbridge*. He started writing it in 1884, and may well have preserved newspaper clippings about "skimmington riding" which was still prevalent in the Dorset countryside. The carnival of anger took place to show communal disgust at behaviour that had offended against the moral code. One of these parades took place through **Melbury Osmond**, Dorset, in November 1865 but the police intervened to prevent effigies being burned.

'Lucy Taylor [1879-1947], living in Stalbridge, recalled a similar procession of local people disguised with sacking over their heads and beating saucepans with tongs and spoons. They escorted a conveyance with caricatures of the guilty pair. The effigies were burned at The Ring, the village green. No one in the village next day was prepared to admit knowing who had taken part in the event.'

Somersett.

To the overseers of the poore of
Mynehead in this County: &

Whereas complaint hath been made unto us that
Henry Gitto otherwise Jenkins of Mynehead is gone
from thence & hath absented himselfe from his
there, and that it is feared his daughter will be
chargable to the parish there unles his [...]
wife whom he hath left his goods take care to
Employ the same for the maintenance of the
child, These are to will & require you to give not[ice]
to the persons who have any goods of the said
Henry Gittoes otherwise Jenkins in their hand[s]
custody to provide & maintaine the said child
the said Henry Gitto therewith & to take care
they be not chargable to the said parish hav[ing]
left sufficient goods to that purpose; And the[y]
not to faile, Given under our hands the 20th
of May 1667:

Wm. Wyndham

John Malet

Instructions to Overseers regarding maintenance of a child, 1667
(case 2).

To the Minister, Constables, Overseers for the poore
and Churchwardens of the towne of Minehead &
all other persons whome this may concerne

Whereas William Godfrey & Hannah Godfrey his wife
Samuell Godfrey his son & Hannah Godfrey his daughter lately liuing in ye street of St Thomas and County
of Cornwall and now for there better liuelywood and preferm[ent]
haue a minde to dwell & Inhabit within your towne
of Minehead in ye County of Summerset We the Inhabitants
of the sd street of St Thomas & County aforesaid whose
names are here subscribed doe promise to take & releaue
the sd persons aboue named if they or either of them shall
become chargeable to yor sd towne or parish And we doe further certifie that the sd William Godfrey hath an Estate
within ye street of St Thomas which will alwaies make
him an undeniable Inhabitant within ye sd street and
that he is alwaies continued to be a payer to ye & ___
poore And further we doe certifie for his behauior
& Carrage when liuing among us in ye sd street to be so
honest & iust so quiet and peaceable towards euery person
& so well able to Instruct & bring up youth that it is a loss
to us by his departure Giuen under ye hands & seals this
eighteenth day of Aprill Anno Domini 1699

ffran: Downing
Mayer

Henry White
Churchwarden

John Bewes

William Parsons

Ruben Kingdom
Overseers

Indemnity Certificate for William Godfrey and family, 1699
[case 8].

The Examination of Robert Henlton of the parish of Mells
in the County of Somersett taken before Henry Fredd and
William Applin Esq two of his Majᵗ Justices of the peace
for the said County the Nine and twentyth day of March
Annoʒ Dom 1717

Who upon his oath saith That he was borne in the parish of Mells in the County of Som̃ersett, lived Somrsett... and wrot att the Cloathing trade Somersett... yeares att
Scribling, and about three yeares last July this Examinant made a Covenant with a
Samuell Allen who lives in the parish of temple in the City of Bristoll a drug...
to serve him one whole yeare as a Covenant servant, and was to have for that...
yeare five pounds a yeare, and this Examinant lived two yeares more with the said Samu...
Allen and had five pounds severapounds a yeare, and during the whole terme of the...
yeares that this Examinant lived in his service the whole... or soever abo...
in the sd County of Somersett and there did look after Somersett work... people...
the said Samuell Allen had at worke upon the Cloathing trade of... And this
Examinant further saith that he never served a Covenant servant to...
person whatsoever but the said Samuell Allen and to this Examinant the...
wages of the said Samuell Allen and nott meate drink waishing or Lodging

Robert Henlton

HENRY FREDD

WM APPLIN

At Michaelmas Sessions 2ᵈ
...... 1717

Upon this Case & Examinaiõn I am of Opinion yt Robt Henl...
can't be Parishioner at Mells, but think from the place of
dwelling, living about againe under Covenant with his mast... and the...
a ..... may find a ..... to ..... his look after his ...
into any Place. In this case it... to Sᵗᵗ from remove, By wch means you c...
take advantage of the Covenant made att Bristoll. Thoˢ Gapper ?g

---

**Examination of Robert Henlton, and Counsel's Opinion, 1717
[case 13].**

County of } To wit The Examination of Thomas Node —
Gloucester }

This Examinant maketh oath that he believes he was
born in the parish of Wells in Somersetshire That he
hath not been a yearly Servant or an apprentice any
where nor by any other means gained any legal
settlement in any other parish or place to the best
of his knowledge and beliefs and for about five years
last past he hath travelled about the country gathering
Raggs and buying and selling Rabit Skins for a livelyhood
and about last monday Seven night he was very Sick
and weak in the parish of Henbury in the said County
and had no money Some persons took care of him and
about Six years ago he was Lawfully marryed in St Mary
Magdalen Church in London to his present
wife mary.

                              The mark of

                                   +

                            Thomas Node

Sworn Before me one of his
majesties Justices of the peace
for the said County the 12th
ffebruary 1745. Ro: Cann

                            a true Copy

Examination of Thomas Node, 1745 (case 36).

County of Somerset }

THE Examination of *William Brookman Labourer* — . n
residing in the Parish of *Road* — — — in
said County of *Somerset*, ———— (touching *his* last legal Settlement) taken upon *his* Oath before us his Majesty's Justices of
Peace in and for the said County this *3?* — Day of *April*
in the Year of our Lord 1772.

Who upon *his* Oath saith, that *he* is about *twenty three* Years old, and
born in the Parish of *Burnet* — — in the County of *Somerset* —
(as *he* hath been informed and believes) that being also the Place of *his*
Father's legal Settlement (as *he* hath also been informed and believes) saith

about two years ago he hired himself to *one Samuel Selway of*
Wellow in the said County Yeoman for a year at the Wages of f
pounds and fifteen Shillings, and Meat Drink Washing & Lodging
Saith that he served about ten Months under the said hiring at
Wellow aforesaid, and then intermarried with his present wife
by whom he hath one Child named Joseph aged about nine mon
Saith that notwithstanding his Marriage he served all the said ye
pursuant to the said hiring and always lodged in the said paris
Wellow, except that after his Marriage he sometimes on a Sa
and Sunday night lodged with his wife in the parish of Roa
aforesaid. That he hath ˄since done no Act to gain a Settleme
to his knowledge or belief.

Sworn the Day & Year first
above written, before us —

H. Edgell

H. Harris

The mark of

✝

William Brookman

Examination of William Brookman, 1772 (case 64).

County of Somerset} THE Examination of *Edward Greenland* now residing in the Parish of *Road* in the said County of *Somerset, Clothworker* (touching *his* last legal Settlement) taken upon *his* Oath before us his Majesty's Justices of the Peace in and for the said County this 3? Day of *April* in the Year of our Lord 1772.

Who upon *his* Oath saith, that *he* is about *twenty seven* Years old, and was born in the Parish of *Road* in the County of *Somerset* (as *he* hath been informed and believes) ~~that being also the Place of Father's legal Settlement (or hath also been informed and believes)~~ saith *that his father Edward Greenland was as to this Exant hath heard & believes a legal Parishioner of the parish of Tellisford in the said County of Somerset. Saith that he when he this Exant was about fourteen years old, he agreed to serve Mr Barnes of Road aforsd Scribler for three years at certain weekly wages then agreed on. Saith that the said Mr Barnes was to teach this Exant to scrible Wool on the working days, and this Exant was to attend on these Mr Barnes to clean his shoes and look after his horse on Sundays, and was to find himself out of his Wages in Meat Drink Washing and Lodging, except on Sundays when he was to have of the said Mr Barnes a Breakfast and Dinner. Saith that he served the sd Mr Barnes under the said Agreemt about two years, and during that time lodged in the said parish of Road. Then the said Mr Barnes died, and this Exant agreed to serve John Wickham of Road aforsd Clothworker for four years. Saith that he was to serve the sd Wickham Sundays as well as working days, and was to receive weekly wages and find himself thereout in Meat Drink Washing & Lodging. Saith that he served the sd Wickham at Road aforsd upwards of a year, and then the said Wickham failed in Trade.* ~~This Exant~~ ~~was agreed and served with the said month~~ *Saith that he hath done no Act to gain a Settlement in any other parish or place to his knowledge or belief; and that he hath a wife named Martha and three children, namely Ann aged five years, Samuel aged two years, and Betty aged four months.*

~~sworn~~ on the Day and Year first above written, before us, }

W Edgell

H. Harris

The mark of

The mark of +

Edward Greenland.

Examination of Edward Greenland, 1772 (case 66).

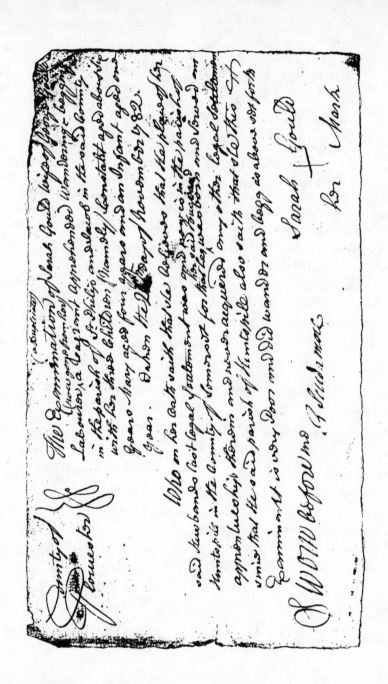

Examination of Sarah Gould and Vagrant's Pass (opposite), 1790 [case 76].

To all Constables and Tythingmen within the said County, and to
every or any of them, to convey; and to all Governors or Maf-
ters of Houfes of Correction; and alfo to all Conftables and
other Officers whom it may concern, to receive and convey; and
to the Churchwardens, Chapelwardens, or Overfeers of the Poor
of the *parish of Kimtspile in the County of Somerset* or either of them to receive and obey.

County of Gloucster

WHEREAS *Sarah Gould wife of George Gould Labourer (now gone from her) and his three Children, Namely, Constant aged about Six years, Mary aged about four years and an Infant aged one year*

apprehended in the Parifh of *St. Philip and Jacob* in the
County *of Glouceſter* aforefaid as a Rogue and Vagabond (videlicet) *Wandering and begging there*

———— || ————

and upon Examination of the faid *Sarah Gould*
taken upon Oath before me one of his Majefty's
Juftices of the Peace for the faid County of *Gloucster*
(which Examination is hereunto annexed) it doth appear, that the Place of the laft legal Settlement of the
faid *Sarah Gould and her said three children was and now is in the parish of Kimtspile aforesaid*

R Seydamor

THESE are therefore to require you the faid
Conftable to convey the faid *Sarah Gould (first
duly Correcting her) and her said three children to
the parish of St. Philip and Jacob in the City of Bristol*
that being the firft *Parish* in the next
Precinct through which they ought to pafs in the direct
Way to the faid *parish of Kimtspill* to which
they are to be fent, and deliver them to the Conftable, or
other proper Officer of fuch *Parish* in fuch next
Precinct together with this Pafs and the Duplicate of
the Examination of the faid *Sarah Gould*
taking his Receipt for the fame, and the faid *Sarah
Gould and her said three children* to be thence conveyed on in like Manner, to the faid *parish of
Kimtspill* to be there delivered to fome
Church-warden, Chapel-warden, or Overfeer of the
Poor of the fame *Parish* to be there provided for according to Law; And you the faid Churchwardens, Chapel-wardens, and Overfeers of the Poor
are hereby required to receive the faid Perfon and
provide for them as aforefaid.
Given under my Hand and Seal, the *Twenty first*
Day of *November* in the Year of our Lord 1782

SOMERSET,
(TO WIT.)
THE Examination of *John Rose, Labourer* [1]
aged *thirty* Years, now residing in the Parish of
Taunton Saint Mary Magdalen in the said County, taken on
Oath before us two of his Majesty's Justices of the Peace,
in and for the said County, the *twenty eight* ____ Day of
June ____ 18*20* - touching the Place of *his* ____
last legal settlement, _____
Who upon oath saith, that he hath heard, and believes
- he was born in the Parish of *Litcheat Bacon near* ____
Poole That about 10 Years ago he agreed with *John Lane* then
Ostler at the Castle Inn in Taunton St Mary Magdalen to
serve him for a Year as under Ostler, at £ 14 *pr* annum
& his board and Lodging & served out the Year & then ____
Agreed for another Year & served about 9 months, That
during that time he slept in the Ostlery at the Castle ____
which situated over the Drain which divides the Parishes
of Taunton St Mary Magdalen and Bishops Hull and the
said Drain divided this Informant's Bed longwise, and
this Informant is therefore uncertain in which Parish he
may be considered to have slept ____ That he hath never since
been in one Service for a Year nor done any other Act
whereby to gain a Settlement ____ That about 8 Years
ago he married Grace Perry at Taunton St James's
& hath two Children John aged 7 Years & William ____
aged 5 Years

Signed { *Webb Stone*
{ *M Blake*

Signed *John Rose*

(margin, printed vertically): MARRIOTT, PRINTER, TAUNTON.

Examination of John Rose, 1820 (case 129).

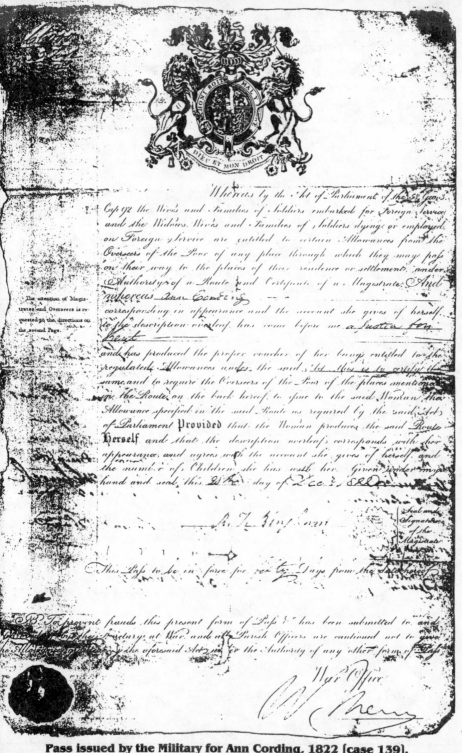

Whereas by the Act of Parliament of the 55 Geo
Cap 92 the Wives and Families of Soldiers embarked for Foreign Service
and the Widows, Wives and Families of Soldiers dying or employed
on Foreign Service are entitled to certain Allowances from the
Overseers of the Poor of any place through which they may pass
on their way to the places of their residence or settlement; under
Authority of a Route and Certificate of a Magistrate. And
whereas Ann Cording
corresponding in appearance and the account she gives of herself,
to the description overleaf, has come before me a Justice for
Kent
and has produced the proper voucher of her being entitled to the
regulated Allowances under the said Act, this is to certify the
same, and to require the Overseers of the Poor of the places mentioned
in the Route on the back hereof, to issue to the said Woman the
Allowance specified in the said Route as required by the said Act
of Parliament **Provided** that the Woman produces the said Route
Herself and that the description overleaf corresponds with her
appearance, and agrees with the account she gives of herself, and
the number of Children she has with her. Given under my
hand and seal, this 28th day of Dec 1822

R. I. Bingham

Seal and
Signature
of the
Magistrate

This Pass to be in force for xxx ty Days from the date hereof

N.B. To prevent frauds this present form of Pass &c has been submitted to and
approved of by the Secretary at War, and all Parish Officers are cautioned not to give
the Allowances granted by the aforesaid Act on the Authority of any other form of Pass

War Office

of George Cook now residing in the In parish of Saint Cuthbert
in the City or Borough of Wells in the County of Somerset
Labourer of and concerning the place of his last legal settlement
taken upon his Oath before us the undersigned Robert Brooks and
Francis Besby Esquires ~~two~~ —
of His Majesty's Justices of the Peace for the said City or Borough this
day of   183 5 —

Who on his Oath saith as follows:

I am the son of Thomas and Amy Cook both now resided
in the In parish of Saint Cuthbert in Wells — I was thirty four
years old the 21st of March last and I was Born in the parish
of Pilton in the County of Somerset, all which I have heard
believe is true — I lived with my Father till the year 1818 when
I went to the Island of Antigua as a plough Boy on Mr
Tudways Estates, I remained there eleven years and returned
to England in the year 1829 from Illness and came to live
with my Father in Queen Street in the said In parish of
Saint Cuthbert in Wells — I have lived in that parish
ever since — When I came home I applied for relief
the Overseers of the parish of Pilton, they allowed me
2s and 6d regular Weekly pay for nearly twelve months
till I got well — I have been ill again since, I believe it was
in the Spring of last year and then I applied again
Pilton Parish for relief and they allowed me 2s and 6d a
for several weeks — About a month ago I received 1s
from the Overseers of Pilton — I never hired myself to any
person for a year nor lived as a Servant with any one
for a Year — I was never Apprenticed to any one —
never rented any House or Land any where — I never was
the owner of any property — I never served any Office
and to the best of my knowledge and belief never did
any Act to gain a Settlement in my own right — I
now actually chargeable to the said In parish of Saint
Cuthbert and have received 7s — relief from the Overseers
of that parish —

Taken and sworn the day and year }
first above written before us — — — }

11 Darlington Street Bath.
December 5th 1837.

My Dear Sir:

At so long a distance of time I cannot take upon myself to speak correctly without reference to my Memorandums which I now cannot lay my hands on, or having some communication with the Pauper himself —

But as it stands at present I am strongly inclined to think that he lived with me under a hiring for a Year, giving him a suit of Drab Livery Breeches & Boots also a Stable dress

Such an agreement I had with a Boy at the time I was constantly residing hunting shooting in Dorsetshire — I perfectly recollect I lodged as well as boarded him.

As it is Parish business I will trouble you in future to pay Postage's & of further commun

I am my D Sir
Yours truly
Wm Pulsford

Letter concerning George Cook, 1837, and his Examination (opposite) of 1835 [case 166].

To the Churchwardens and Overseers of the Poor of the
Parish of *Llangynider* in the said County of
COUNTY OF Brecon, and to the Churchwardens and Overseers of the Poor
of the Parish of *High Littleton*
BRECON. in the County of *Somerset* and to each
and every of them.

UPON the complaint of the Churchwardens and Overseers of the Poor of the
Parish of *Llangynider* aforesaid, in the said County of
Brecon, unto us whose names and seals are hereunto subscribed and set, being
two of her Majesty's Justices of the Peace, in and for the said County of
Brecon, and one of us of the Quorum, that *John Smith and Jane
his wife, and their four children namely Silas aged
ten years or thereabouts, Charlotte aged seven years
or thereabouts, Ann aged five years or thereabouts
and Martha aged eighteen months, or thereabouts*
ha*ve* come to inhabit in the said Parish of *Llangynider* not
having gained a legal settlement there, nor produced any certificate, owning
them or either of them to be settled elsewhere, and that the said *John
Smith and Jane his wife, Silas, Charlotte, Ann
and Martha are now*
actually chargeable to the said Parish of *Llangynider*
WE the said Justices, upon due proof made thereof, as well upon the examination
of the said *John Smith*
on oath as otherwise
and likewise upon due consideration had of the Premises, do adjudge the same to
be true, and WE do likewise adjudge that the lawful settlement of the said *John
Smith and Jane his wife and their four
children Silas, Charlotte, Ann, and Martha*

is in the Parish of *High Littleton* aforesaid, in the said County
of *Somerset* WE do therefore require you the said Churchwardens
and Overseers of the Poor of the said Parish of *Llangynider*
or some or one of you to convey the said *John Smith and Jane
his wife Silas, Charlotte, Ann and Martha*

from and out of the said Parish of *Llangynider* to the said
Parish of *High Littleton* and *them* to deliver to the
Churchwardens and Overseers of the Poor there or to some or one of them,
together with this our order, or a true copy thereof, at the same time shewing to
them the original. And WE do also hereby require you the said Churchwardens
and Overseers of the Poor of the said Parish of *High Littleton*
to receive and provide for *them as* inhabitant*s* of your Parish.

GIVEN under our hands and Seals, *this* 19*th* day of *April*
in the *fourth* Year of the Reign of Her Majesty Queen Victoria, and in
the Year of our Lord One Thousand Eight Hundred and Forty *one.*

Removal Order in respect of John Smith (case 170).

LANGPORT UNION.

The Board of Guardians of the Langport Union, in the County of Somerset, do hereby certify, that *on the* previously to the first day of *July* — one thousand eight hundred and *forty nine* *Sarah* ——— the *said late* Wife of *Mitchell* and *her* Children *James, Rosina, Charlotte, Mary, Frederic, Edwin, Herbert, Reuben*

became chargeable to the Parish of *Curry Rivell* ——— in the said Union and County, and still continue chargeable thereto.

In testimony whereof the common seal of the said Guardians *is hereunto* affixed at a meeting of their Board this *twenty fourth* — day of *July* ——— *1849*-

{ Presiding Chairman of the said Board.

{ Clerk (or acting as Clerk) to the Board of Guardians of the Langport Union.

The above is the Certificate of Chargeability mentioned and referred to in the *against* of Sarah Mitchell taken before us the *25th* day of July 1849 ———

William Speke

Thos. B. Ottermoore

Notice of Chargeability regarding Sarah Mitchell, 1849 (Appendix).

INDEX OF EXAMINEES

INDEX OF PLACES IN BOLD TYPE

Thorncombe (Devon, Dorset 1844)
    87 134 182
Thornford, Dorset 56
Thringstone, Leicestershire 128
Thurloxton 180
Tilehurst, Berkshire 66
Timsbury 147 157
Tiverton, Devon 45 142
Towcester, Northamptonshire 103
Tring, Hertfordshire 142
Trowbridge, Wiltshire 85
Twyning, Gloucestershire 85

Uphill 102
Upwey, Dorset 87

Varleg Iron Works 153
Vigo in Spain 44
Vitry-le-Francois (Vitre) 55
Voale, Mark 105
Vobster, Mells 89

Wakefield, Yorkshire 91
Walcot 116 137 166
Wales 92 102
Wambrook (Dorset,
    Somerset 1896) 134
Warmwell, Derbyshire 43
Watchet 127
Wedmore 50 85 118 119 166
Wellington 154 155
Wellow 76
Wells 39 51 68 70 86 128 153
Wells Asylum 164
Wenesley Farm, Wells 118
West Buckland 156
Westbury Leigh, Wiltshire 154
Westbury-on-Trym, Gloucestershire
    86 114
West Coker 93 100 121

West Harptree 128
West Hatch 109
West Indies 73 136
West Leigh, Ash Priors 162
Westminster, Middlesex 70 78 93
West Monkton (Monckton) 80 91
Westonzoyland 43
Whatley 96
Whitby, Yorkshire 86
Whitechapel, London 114 116
Whitelackington 109
White Waltham, Berkshire 66
Whitwick, Leicestershire 128
Wick St Lawrence 139
Wicksworth (Waxworth) 43
Widcombe see Lyncombe
Wilkinthroop, Horsington 96
Williton 127
Wilton Gaol, Taunton 135 167
Wincanton 49 63 127
Windsor, Berkshire 50
Winsford 150
Winsham 90 123 124
Witham Friary (Witham Frary) 85
Witheridge, Devon 142
Withypool 69
Wiveliscombe 103 145 150 162
Wonersh, Surrey 142
Wookey 119
Wookey Hole 75
Wootton Fitzpaine, Dorset 136
Worcester (Woster)53
Worle 139
Wrington 41

Yard, Watchet 128
Yatton 114
Yeovil 94 130
Yorkshire 110